Let's Study!

The Grammar School 2

I am books

Contents

Features

새로운 중학교 교과 과정 반영

자기주도 학습을 통한 내신 완벽 대비

내신 기출문제 분석

명확한 핵심 문법 해설

Workbook – 다양하고 풍부한 문법문제 수록

Unit 문법 설명

· 새로운 교과 과정이 반영된 교과서를 분석하여 꼭 알아야 할 문법 사항을 예문과 함께 정리하였습니다.

· 쉬운 설명으로 문법의 기초를 다질 수 있습니다.

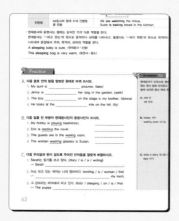

Practice

· 다양한 주관식 문법 문제를 통해 배운 문법 사항을 문제로 풀어보며 익히도록 하였습니다.

· 핵심 문법 설명을 토대로 배운 문법 사항을 Practice를 통해 확실하게 점검할 수 있습니다.

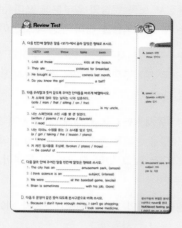

Review Test

· 해당 Chapter에서 배운 문법 사항을 통합하여 다양한 주관식 문제를 통해 복습하며 점검하도록 하였습니다.

· 학습 내용을 바탕으로 문제를 해결하며 응용력을 키울 수 있도록 하였습니다.

Chapter Test

· 해당 Chapter에서 배운 내용들을 학교 시험 유형으로 구성하였으며 출제 비율이 높은 문제를 선별하여 종합 문제로 제시하였습니다.

· 학교 시험에 나올만한 내신 대비 문제와 주관식 문제를 수록하여 내신을 완벽하게 대비하도록 하였습니다.

· 종합문제를 통해 자신의 실력을 점검하도록 하였습니다.

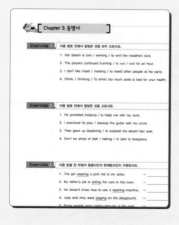

Workbook

· 해당 Chapter에서 배운 문법 사항과 관련된 추가 문법 문제로 구성하였습니다.

· 주관식 문제를 대폭 수록하여 많은 문제를 풀어보며 실력을 쌓을 수 있도록 하였습니다.

문법 용어 정리

가정법 사실이 아닌 것을 가정하거나 상상하여 나타내는 표현법. 동사의 형태에 따라 가정법 과거, 가정법 과거완료, 가정법 미래로 나타낸다.

가주어 문장의 주어가 부정사구이거나 that절일 경우 문장의 균형을 맞추기 위해 그 주어를 대신하여 it을 쓰는데, 이때의 it을 가주어라고 한다.

간접의문문 「의문사/if[whether]+주어+동사」의 형태. 의문문이 다른 문장의 일부분이 될 때 이것을 간접의문문이라고 한다.

간접화법 다른 사람의 말을 자신의 말로 고쳐서 전달하는 방법이다.

감탄문 문장 끝에 감탄 부호(!)를 붙이며 기쁨, 슬픔, 놀람 등의 감정을 나타내는 문장. what으로 시작하는 형태와 how로 시작하는 형태가 있다.

과거분사 「동사원형+-ed」의 형태를 원칙으로 하며 불규칙 동사는 불규칙적으로 변한다. 명사 앞, 뒤에서 명사를 수식하며 완료나 수동의 의미를 담고 있다.

관계대명사 「접속사+대명사」의 역할. 앞에 오는 명사(사람, 사물, 동물)를 꾸며 주는 문장을 이끌어 준다.

관계부사 「접속사+부사」의 역할. 앞에 오는 명사(장소, 시간, 이유, 방법)를 꾸며 주는 문장을 이끌어 준다.

관사 a(n), the를 관사라고 하는데 이들은 항상 명사 앞에 쓰이므로 마치 단어(명사)에 모자를 씌운 것 같다 하여 관사라고 부른다.

구 「주어+동사」의 형태를 포함하지 않고 2개 이상의 단어가 모여 하나의 품사 역할을 하는 것을 말한다.

능동태 '…이 ~을 하다'라는 주어가 목적어에게 행위를 가하는 문장을 말한다.

대동사 앞에 나온 동사(구)가 반복적으로 나오는 것을 피하기 위해 do나 does와 같은 말을 대신 사용하는데 이를 대동사라고 한다.

도치 문장은 일반적으로 「주어+동사+목적어/보어」의 어순이 되는데, 이와 같은 어순에서 동사나 목적어/보어 등이 주어 앞에 놓이는 것을 도치라고 한다. 의문문, 감탄문이 그 대표적인 예인데 평서문에서도 도치가 되는 경우가 많다.

독립부정사 보통 문장의 앞부분에 쓰여 문장 전체를 수식하는 부사구 역할을 하며 관용적 표현이 많다.

독립분사구문 분사구문의 의미상 주어와 문장의 주어가 다를 경우 분사구문의 주어를 생략하지 않고 분사 앞에 그대로 둔다.

동명사 「동사원형+-ing」의 형태. 동사가 형태를 바꾸어 명사 역할을 한다는 뜻으로 붙여진 이름이다. 동사의 성질을 그대로 갖고 있어 그 자체의 목적어, 보어, 수식어구를 취한다.

동사원형 동사의 기본형(원형). 조동사 뒤에 쓰이거나 명령문의 동사로 사용한다.

등위접속사 단어와 단어, 구와 구, 절과 절을 대등한 관계로 연결시켜 주는 역할을 한다.

명령문 명령, 요구, 금지 등을 나타내는 문장이며 보통 주어 You를 생략하고 동사원형으로 시작한다.

명사절 접속사, 의문사, 관계대명사(what)가 이끄는 절. 문장에서 명사 역할(주어, 보어, 목적어 역할)을 한다.

문장 요소 문장을 이루는데 반드시 필요한 주요소(주어, 동사, 목적어, 보어)와 주요소를 꾸미는 수식 요소가 있다.

복문 「주어+동사」 형태의 절이 둘 이상인 문장. 그 중 하나의 절이 의미상 중요한 절이 되며 나머지 절이 그 절에 종속되어 있는 문장이다.

부대상황 분사구문의 한 종류로서, 주절의 동작과 동시에 일어나는 동작이나 사건이 잇따라 일어나는 경우를 나타낸다.

부분 부정 all, both, every가 부정문에 사용되면 일부분만 부정하는 말이 되는데 이를 부분 부정이라고 한다.

부사절 「접속사+주어+동사」 형태. 문장에서 장소, 시간, 원인, 목적, 결과, 조건, 양보 등의 의미를 나타내는 부사 역할을 하는 절을 말한다.

부정대명사 some, any, one, other, another과 같은 단어가 특정한 사람이나 사물을 가리키지 않고 막연히 어떤 사람이나 사물 또는 수량을 가리키는 대명사를 말한다.

부정사 부정사는 품사가 정해지지 않았다는 말로 「to+동사원형」의 형태가 일반적이지만, to가 없는 부정사도 있다. 부정사는 동사 본래의 성질을 가지고 있으므로 그 자체의 목적어, 보어, 수식어구를 취하며 문장에서 명사, 형용사, 부사의 역할을 한다.

분사구문 때, 이유, 조건, 양보 등을 나타내는 부사절을 분사로 시작하는 분사구로 간결하게 나타내는 구문을 말한다.

비교급 형용사나 부사는 원급, 비교급, 최상급으로 변하는데 비교급은 '더 ~한, 더 ~하게'의 뜻으로 원급에 -er를 붙이는 규칙 변화와 그렇지 않은 불규칙 변화가 있다.

비인칭 주어 it 시간, 거리, 요일, 명암, 날씨 등을 나타낼 때 문장의 주어로 it이 사용된다. '그것'이라고 해석되는 대명사 it과는 다르다.

빈도부사 동사를 수식하여 얼마만큼 자주 행해지는가를 나타내는 부사. be동사나 조동사 뒤에, 일반동사 앞에 놓인다.

사역동사 '…에게 ~을 시키다'라는 의미를 가진 동사로 let, make, have 등이 있다.

상관 접속사 단어와 단어, 구와 구, 절과 절을 연결하는 말로 전후 두 요소가 짝이 되어 쓰이는 접속사이다.

선택의문문 두 개 이상 중에서 상대방의 선택을 묻는 의문문이며 Yes나 No를 사용하여 대답하지 않는다.

선행사 「접속사+대명사」의 역할을 하는 관계대명사나 「접속사+부사」의 역할을 하는 관계부사가 수식하는 앞 문장의 명사나 대명사를 말한다.

수동태 「be동사+과거분사」의 형태. 능동태의 목적어를 주어로 삼아 '~이 되다' 또는 '~되어 있다'라고 해석되며, 주어가 어떤 일을 당한다는 의미의 문장을 말한다.

수여동사 '…에게 ~을 주다'라는 의미를 지닌 동사로 목적어 2개를 취하는 4형식 문장을 만든다.

시제 동사가 나타내는 동작 또는 상태가 일어난 시간적 위치. 시제는 크게 기본시제(현재, 과거, 미래), 완료시제(현재완료, 과거완료, 미래완료), 진행시제(현재진행, 과거진행, 미래진행, 현재완료진행, 과거완료진행, 미래완료진행)로 나눌 수 있다.

원급 형용사나 부사는 원급, 비교급, 최상급으로 변하는데 원급은 다른 것과 비교하지 않는 형용사, 부사의 원래 형태를 말한다.

원형부정사 to가 붙지 않은 부정사를 말한다. 주로 지각동사나 사역동사의 목적격보어로 쓰인다.

의미상 주어 to부정사는 동사의 성질을 가지고 있기 때문에 내용상 주어(=의미상 주어)가 필요하며 보통 「for+목적격」으로 나타낸다. 단, 사람의 성격을 나타내는 형용사와 뒤에는 「of+목적격」을 사용한다.

의지미래 주어의 강한 의지나 고집을 나타낼 때 사용하는 시제이며 조동사 will을 사용한다.

이중소유격 소유격은 a(n), the, this, that, any, every, some, no 등과 나란히 사용할 수 없으므로 소유의 관계를 나타내는 전치사 of를 함께 써서 「of+소유대명사」의 형태로 나타낸다.

재귀대명사 인칭대명사의 소유격 또는 목적격에 -self나 -selves를 붙여서 '~ 자신'이라는 뜻을 나타내는 대명사이다.

준동사 동사의 본래의 기능을 가지고 있으면서 다른 품사의 구실을 하는 동사형을 준동사라고 한다. 준동사에는 부정사, 동명사, 분사가 있다.

지각동사 '보다, 듣다, 냄새를 맡다' 등의 감각 기관을 통하여 대상을 인식함을 나타내는 동사이다.

진주어 to부정사나 명사절과 같이 문장이 길 때에는 그 자리에 대신 It을 쓰고 to부정사나 명사절을 문장 뒤에 두기도 하는데, 이때의 to부정사나 명사절을 진주어라고 한다.

최상급 형용사나 부사는 원급, 비교급, 최상급으로 변하는데 최상급은 '가장 ~한, 가장 ~하게'의 뜻으로 원급에 -est를 붙이는 규칙 변화와 그렇지 않은 불규칙 변화가 있다.

형용사절 「접속사+대명사」의 역할을 하는 관계대명사와 「접속사+부사」의 역할을 하는 관계부사가 이끄는 문장을 형용사절이라고 한다.

문장의 형식이란 무엇인가?
문장을 이루는 중심 요소인 주어, 동사, 목적어, 보어의 구성에 따라 문장의 형식을 구분하여 분류한 것으로 1~5형식으로 나타낼 수 있다.

문장의 형식은 어떻게 구분하는가?
– 1형식 : 「주어+동사」로 이루어진 문장
– 2형식 : 「주어+동사+보어」로 이루어진 문장
– 3형식 : 「주어+동사+목적어」로 이루어진 문장
– 4형식 : 「주어+동사+간접목적어+직접목적어」로 이루어진 문장
– 5형식 : 「주어+동사+목적어+목적격보어」로 이루어진 문장

Chapter 1. 문장의 형식

01 | 1형식과 2형식 문장

- 1형식 문장은 「주어+동사」로 이루어진 문장으로 부사(구)와 함께 쓸 수 있다.

  Thomas runs.　　　　The bus arrived in front of the store.

- 2형식 문장은 「주어+동사+**보어**」로 이루어진 문장으로 동사 뒤에 보어는 주어의 상태나 성질을 설명한다. 감각동사(look, sound, smell, taste, feel)는 보어로 형용사를 쓴다.

  My teacher is **kind**.　　　　The leaves turn **red**.　　　　The bread smelled **good**.

2형식 동사의 종류	
상태(~이다)	be(am, are, is), keep, stay ...
상태의 변화(~되다)	become, go, grow, get, turn ...
감각동사	look(~하게 보이다), sound(~하게 들리다), smell(~한 냄새가 나다), taste(~한 맛이 나다), feel(~하게 느껴지다)

Practice

A. 다음 문장의 형식을 쓰시오.

1. She looks upset today.　　　_____
2. The baby cried at night.　　　_____
3. Her face turned red.　　　_____
4. The song sounds sweet.　　　_____
5. Brian jogs every morning.　　　_____

B. 다음 괄호 안에서 알맞은 것을 고르시오.

1. The story sounds (strange / strangely).
2. The silk feels (soft / softly).
3. The pie tastes (deliciously / delicious).
4. These cookies smell very (well / good).
5. My father looks (busy / busily).

C. 다음 우리말과 뜻이 같도록 주어진 단어들을 알맞게 배열하시오.

1. 그녀는 학교로 걸어갔다. (school, she, to, walked)

   → _____

2. 그는 문 옆에 서 있다. (is, next to, standing, the, door, he)

   → _____

3. 그 약은 쓴맛이 난다. (bitter, the, medicine, tastes)

   → _____

4. 너의 계획은 가능해 보인다. (possible, plan, your, looks)

   → _____

Grammar Tip

A. upset 화난
　　turn ~ 되다

주어와 감각동사만으로는 의미가 불완전하므로 감각동사 다음에는 형용사가 필요하다.

B. strange 이상한

목적어를 필요로 하지 않는 동사를 자동사라고 하므로 1형식과 2형식 문장의 동사는 자동사이다.

C. next to ~ 옆에
　　medicine 약
　　possible 가능한

02 3형식과 4형식 문장

- 3형식 문장은 「주어+동사+**목적어**」로 이루어진 문장으로 목적어는 '~을(를)'로 해석한다.

  She likes **flowers**.

  Tom wants **to buy the bike**.

  * 목적어가 동작이나 행위를 나타낼 때, 목적어는 to부정사나 동명사가 온다.

- 4형식 문장은 「주어+동사+**간접목적어**+**직접목적어**」로 이루어진 문장으로 간접목적어는 '~에게', 직접목적어는
  '~을(를)'로 해석한다. 목적어를 2개 가지는 4형식 동사를 수여동사라고 한다.

  Carol gave **her a gold ring**.

수여동사란?	의미상 2개의 목적어를 필요로 하는 동사
수여동사의 종류	give(주다), buy(사 주다), show(보여 주다), send(보내다), make(만들어 주다), teach(가르치다), lend(빌려주다), ask(물어보다) ...

Practice

A. 다음 문장의 형식을 쓰시오.

1. He played the flute on the stage. _____
2. I enjoy listening to music. _____
3. Sarah found him his key. _____
4. Bill entered the office fast. _____
5. We decided to buy a camera. _____

B. 다음 문장에서 목적어를 모두 찾아 동그라미 하시오.

1. He loves basketball.
2. I can't remember her name.
3. She is making her daughter a doll.
4. The child kicked a big ball.
5. I sent him the letter.

C. 다음 우리말과 뜻이 같도록 주어진 단어들을 알맞게 배열하시오.

1. Paul은 그 지갑을 찾았다. (found, the, purse, Paul)

   → _____

2. 우리는 런던을 5시에 떠났다. (at, five, London, we, left)

   → _____

3. 그녀는 그들에게 수학을 가르친다. (she, math, them, teaches)

   → _____

4. 나는 그녀에게 내 앨범을 보여줬다. (showed, I, my, album, her)

   → _____

Grammar Tip

목적어를 필요로 하는 동사를 타동사라고 하므로 3형식(목적어 1개)과 4형식(목적어 2개) 문장의 동사는 타동사이다.

A. enter 들어가다

B. remember 기억하다
   kick 차다

C. purse 지갑
   left 떠났다(leave의 과거형)
   album 앨범

03 4형식 문장의 3형식 전환

• 4형식 문장은 간접목적어와 직접목적어의 순서를 바꾸고 간접목적어 앞에 전치사 to, for, of를 써서 3형식 문장으로 나타낼 수 있다.

4형식 문장	주어＋수여동사＋간접목적어＋직접목적어
3형식 문장	주어＋수여동사＋직접목적어＋전치사(to, for, of)＋간접목적어

He sent me an email. = He sent an email **to me**.

I bought my son a toy. = I bought a toy **for my son**.

She asked me a question. = She asked a question **of me**.

to를 쓰는 동사	give, send, bring, teach, show, read, tell, write, lend ...
for를 쓰는 동사	make, buy, get, cook, find ...
of를 쓰는 동사	ask, inquire ...

Practice

A. 다음 빈칸에 to, for, of 중 알맞은 것을 쓰시오.

1. Mom bought pants _____ me yesterday.
2. Peter told the story _____ the children.
3. Jake will make a chair _____ you.
4. I asked some advice _____ my friends.
5. Jason teaches history _____ students.

B. 다음 두 문장의 뜻이 같도록 빈칸에 알맞은 말을 쓰시오.

1. She cooked pizza for us every Sunday.

   = She cooked _____ _____ every Sunday.

2. The man gave a card to her.

   = The man gave _____ _____ _____.

3. Can I ask you a favor?

   = Can I ask _____ _____ _____ _____?

C. 다음 4형식 문장을 3형식 문장으로 바꾸어 쓰시오.

1. Susan made her brother a suit.

   → _____

2. He didn't lend her his laptop.

   → _____

3. I will ask him his name.

   → _____

Grammar Tip

4형식 문장을 3형식으로 바꿀 때 동사에 따라서 전치사 to, for, of가 필요하다.

A. advice 충고
history 역사

B. favor 호의, 부탁

4형식 문장을 3형식 문장으로 바꿀 때 직접목적어가 대명사인 경우에는 4형식을 쓸 수 없고 3형식으로 쓴다.
He gave it to her. (3형식 O)
→ He gave her it. (4형식 ×)

C. suit 정장
lend 빌려주다

Unit 04 | 5형식 문장

· 5형식 문장은 「주어+동사+목적어+**목적격보어**」로 이루어진 문장으로 목적격보어로는 명사, 형용사, to부정사 등 이 올 수 있으며 목적어를 뒤에서 설명해 준다.

목적격보어가 **명사**인 경우	명사인 경우는 목적어와 목적격보어가 동격이다. She made <u>her son</u> **a pianist**.
목적격보어가 **형용사**인 경우	형용사인 경우는 목적어의 상태를 설명한다. I found <u>the exam</u> **easy**.
목적격보어가 to부정사 경우	to부정사인 경우는 목적어의 상태나 동작을 설명한다. I want <u>you</u> **to go** home early.

· 5형식 문장은 동사에 따라 어울리는 목적격보어가 따로 있다.

목적격보어로 **명사**가 오는 동사	make, call, name, think, elect ...
목적격보어로 **형용사**가 오는 동사	make, keep, find, leave, think ...
목적격보어로 **to부정사**가 오는 동사	want, ask, tell, order, advise, allow, expect ...

Practice

A. 다음 괄호 안에서 알맞은 것을 고르시오.

1. My sister asked me (to stay / stay) at home.
2. Jack made his friends (happy / happiness).
3. Sweaters keep us (warm / warmly).
4. People call the woman (kind / Angel).

B. 다음 빈칸에 알맞은 말을 〈보기〉에서 골라 쓰시오.

> 〈보기〉 expected   thought   allowed   named

1. We _____ the project Super K.
2. I _____ him a good teacher.
3. She _____ me to play computer games.
4. We _____ her to pass the exam.

C. 다음 우리말과 뜻이 같도록 주어진 단어를 이용하여 문장을 완성하시오.

1. 그 TV 쇼는 그녀를 스타로 만들었다. (her, a star)
   → The TV show made _____ _____.

2. 우리는 교실을 깨끗하게 유지했다. (clean, the classroom)
   → We kept _____ _____.

3. 나는 네가 공부를 열심히 하기를 원한다. (to, hard, study)
   → I want you _____ _____ _____.

Grammar Tip

5형식 문장은 동사에 따라 목적격보어에 명사, 형용사, to부정사가 온다.

A. stay 머무르다
   happiness 행복
   keep 유지하다

B. expect 기대하다
   name 이름을 지어주다
   allow 허락하다

C. clean 깨끗한

05 지각동사와 사역동사

· 5형식 문장에서 지각동사나 사역동사가 쓰이면 목적격보어로 동사원형을 쓴다.

지각동사란?	보고, 듣고, 냄새를 맡고, 느끼는 감각을 나타내는 동사 → '(목적어가) ~하는 것을 보다[듣다, 느끼다]'
지각동사의 종류	see, watch, hear, smell, feel ...

She **heard** someone **call** her name.

I **saw** you **running** to the cinema.

* 진행 중인 동작을 강조할 때는 동사원형 대신 현재분사를 쓸 수 있다.

사역동사란?	'(목적어가) ~하게 하다, ~하도록 시키다'라는 뜻을 가진 동사
사역동사의 종류	make, have, let ...

She **made** her children **brush** the teeth.   Let me **introduce** myself.

He **had** the cat **sleep** on his bed.

* help는 목적격 보어로 to부정사와 동사원형을 둘 다 쓸 수 있다.

   She **helped** me **(to) get** some information.

Practice

A. 다음 문장에서 <u>틀린</u> 부분을 찾아 동그라미 하고 바르게 고치시오.

1. She saw the sun to rise.　　　　　　　　_____

2. He heard a baby to cry.　　　　　　　　_____

3. My mom made me cleaning the house.　_____

4. Let me introducing her to you.　　　　　_____

5. She had her grandson playing outside.　_____

B. 다음 괄호 안에서 알맞은 것을 고르시오.

1. He let me (realize / to realize) the truth.

2. Ann smelled firewood (to burn / burn).

3. He watched her (to dance / dancing) on the street.

4. His kindness made everybody (smile / smiling).

C. 다음 빈칸에 알맞은 말을 〈보기〉에서 골라 쓰시오.

〈보기〉	use	touch	sit	fly

1. The teacher made a student _____ down.

2. Mr. Jason let her _____ his laptop.

3. She saw the balloon _____ in the sky.

4. I felt someone _____ my bag.

Grammar Tip

5형식 문장에서 동사자리에 지각동사나 사역동사가 오면 목적격보어는 동사원형이 온다. 지각동사의 경우 의미에 따라 현재분사가 올 수도 있다.

A. rise 뜨다, 솟다
　 grandson 손자

B. realize 실현하다, 깨닫다
　 burn 타다
　 kindness 친절함

C. laptop 노트북
　 balloon 풍선

 **Review Test**

A. 다음 문장을 바르게 해석하시오.

1. My friend wrote me a letter.

2. I found the box empty.

3. Joe thinks her beautiful.

B. 다음 우리말과 뜻이 같도록 빈칸에 알맞은 말을 쓰시오.

1. 그 운동화는 더러워 보인다.
   → The sneakers _____ _____.

2. Dave는 운동 후에 피곤하다고 느꼈다.
   → Dave _____ _____ after exercise.

3. 그 우유는 나쁜 냄새가 난다.
   → The milk _____ _____.

4. 그 동화는 흥미롭게 들렸다.
   → The fairy tale _____ _____.

C. 다음 빈칸에 알맞은 말을 <보기>에서 골라 쓰시오.

<보기>	wants	bought	became	passed

1. We _____ teachers.

2. Julie _____ me to ask his name.

3. I _____ him the salt.

4. He _____ a new car.

D. 다음 두 문장의 뜻이 같도록 빈칸에 알맞은 말을 쓰시오.

1. She gave me a handkerchief.
   = She gave a handkerchief _____ _____.

2. My mom bought me a present.
   = My mom bought a present _____ _____.

3. He asked her a question.
   = He asked a question _____ _____.

E. 다음 밑줄 친 부분을 바르게 고치시오.

1. My teacher made us to do the project. _____

2. I let her knowing my phone number. _____

3. The girl watched him to sing a song. _____

Grammar Tip

A. letter 편지
   empty 빈, 비어 있는
   beautiful 아름다운

감각동사가 있는 경우 부사처럼 해석하지만 뒤에는 형용사가 와야 한다.

B. dirty 더러운
   tired 피곤한
   fairy tale 동화

C. bought 샀다(buy의 과거형)
   became 되었다(become의 과거형)
   pass 건네주다
   salt 소금

D. handkerchief 손수건
   present 선물

지각동사나 사역동사 뒤에 목적격보어는 동사원형이 온다. 지각동사의 경우에는 진행을 강조할 때 현재분사가 올 수도 있다.

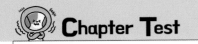

1. 다음 빈칸에 알맞지 <u>않은</u> 것은?

   > Peter looks _____ today.

   ① upset ② happy
   ③ sadly ④ nervous
   ⑤ pleasant

2. 다음 중 문장의 형식이 <u>다른</u> 하나는?
   ① She cooks in the kitchen.
   ② They run in the park.
   ③ The boy looks very handsome.
   ④ Birds sing in the tree.
   ⑤ The baby sleeps on the bed.

3. 다음 중 밑줄 친 부분의 문장 요소가 <u>다른</u> 것은?
   ① Mr. Jason likes <u>chess</u>.
   ② The book made us <u>happy</u>.
   ③ She wanted me <u>to play tennis</u>.
   ④ I found the test <u>difficult</u>.
   ⑤ She called me <u>a genius</u>.

4. 다음 중 밑줄 친 fun과 쓰임이 같은 것은?

   > My parents make me <u>fun</u>.

   ① Are you having <u>fun</u>?
   ② He found the game <u>fun</u>.
   ③ Dan knows many <u>fun</u> stories.
   ④ His story sounds <u>fun</u>.
   ⑤ There are many <u>fun</u> things here.

5. 다음 문장의 빈칸에 들어갈 알맞은 것은?

   > I wanted my dad _____ a new watch.

   ① to buy ② buy
   ③ buying ④ bought
   ⑤ has bought

6. 다음 중 어법상 어색한 것은?
   ① He gave flowers to his wife.
   ② Olive asked a question of me.
   ③ She made spaghetti of her son.
   ④ I sent a message to my teacher.
   ⑤ He bought a robot for his brother.

[7-8] 다음 우리말과 뜻이 같도록 단어들이 바르게 배열된 문장을 고르시오.

7.
   > 그는 우리에게 영화를 보여 주었다.
   > (showed, he, us, a movie)

   ① He showed a movie us.
   ② He a movie us showed.
   ③ He showed a movie us.
   ④ He showed us a movie.
   ⑤ He us a movie showed.

8.
   > 그녀는 나에게 헤어핀을 사 주었다.
   > (for, she, a hairpin, me, bought)

   ① She bought me a hairpin for.
   ② She bought a hairpin for me.
   ③ She bought a hairpin me for.
   ④ She bought for a hairpin me.
   ⑤ She bought me for a hairpin.

9. 다음 문장의 빈칸에 들어갈 알맞은 것을 두 개 고르시오.

> He saw her _____ down the street.

① walk
② walked
③ walking
④ to walking
⑤ to walk

10. 다음 밑줄 친 부분 중 문장 내에서 역할이 다른 것은?

① She feels <u>bored</u>.
② They took <u>pictures</u>.
③ I know <u>the answer</u>.
④ He used <u>the machine</u> for work.
⑤ Joe read <u>a book</u> yesterday.

11. 다음 빈칸에 공통으로 알맞은 전치사는?

> · She sent a letter _____ me.
> · I expected you _____ win the game.

① on
② of
③ for
④ in
⑤ to

12. 다음 빈칸에 가장 알맞은 것은?

> A: I bought this scarf last weekend.
>   What do you think?
> B: Wow, it _____ so pretty!

① feels
② tastes
③ looks
④ smells
⑤ sounds

[13-14] 다음 두 문장의 뜻이 같도록 빈칸에 알맞은 단어를 쓰시오.

13.

> She didn't tell me the truth.

= She didn't tell the truth _____ _____.

14.

> Who made you this chair?

= Who made this chair _____ _____?

15. 다음 대화의 빈칸에 들어갈 가장 알맞은 질문은?

> A: _____
> B: I advised him to keep his promise.

① Did he do the homework?
② Can you ask me a favor?
③ Where is he now?
④ What did you tell him to do?
⑤ Do you need some advice?

16. 다음 빈칸에 들어갈 말이 나머지와 다른 것은?

① He asked Anna _____ marry him.
② She told her sister _____ have dinner.
③ He allowed me _____ use the Internet.
④ She wants her son _____ be patient.
⑤ I asked a favor _____ Jay.

[17-18] 다음 문장에서 틀린 부분을 찾아 바르게 고치시오.

17.

She heard someone to call her.

_____ → _____

18.

Bill had the men to clean the park.

_____ → _____

19. 다음 대화의 빈칸에 알맞은 전치사는?

A: Do you have board games?
B: Yes, I do. My aunt bought one _____ me last month.

① to   ② for
③ about   ④ of
⑤ on

20. 다음 중 어법상 알맞은 것은?

① We found the movie sadly.
② His story sounds interesting.
③ Can you show the way the people?
④ Chris made me to feel comfortable.
⑤ My mom will buy me for sandals.

〈서술형 문제〉

[21-22] 다음 우리말과 뜻이 같도록 주어진 단어들을 이용하여 영어 문장을 쓰시오.

21.

나는 그녀가 상자를 옮기는 것을 도와주었다.
(help, move, the box)

→ _____

22.

그녀는 나에게 자전거를 고쳐 달라고 부탁했다.
(ask, fix, the bike)

→ _____

23. 다음 밑줄 친 부분 중에서 어법상 어색한 것을 찾아 바르게 고쳐 쓰시오.

My grandfather bought a new swim suit for me. I like the suit because it feels well. So I always wear it when I go swimming.

_____ → _____

[24-25] 다음 〈보기〉를 참고하여 괄호 안에 주어진 단어를 이용하여 문장을 완성하시오.

〈보기〉
My mom tells me, "Go to bed early."
= My mom wants me to go to bed early. (want)

24. She told me her phone number, so I know her number.
 = She _____.
   (let)

25. I was sick. My teacher told me, "You can go back home."
 = My teacher _____.
   (allow)

to부정사란 무엇인가?
to부정사는 「to+동사원형」의 형태로 문장에서 동사가 명사, 형용사, 부사로 쓰이며 '~하기, ~하는 것' 등으로 해석한다.
I like **to watch** movies.

to부정사의 역할은 무엇인가?
to부정사는 문장에서 명사, 형용사, 부사의 역할을 하는데, 명사 역할을 할 경우에는 명사처럼 주어, 목적어, 보어로 쓰이며 형용사로 쓰일 경우에는 명사를 꾸며준다. 또한 부사로 쓰일 경우에는 부사처럼 동사, 형용사, 다른 부사 등을 꾸며준다.

Chapter 2. to부정사

06 명사적 용법 1

- to부정사가 명사처럼 쓰이는 경우에는 주어, 보어, 목적어 역할을 한다. 문장에서 주어로 쓰이면 '~하는 것은, ~하기는'의 뜻이고, 보어로 쓰이는 경우에는 '~하는 것이다'의 뜻이다.

주어 역할	~하는 것은, ~하기는	To make a movie is not easy. To exercise regularly is important.
보어 역할	~하는 것이다	My hope is to be a great doctor. His plan is to travel around the world.

＊to부정사가 보어로 쓰인 경우에는 보통 be동사 뒤에 온다.

- to부정사가 주어로 쓰인 경우에는 주어 자리에 가주어 it을 쓰고 to부정사를 뒤로 보내는 것이 자연스럽다.

    To make a movie is not easy.
    = It is not easy **to make a movie.** 〈It → 가주어 / to make a movie → 진주어〉

Practice

A. 다음 밑줄 친 부분을 바르게 해석하시오.

1. To swim is very exciting. _____

2. To drink enough water is necessary. _____

3. My plan is to learn Chinese. _____

4. Her dream is to be a designer. _____

B. 다음 문장을 it을 주어로 하는 문장으로 다시 쓰시오.

1. To eat vegetables is important for health.
   → _____

2. To bake bread is interesting.
   → _____

3. To go to bed early is good for you.
   → _____

C. 다음 우리말과 뜻이 같도록 to부정사를 이용하여 문장을 완성하시오.

1. 나의 꿈은 아픈 사람들을 돕는 것이다. (help)
   → My dream _____ _____ _____ sick people.

2. 기타를 연주하는 것은 재미있다. (play)
   → _____ _____ the guitar is fun.

3. 나의 취미는 오래된 동전들을 모으는 것이다. (collect)
   → My hobby _____ _____ _____ old coins.

4. 미래를 준비하는 것은 어렵다. (prepare)
   → _____ is difficult _____ _____ for the future.

Grammar Tip

to부정사가 be동사 뒤에 오는 경우는 보어 역할을 하며 '~하는 것이다'라고 해석한다.

A. enough 충분한
   necessary 필요한
   designer 디자이너

B. important 중요한
   health 건강
   early 일찍

C. sick 아픈
   hobby 취미
   prepare 준비하다
   future 미래

07 명사적 용법 2

· to부정사가 명사처럼 쓰여 목적어 역할을 하는 경우에는 '~하는 것을, ~하기를'의 뜻이다. 또한 문장에서 to부정사를 목적어로 취하는 동사들이 있다.

목적어 역할	~하는 것을, ~하기를	I like **to play** soccer. She wanted **to buy** the skirt.

* to부정사를 목적어로 취하는 동사 : like, love, hate, want, hope, start, decide, expect, need, begin, wish

· 「의문사+to부정사」는 명사 역할을 하는데, 주로 동사의 목적어로 쓰인다.

what+to부정사	무엇을 ~할지	where+to부정사	어디서 ~할지
how+to부정사	어떻게 ~할지, ~하는 방법	when+to부정사	언제 ~할지

I don't know **what to do** now. Can you tell me **how to get** there?

Practice

A. 다음 괄호 안의 동사를 알맞은 형태로 쓰시오.

1. He wants _____ at the hotel. (stay)

2. Tom started _____ English in Korea. (teach)

3. My sister decides _____ a skateboard. (ride)

B. 다음 빈칸에 알맞은 말을 〈보기〉에서 골라 쓰시오.

〈보기〉	where to buy	what to do
	when to start	how to bake

1. Let's ask him _____ the ingredients.

2. I don't know _____ the project.

3. She explained me _____ cookies.

4. He will tell you _____ in the evening.

C. 다음 우리말과 뜻이 같도록 to부정사를 이용하여 문장을 완성하시오.

1. 그녀는 그 물건을 어디에 놓아야 할지 몰랐다. (put)
   → She didn't know _____ the thing.

2. 우리는 그때 성공하기를 기대했다. (succeed)
   → We expected _____ at that time.

3. 그는 나에게 그 기계를 사용하는 방법을 보여줬다. (use)
   → He showed me _____ the machine.

Grammar Tip

A. skateboard 스케이트보드

「의문사+to부정사」는 문장에서 명사 역할을 하며 주로 know, tell, ask 등의 목적어로 쓰인다. 단, 「why+to부정사」의 표현은 없다.

B. ingredient 재료
project 연구 과제
explain 설명하다

C. put 두다
succeed 성공하다
expect 기대하다
machine 기계

08 형용사적 용법

• to부정사가 형용사처럼 쓰이는 경우에는 '~하는, ~할'의 뜻으로 앞의 명사나 대명사를 수식하는 역할을 한다.

I have some photos to show you. 보여줄 몇 장의 사진들

It's time to say goodbye. 인사할 시간

He has something to tell me. 말할 것

• to부정사 앞에 쓰인 명사가 전치사의 목적어가 될 경우, to부정사 뒤에 전치사를 반드시 쓴다.

He has a house to live in. 살 집   (live in a house → a house to live in)

I have a pencil to write with. 쓸 연필   (write with a pencil → a pencil to write with)

She saw a chair to sit on. 앉을 의자   (sit on a chair → a chair to sit on)

He looked for paper to write on. 쓸 종이   (write on paper → paper to write on)

Practice

A. 다음 밑줄 친 부분을 바르게 해석하시오.

1. It's time to get up for school. _____

2. Do you have money to buy it? _____

3. She has a lot of homework to do. _____

4. They have a key to open the door. _____

5. I want something to eat now. _____

6. We have no place to sleep in. _____

B. 다음 빈칸에 알맞은 말을 〈보기〉에서 골라 쓰시오.

〈보기〉   with   on   about   in   to

1. Jamie found a sofa to sit _____.

2. I will buy a pen to write _____.

3. She lent a house to live _____.

4. What is the topic to think _____ now?

5. I have many friends to talk _____.

C. 다음 밑줄 친 부분을 바르게 고치시오.

1. The boy has colored pencils to write on. _____

2. We have enough time to had lunch. _____

3. Do you have anything ask me? _____

4. What is the name of the city to arrive now? _____

5. She wants cold something to drink. _____

09 부사적 용법 I

· to부정사가 부사처럼 쓰이는 경우는 목적, 감정의 원인, 결과의 의미 등을 나타낸다.
· to부정사가 목적을 나타낼 때는 '~하려고, ~하기 위해서'라는 뜻으로 쓰인다.
· 감정의 원인을 나타낼 때는 감정을 나타내는 형용사 뒤에 to부정사가 쓰여 '~해서, ~하다니'의 뜻으로 쓰인다.

목적	~하려고, ~하기 위해서	I do exercise **to keep** healthy. He turned on the TV **to watch** the news.
감정의 원인	~해서, ~하다니	We were <u>excited</u> **to see** the baseball game. You are <u>lucky</u> **to pass** the exam.

* 목적으로 쓰인 경우에 to부정사는 in order to나 so as to로 바꾸어 쓸 수 있다.
　She visited Paris **to travel**. = She visited Paris **in order to**[**so as to**] travel.

Practice

A. 다음 밑줄 친 부분을 바르게 해석하시오.

1. We went to the restaurant <u>to eat pizza</u>. ＿＿＿＿＿＿＿

2. She bought detergent <u>to do the laundry</u>. ＿＿＿＿＿＿＿

3. We sat there <u>to take a picture</u>. ＿＿＿＿＿＿＿

B. 다음 우리말과 뜻이 같도록 주어진 단어들을 알맞게 배열하시오.

1. 나는 사과를 사기 위해 시장에 갔다. (buy, to, apples)
　→ I went to the market ＿＿＿＿＿＿＿＿＿＿＿＿.

2. Jason은 그 버스를 타기 위해 빨리 달렸다. (catch, the bus, to)
　→ Jason ran fast ＿＿＿＿＿＿＿＿＿＿＿＿.

3. 그는 역사를 공부하기 위해 그 책을 샀다. (history, study, to)
　→ He bought the book ＿＿＿＿＿＿＿＿＿＿＿.

C. 다음 빈칸에 알맞은 말을 〈보기〉에서 골라 쓰시오.

〈보기〉	angry	pleased	surprised	sad

1. 우리는 함께 노래를 불러서 기뻤다.
　→ We were ＿＿＿＿＿＿＿ to sing together.

2. 나는 그 뉴스를 들으니 화가 난다.
　→ I am ＿＿＿＿＿＿＿ to hear the news.

3. 그녀는 그녀의 집을 떠나야 해서 슬펐다.
　→ She was ＿＿＿＿＿＿＿ to leave her house.

4. 그들은 거대한 동굴을 보고 놀랐다.
　→ They were ＿＿＿＿＿＿＿ to see a huge cave.

Grammar Tip

부사적 용법 : 목적의 의미로 쓰인 to부정사는 앞에 있는 동사를 꾸며주며 '~하기 위해서'라고 해석한다.

A. detergent 세제
　do the laundry 빨래하다

B. market 시장
　catch 잡다, 타다
　history 역사

감정을 나타내는 형용사에는 happy, glad, pleased, lucky, surprised, bored, sad, sorry, angry, upset 등이 있다.

C. hear 듣다
　leave 떠나다
　huge 거대한
　cave 동굴

Unit 10 부사적 용법 2

- 부사적 용법은 목적, 감정의 원인뿐만 아니라 결과나 형용사 수식을 나타낸다.
- to부정사가 결과를 나타낼 때는 '(결과적으로, 결국 …해서) ~하다'라는 뜻으로 쓰이며, to부정사가 앞에 오는 형용사를 수식하는 경우에는 '~하기에 …한'이라는 뜻으로 쓰인다.

결과	(결과적으로, 결국 …해서) ~하다	The boy grew up **to be** an actor. My dog lived **to be** 17 years old.
형용사 수식	~하기에 …한	This machine is <u>easy</u> **to use**. He is <u>young</u> **to know** the meaning.

* 결과로 사용되는 경우에는 live, grow up 등 무의지 동사와 자주 쓰인다.

Practice

A. 다음 밑줄 친 부분을 바르게 해석하시오.

1. The water in the spring is safe <u>to drink</u>. _____

2. The poem is easy <u>to understand</u>. _____

3. The little boy grew up <u>to be a lawyer</u>. _____

B. 다음 우리말과 뜻이 같도록 밑줄 친 부분을 바르게 고치시오.

1. 그는 자라서 유명한 축구 선수가 되었다.
   → He grew up <u>be</u> a famous soccer player. _____

2. 그 규칙들은 기억하기가 어렵다.
   → The rules are hard <u>remember</u>. _____

3. 이 드레스는 파티에서 입기에 적당하다.
   → This dress is suitable <u>for wear</u> at the party. _____

C. 다음 주어진 동사를 이용하여 문장을 완성하시오.

1. 나의 할아버지는 80세까지 사셨다. (is)
   → My grandfather lived _____ 80 years old.

2. 이 호수는 수영하기에 매우 위험하다. (swim)
   → This lake is very dangerous _____ in.

3. 그 소녀는 자라서 위대한 작가가 되었다. (was)
   → The girl grew up _____ a great writer.

4. 그 문제는 풀기에 어렵다. (solve)
   → The problem is difficult _____.

Grammar Tip

grow up to be는 grow up and became으로 바꾸어 쓸 수 있다.

A. spring 샘
poem 시
lawyer 변호사

B. famous 유명한
rule 규칙
suitable 적당한, 알맞은

to부정사 앞에 감정을 나타내는 형용사 외에 다른 형용사가 오면 '~하기에 …한'이라고 해석한다.

C. dangerous 위험한
writer 작가
solve 풀다

11 | to부정사의 의미상 주어

· to부정사가 나타내는 동작, 상태의 주체를 to부정사의 '의미상의 주어'라고 한다.
· to부정사의 의미상 주어가 문장의 주어와 일치하지 않는 경우, to부정사 앞에 「for+목적격」 혹은 「of+목적격」을 붙여 to부정사의 의미상 주어를 표현한다.

「for+목적격(행위자)」	It is easy **for her** to solve this problem. 가주어 의미상 주어 진주어 It is surprise **for Bill** to lose his weight.
「of+목적격(행위자)」 사람의 성격이나 태도를 나타내는 형용사 뒤에 붙인다.	It is **nice of you** to help me. 가주어 의미상 주어 진주어 It is <u>foolish</u> **of him** to buy the book.

* 「It is+형용사+of 행위자+to부정사」의 유형에 쓰이는 형용사 : kind, wise, smart, foolish, stupid, brave, careful, nice 등
· 의미상의 주어가 막연한 일반인(people, we 등)일 때는 의미상의 주어를 쓰지 않는다.
  It is impossible (for us) to walk in the sky.

Practice

A. 다음 괄호 안에서 알맞은 것을 고르시오.

1. It was stupid (for, of) you to miss the good chance.
2. It was difficult for (she, her) to answer the question.
3. It is very kind (for, of) him to help the people.
4. It is impossible (for, of) them to win the game.

B. 다음 주어진 단어를 이용하여 문장을 완성하시오.

1. It was smart _____ _____ to discover the answer. (she)
2. It is dangerous _____ _____ to climb a mountain. (you)
3. It was rude _____ _____ to say so. (he)
4. It is good _____ _____ to jog every morning. (they)
5. It is important _____ _____ to have a dream. (Amy)

C. 다음 우리말과 뜻이 같도록 주어진 단어를 이용하여 문장을 완성하시오.

1. 우리가 규칙적으로 운동하는 것은 중요하다. (exercies)
   → It is important _____ _____ _____ _____ regularly.

2. 그녀가 그 돈을 저축하다니 매우 현명했다. (save)
   → It was very wise _____ _____ _____ _____ the money.

3. 네가 혼자 그 시장에 가는 것은 위험하다. (go)
   → It is dangerous _____ _____ _____ _____ to the market alone.

4. 그가 그 도둑을 잡다니 아주 용감했다. (catch)
   → It was so brave _____ _____ _____ _____ the thief.

Grammar Tip

의미상의 주어는 「for+행위자」로 나타내며 행위자는 목적격으로 나타낸다.

A. stupid 어리석은
   miss 놓치다
   impossible 불가능한

사람의 성격이나 태도를 나타내는 형용사 뒤에는 「of+목적격(행위자)」의 형태로 쓴다.

B. discover 발견하다, 찾아내다
   rude 무례한
   climb 오르다

C. regularly 규칙적으로
   save 저축하다
   alone 홀로
   thief 도둑

12 | too~to, enough to

- 「too+형용사/부사+to부정사」: '~하기에는 너무 …한/하게'라고 해석한다.

too+형용사/부사+to부정사 = so+형용사/부사+that+주어+can't/couldn't+동사원형	She is lazy. She can't get up early. → She is **too** lazy **to** get up early. = She is **so** lazy **that** she **can't** get up early. 그녀는 너무 게을러서 일찍 일어날 수 없다.

- to부정사의 의미상의 주어가 문장의 주어와 다를 경우, to부정사 앞에 의미상의 주어를 「for+목적격」의 형태로 쓴다.
  The book is too difficult **for me** to understand.
- 「형용사/부사+enough+to부정사」: '~할 만큼 충분히 …한/하게'라고 해석한다.

형용사/부사+enough+to부정사 = so+형용사/부사+that+주어+can/could+동사원형	He is rich. He can buy a new car. → He is rich **enough to** buy a new car. = He is **so** rich **that** he **can** buy a new car. 그는 아주 부자여서 새 차를 살 수 있다.

Practice

A. 다음 괄호 안에서 알맞은 것을 고르시오.

1. It is warm (enough, too) to play baseball outside.

2. The suitcase was (enough, too) heavy to carry.

3. The tomato became big (enough, too) to eat.

B. 다음 두 문장의 뜻이 같도록 빈칸에 알맞은 말을 쓰시오.

1. My sister's hair is so long that she can tie it.
   = My sister's hair is long _____ _____ tie.

2. The room was too dirty for me to get in.
   = The room was so dirty _____ I _____ get in.

3. He is kind enough to help with my homework.
   = He is _____ _____ that he can help with my homework.

4. I was so busy that I couldn't have time for a conversation.
   = I was _____ busy _____ have time for conversation.

C. 다음 우리말과 뜻이 같도록 주어진 단어들을 알맞게 배열하여 문장을 완성하시오.

1. 그 케이크는 내가 먹기에는 너무 달다. (too, to, sweet, eat, me, for)
   → The cake is _____.

2. 바다에서 수영할 수 있을 만큼 충분히 덥다. (to, enough, swim, hot)
   → It is _____ in the sea.

3. 그 가방은 충분히 커서 내 물건들을 넣을 수 있다.
   (big, can, that, so, I, in, put)
   → The bag is _____ my stuff.

Grammar Tip

A. suitcase 여행 가방
picnic 소풍

too ~ to와 enough to는 so ~ that
을 사용하여 바꿀 수 있는데 문장의
시제에 따라서 that절의 시제도 일치
시킨다.

B. tie 묶다
dirty 더러운
conversation 회화, 대화

C. understand 이해하다
stuff 물건

A. 다음 우리말과 뜻이 같도록 주어진 단어들을 알맞게 배열하시오.

1. 그 어린이는 피자를 먹는 것을 원했다.
   (wanted, eat, to, pizza, the, child)
   → _____

2. 그는 그 이메일을 확인하기 위해 컴퓨터를 켰다.
   (the, he, computer, to, check, turned on, the, email)
   → _____

3. 내 계획은 매일 조깅을 하는 것이다.
   (every day, to, is, plan, my, jog)
   → _____

4. Rebecca는 비행기를 타기 위해 서둘렀다.
   (an, to, airplane, hurried, Rebecca, take)
   → _____

B. 다음 빈칸에 알맞은 말을 <보기>에서 골라 쓰시오. (단, 한 번씩만 쓸 수 있음)

| <보기> | where to put | how to raise | what to buy | when to meet |

1. I told Mom _____ for Dad.
2. She didn't know _____ a dog.
3. They can't decide _____ together.
4. He asked me _____ his bag.

C. 다음 문장에서 틀린 부분을 찾아 동그라미 하고 바르게 고치시오.

1. This is dangerous to swim in the deep sea. _____
2. It was hard of me to find a way with a map. _____
3. It is very kind of you help to me. _____
4. It was interesting for us to painting a wall. _____

D. 다음 문장이 자연스럽게 완성되도록 빈칸에 들어갈 알맞은 것을 고르시오.

| (a) to understand the book | (b) to do exercise regularly |
| (c) for me to watch again | (d) for me to say anything |

1. The boy was too young _____.
2. The movie is great enough _____.
3. The library was too quiet _____.
4. She is diligent enough _____.

[1-2] 다음 빈칸에 알맞은 것을 고르시오.

1.
> She was excited _____ watch the show.

① of ② at
③ to ④ for
⑤ on

2.
> It was fun _____ him to observe plants.

① to ② into
③ of ④ from
⑤ for

3. 다음 중 to의 쓰임이 다른 것은?
① I am sorry to hear that.
② I know what to do.
③ They went to the museum.
④ He was to become the next king.
⑤ Michael came here to see you.

4. 다음 중 어법상 옳은 문장은?
① I will study passing the exam.
② She likes eat chocolate cake.
③ They promised stay here until five.
④ Jamie was at the park to take photos.
⑤ He went to a concert to saw the band.

5. 다음 우리말과 뜻이 같도록 빈칸에 알맞은 것은?
> 그 칼은 사용하기에는 너무 위험하다.
> → The knife is _____ dangerous to use.

① enough ② to
③ many ④ too
⑤ never

6. 다음 중 밑줄 친 to부정사의 쓰임이 다른 것은?
① I love to go shopping.
② She wanted to travel.
③ Naomi wished to get an A.
④ He worked hard to make money.
⑤ Did you start to compose a song?

7. 다음 밑줄 친 부분의 쓰임이 <보기>와 같은 것은?

> <보기>
> It was easy for her to solve the problems.

① We called it Nana.
② It is stormy in Japan.
③ It is 11:30 in the morning.
④ I sent it to the man yesterday.
⑤ It was difficult to move the luggage.

[8-9] 다음 빈칸에 공통으로 알맞은 것을 고르시오.

8.
> · _____ is cloudy today!
> · _____ is important to be honest.

① It ② They
③ What ④ This
⑤ That

9.
> · I don't know _____ to put the box.
> · _____ are we going right now?

① when ② where
③ what ④ who
⑤ how

10. 다음 두 문장의 뜻이 같도록 빈칸에 알맞은 것은?

> The ground was so big that we could play soccer.
> = The ground was big _____ for us to play soccer.

① enough   ② many
③ much   ④ too
⑤ so

[11-12] 다음 대화의 빈칸에 알맞은 것을 고르시오.

11.
> A: Can you tell me _____ close the door?
> B: At seven in the evening.

① what to   ② how to
③ why to   ④ when to
⑤ where to

12.
> A: I traveled the whole country last year.
> B: Oh, I'm surprised _____ that.

① to hear   ② to hearing
③ to heard   ④ too hear
⑤ hear about

13. 다음 우리말과 뜻이 같도록 빈칸에 알맞은 것은?

> 그 신발은 신기에 편안했다.
> → The shoes were _____.

① comfortable put on
② comfortable to put on
③ comfortable put to on
④ to put on uncomfortable
⑤ to put comfortable on

14. 다음 밑줄 친 to부정사의 쓰임이 <보기>와 같은 것은?

> <보기> I have a plan to learn tennis.

① I am happy to help you.
② She bought a book to read.
③ The boy grew up to be a police officer.
④ He woke up early to get the train.
⑤ We hated to do the work at that time.

15. 다음 우리말과 뜻이 같도록 빈칸에 알맞은 전치사는?

(1) Sam이 그 창문을 깨다니 정말 어리석었다.
   → It was so stupid _____ Sam to break the window.

(2) Lisa가 자전거를 타는 것은 불가능했다.
   → It was impossible _____ Lisa to ride a bicycle.

16. 다음 두 문장의 뜻이 같도록 빈칸에 알맞은 것은?

> Bill is tall enough to reach to the ceiling.
> = Bill is _____.

① too short to reach to the ceiling
② so tall that reach to the ceiling
③ too tall that reach to the ceiling
④ so tall that he can reach to the ceiling
⑤ so tall that he can't reach to the ceiling

17. 다음 우리말과 뜻이 같도록 빈칸에 알맞은 말을 쓰시오.

> 나는 거기에 너무 늦게 도착해서 그를 만나지 못했다.
> → I arrived there (a) late to meet him.
>   = I arrived so late (b) I couldn't meet him.

(a) _____   (b) _____

18. 다음 빈칸에 알맞은 것은?

> She came out at night _____.

① to watch the great opera
② to watching the great opera
③ for watch the great opera
④ for to watch the great opera
⑤ to watched the great opera

19. 다음 빈칸에 알맞은 전치사는?

> We met some friends to chat _____.

① about ② in
③ for ④ with
⑤ on

20. 다음 빈칸에 enough가 어색한 것은?

① She is not old _____ to go to school.
② Peter is brave _____ to go there alone.
③ This problem is _____ difficult to solve.
④ The young man is kind _____ to take care of them.
⑤ Carol is very healthy _____ to run in the marathon.

21. 다음 밑줄 친 부분 중 어법상 어색한 것은?

> Today ①was my birthday. My mom and dad gave a present ②to me. I opened it. ③It was an expensive purse! I was surprised ④seeing it.
> I am very happy ⑤to get the purse.
> I love you, mom and dad!

〈서술형 문제〉

22. 다음 두 문장의 뜻이 같도록 빈칸에 알맞은 말을 쓰시오.

> To sit on a chair all day is bad.

= _____ is bad _____.

23. 다음 우리말과 뜻이 같도록 주어진 단어들을 활용하여 영어 문장을 쓰시오.

> 나의 아버지는 나에게 스케이트 타는 방법을 가르쳐 주셨다.
> (how, me, taught, to, skate)

→ My father _____.

24. 다음 두 문장을 같은 뜻이 되도록 한 문장으로 바꾸시오.

> Cindy wants to get a cat.
> + She wants to play with the cat.

= Cindy wants to get _____.

25. 다음 〈보기〉와 같이 두 문장이 같도록 문장을 완성하시오.

> 〈보기〉
> The rabbit is too fast for me to catch.
> = The rabbit is so fast that I can't catch it.

The system was too hard for me to handle.
= The system _____
_____.

동명사란 무엇인가?
동명사는 「동사원형+-ing」의 형태로 문장에서 명사로 쓰인다.
I enjoy **playing** soccer.

동명사의 역할은 무엇인가?
동명사는 문장에서 명사의 역할을 하여 주어(~하기는, ~하는 것은), 동사나 전치사의 목적어(~하기를, ~하는 것을), 보어(~하는 것이다)로 쓰인다.

Chapter 3. 동명사

Unit

13 동명사의 역할 1

• 동명사는 문장에서 주어나 보어로 쓸 수 있는데 주어로 쓰일 때는 '~하기는, ~하는 것은'의 뜻이고 보어로 쓰일 때는 '~하는 것이다'의 뜻이다.

주어 역할	~하는 것은, ~하기는	Getting up early is not easy. Doing your best is important.
보어 역할	~하는 것이다	My hobby is **cooking**. Her job is **writing** books.

• 주어나 보어로 쓰이는 동명사는 to부정사로 바꿔 쓸 수 있다.

Eating vegetables makes you healthy. = **To eat** vegetables makes you healthy.

Practice

A. 다음 밑줄 친 부분을 바르게 해석하시오.

1. <u>Swimming at night</u> is dangerous. _____

2. <u>Taking a walk</u> is good for your health. _____

3. His dream is <u>being a singer</u>. _____

4. The best way is <u>taking a taxi</u>. _____

B. 다음 두 문장의 뜻이 같도록 빈칸에 알맞은 말을 쓰시오.

1. Being honest is important.

   = _____ _____ honest is important.

2. My plan is inviting my grandparents.

   = My plan is _____ _____ my grandparents.

3. His job is making dolls for kids.

   = His job is _____ _____ dolls for kids.

C. 다음 우리말과 뜻이 같도록 동명사를 이용하여 문장을 완성하시오.

1. 내가 가장 좋아하는 활동은 농구하는 것이다. (play)

   → My favorite activity _____ _____ basketball.

2. 스페인어를 배우는 것은 어렵다. (learn)

   → _____ Spanish is difficult.

3. 가장 중요한 것은 다른 사람들의 말을 듣는 것이다. (listen)

   → The most important thing _____ _____ to others.

4. 새 책을 읽는 것은 흥미롭다. (read)

   → _____ a new book is interesting.

Grammar Tip

동명사가 주어로 쓰일 때는 단수 취급하여 동사도 단수형으로 써야 한다.

A. take a walk 산책하다
   way 방법

B. honest 정직한
   invite 초대하다
   doll 인형

C. activity 활동
   Spanish 스페인어
   listen to ~을 듣다
   others 다른 사람들

unit 14 동명사의 역할 2

- 동명사는 동사나 전치사의 목적어로 쓰여 '~하기를, ~하는 것을'이라는 뜻이 된다.

동사의 목적어	~하기를, ~하는 것을	Tony finished **washing** the dishes. My dad and I enjoyed **jogging**.
전치사의 목적어		She is interested in **swimming**. Lisa and her friends are afraid of **climbing** mountains.

- 전치사 뒤에는 명사나 대명사가 와야 하므로 전치사 뒤의 동사는 동명사의 형태로 쓴다. to부정사는 전치사의 목적어가 될 수 없다.

  She is good at **speaking** English. (O)   She is good at **to speak** English. (×)

Practice

A. 다음 괄호 안의 동사를 알맞은 동명사 형태로 쓰시오.

1. She doesn't like _____. (cook)

2. My uncle enjoys _____ computer games. (play)

3. I'm sorry for _____ late. (be)

4. Roy gave up _____ the problem. (solve)

B. 다음 빈칸에 알맞은 말을 〈보기〉에서 골라 동명사 형태로 쓰시오.

〈보기〉 help   turn   eat   win

1. Mike is proud of _____ in the contest.

2. Do you mind me _____ the light on?

3. Jenny hates _____ spicy food.

4. Thank you for _____ me.

C. 다음 우리말과 뜻이 같도록 주어진 단어들을 이용하여 문장을 완성하시오.

1. 나는 바이올린 연주하는 것을 잘한다. (good, play)
   → I'm _____ _____ _____ the violin.

2. 너는 식물 키우는 것을 즐기니? (enjoy, grow)
   → Do you _____ _____ plants?

3. Brian은 실수하는 것을 두려워한다. (afraid, make)
   → Brian is _____ _____ _____ mistakes.

Grammar Tip

A. cook 요리하다
late 늦은
solve 풀다

동명사의 주어가 문장의 주어와 다를 경우 의미상의 주어를 쓰는데, 동명사 앞에 소유격 또는 목적격으로 쓴다.
Would you mind **my[me]** opening the window?

B. mind 꺼리다
turn on 켜다
spicy 매운

C. be good at ~을 잘하다
grow 재배하다
plant 식물
be afraid of ~을 두려워하다
mistake 실수

unit 15 동명사와 현재분사

• 동명사와 현재분사는 형태는 같지만 문장에서의 역할과 의미가 다르다.

① 보어 역할을 하는 동명사와 진행형의 현재분사

동명사	보어 역할	~하는 것이다	Her job is **teaching** science to children.
현재분사	be동사와 함께 쓰여 진행형을 만드는 역할	~하고 있다	I'm **teaching** science to children.

② 목적, 용도를 나타내는 동명사와 명사를 수식하는 현재분사

동명사	목적, 용도를 나타냄	~하기 위한	I want to buy **dancing** shoes.
현재분사	명사를 수식하는 역할	~하고 있는	Do you know the girl **dancing** over there?

Practice

A. 다음 밑줄 친 부분이 동명사인지 현재분사인지 쓰시오.

1. My hobby is <u>collecting</u> old stamps. _____

2. Sue is <u>taking</u> pictures. _____

3. I want to buy a <u>sleeping</u> bag. _____

4. The boy <u>sitting</u> on a red chair is my son. _____

B. 다음 밑줄 친 부분을 바르게 해석하시오.

1. <u>Eating food</u> is not allowed here. _____

2. Be quiet. The baby <u>is sleeping</u>. _____

3. My plan is <u>writing a diary</u> every day. _____

4. Look at the <u>dancing bear</u> on the stage. _____

C. 다음 우리말과 뜻이 같도록 동명사 또는 현재분사를 이용하여 문장을 완성하시오.

1. Sally는 한국 대중음악을 듣는 것을 즐긴다. (listen)
   → Sally enjoys _____ K-pop.

2. 대기실은 2층에 있다. (wait)
   → There is a _____ on the second floor.

3. Nick은 지금 축구를 하고 있다. (play)
   → Nick _____ now.

4. 그는 길에서 울고 있는 소녀를 보았다. (cry)
   → He saw a _____ on the street.

Grammar Tip

「동사원형+-ing형」이 용도의 의미로 쓰이면 동명사이다. (~하기 위한)

A. collect 모으다, 수집하다
   sleeping bag 침낭

B. allow 허락하다
   quiet 조용한
   write a diary 일기 쓰다
   stage 무대

현재분사가 단독으로 명사를 수식할 때는 명사 앞에 오지만, 목적어나 부사구 등과 함께 쓰일 때는 명사 뒤에 위치한다.
the **crying** baby
the baby **wearing a hat**

C. K-pop 한국 대중음악
   waiting room 대기실
   second floor 2층

Unit

16 동사의 목적어 1

· 동명사와 to부정사 모두 동사의 목적어로 쓰이는데 동사에 따라 구분하여 쓸 때가 있다.

동명사를 목적어로 취하는 동사	enjoy, finish, avoid, give up, mind, keep, imagine, practice ...
	Do you <u>enjoy</u> **eating** chocolate? I <u>keep</u> **learning** English.
to부정사를 목적어로 취하는 동사	want, hope, wish, expect, decide, plan, need, agree, promise, learn ...
	She <u>expects</u> **to see** Chris again. I <u>plan</u> **to make** cookies for my friends.

Practice

A. 다음 괄호 안의 말을 알맞은 형태로 쓰시오.

1. Sam imagines _____ around the world. (travel)

2. I decided _____ the new machine. (use)

3. He avoided _____ the question. (answer)

4. Judy hopes _____ some skills for the job. (learn)

B. 다음 밑줄 친 부분을 바르게 고치시오.

1. My mom enjoys <u>to take</u> pictures of flowers. _____

2. Do you want <u>eating</u> some Italian food? _____

3. He finished <u>to build</u> the tree house. _____

4. Lisa promised <u>coming</u> home at five. _____

C. 다음 우리말과 뜻이 같도록 빈칸에 알맞은 말을 쓰시오.

1. 그녀는 중국어 배우는 것을 포기했다.
   → She gave up _____ Chinese.

2. 나는 그 벽을 칠하기로 결정했다.
   → I decided _____ the wall.

3. Jessy는 운동장을 청소하는 것을 마쳤다.
   → Jessy finished _____ the playground.

4. 그들은 새 차를 사는 것에 동의한다.
   → They agree _____ a new car.

Grammar Tip

동명사나 to부정사가 주어나 보어의 역할을 할 때는 서로 바꿔 쓸 수 있지만 목적어 역할을 할 때는 동사에 따라 달라진다.

A. imagine 상상하다
machine 기계
skill 기술

B. build 짓다, 만들다
promise 약속하다

C. wall 벽
agree 동의하다

Unit 17 | 동사의 목적어 2

- 동명사와 to부정사 모두 목적어로 취하는 동사들도 있다.

동명사와 to부정사를 모두 목적어로 취하는 동사	begin, start, like, love, hate, continue ...
	His daughter began **crying**. = His daughter began **to cry**.

- 동명사와 to부정사를 모두 목적어로 취할 수 있지만, 의미가 달라지는 동사들도 있다.

forget/remember+동명사	~했던 것을 잊다 / 기억하다	My dad forgot **locking** the door. (잠근 것을) I remember **meeting** her yesterday. (만난 것을)
forget/remember+to부정사	~할 것을 잊다 / 기억하다	Don't forget **to lock** the door. (잠그는 것을) Do you remember **to meet** her? (만나는 것을)
try+동명사	시험 삼아 ~해보다	I tried **cooking** steak. (시험삼아 요리해 봤다)
try+to부정사	~하려고 노력하다	I tried **to cook** steak. (요리하려고 노력했다)
stop+동명사(stop의 목적어)	~하는 것을 멈추다	He stopped **talking** to us. (말하는 것을 멈추다)
stop+to부정사(to부정사의 부사적 용법)	~하기 위해 멈추다	He stopped **to talk** to us. (말하기 위해 멈추다)

Practice

A. 다음 주어진 동사를 이용하여 문장을 완성하시오.

1. 갑자기 비가 내리기 시작했다. (rain)

   → It started _____ suddenly.

2. Jan은 우유를 넣어 차를 마시는 것을 정말 좋아한다. (have)

   → Jan loves _____ tea with milk.

3. 그들은 다음 주까지 그 그림 그리는 것을 계속 할 것이다. (draw)

   → They will continue _____ the picture until next week.

B. 다음 주어진 동사를 알맞은 형태로 쓰시오.

1. I'll never forget _____ him last year. (meet)

2. My brother hates _____ the yellow cap on. (put)

3. The students began _____ chess. (play)

C. 다음 밑줄 친 부분을 바르게 해석하시오.

1. Don't <u>forget to bring</u> your umbrella. _____

2. Do you <u>remember sending</u> a message to Bob? _____

3. They <u>stopped singing</u> when the door opened. _____

4. Max <u>tried to pass</u> the exam. _____

A. 다음 빈칸에 알맞은 말을 <보기>에서 찾아 알맞은 형태로 쓰시오. (단, 한 번씩만 쓸 수 있음)

<보기>   visit   drive   eat   run   be

1. _____ vegetables is good for your health.

2. My wish is _____ Greece someday.

3. Justin enjoys _____ his new car.

4. She is afraid of _____ in a dark room.

5. Jamie wants to buy _____ shoes.

B. 다음 우리말과 같도록 주어진 단어를 이용해서 문장을 완성하시오.

1. 그는 만화책 읽는 것을 매우 좋아한다. (comic books, read, love)
   → He _____.

2. Jack은 산에 오르는 것을 포기했다.
   (give up, climb, the mountain)
   → Jack _____.

3. 그 학생들은 도서관에서 말하는 것을 멈췄다. (stop, at the library, talk)
   → The students _____.

4. Sally는 다른 사람들을 이해하려고 노력했다.
   (other people, understand, try)
   → Sally _____.

C. 다음 괄호 안의 말을 알맞은 형태로 쓰시오.

1. Robert wants _____ a singer when he grows up. (be)

2. I remember _____ Nick last night. (meet)

3. Thank you for _____ me to lunch. (invite)

4. Judy continued _____ history. (study)

D. 다음 밑줄 친 부분을 바르게 해석하시오.

1. The woman playing the piano is my teacher.

2. I like riding a bike.

3. Don't forget to close the window when you go out.

4. She stopped to save the poor dog.

37

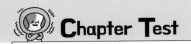

[1-2] 다음 빈칸에 알맞은 것을 고르시오.

1.
My wish is _____ an engineer.

① become
② becomes
③ becoming
④ to becoming
⑤ became

2.
I'm sorry for _____ noise.

① make
② makes
③ made
④ to make
⑤ making

3. 다음 빈칸에 알맞지 않은 것은?

David _____ watching horror movies.

① enjoyed
② avoided
③ gave up
④ forgot
⑤ planned

4. 다음 밑줄 친 동명사의 쓰임이 <보기>와 같은 것은?

<보기> Dan enjoys reading science books.

① His job is driving a taxi.
② I'm interested in writing poems.
③ Writing a diary in English is not easy.
④ My plan is visiting Mexico again.
⑤ Listening to classical music makes me relax.

5. 다음 밑줄 친 부분을 to부정사로 바꿔 쓸 수 없는 것은?

① Eric hates eating carrots.
② My son gave up finishing the project.
③ She started cleaning the room.
④ Do you like listening to music?
⑤ We began making dinner at that time.

6. 다음 밑줄 친 부분의 쓰임이 다른 것은?

① Growing plants is not easy.
② My job is helping poor animals.
③ I'm good at cooking Italian food.
④ Do you enjoy skating in winter?
⑤ He is having dinner with his family.

7. 다음 빈칸에 알맞은 말이 순서대로 짝지어진 것은?

· _____ before other people is hard.
· Sam is interested in _____ African culture.

① Speak – study
② Speak – studying
③ Speaking – studying
④ Speaking – to study
⑤ To speak – to study

8. 다음 중 어법상 어색한 것은?

① Learning French is not easy.
② My dad promises buying me a toy.
③ Henry wants to be a pianist.
④ She is proud of winning first prize.
⑤ Do you mind opening the window?

9. 다음 빈칸에 공통으로 알맞은 것은?

> · _____ basketball is fun.
> · I finished _____ computer games.
> · Ben is good at _____ the guitar.

① play
② playing
③ being play
④ to play
⑤ plays

10. 다음 중 밑줄 친 부분이 어색한 것은?
① I'm thinking of buying a new bag.
② She avoided answering the question.
③ I don't agree to join the sports club.
④ We kept to talk about the movie.
⑤ They need to take a rest.

11. 다음 두 문장을 같은 뜻이 되도록 한 문장으로 바꾸시오.

> I saw the accident this morning.
> + I remember it.

= I remember _____ the accident this morning.

12. 다음 문장에서 어법상 어색한 부분을 찾아 바르게 고치시오.

> I expect meet you again.

_____ → _____

13. 다음 밑줄 친 부분과 바꿔 쓸 수 있는 것은?

> She wanted to learn tennis.

① finished
② hoped
③ minded
④ kept
⑤ gave up

14. 다음 우리말과 뜻이 같도록 괄호 안의 말을 알맞은 형태로 바꾸시오.

> 그녀는 제시간에 거기에 도착하려고 노력했다.

→ She tried _____ there in time. (arrive)

15. 다음 밑줄 친 부분의 쓰임이 <보기>와 다른 것은?

> <보기> He is looking for a sleeping bag.

① Where is the waiting room?
② My mom bought me dancing shoes.
③ The baby sleeping in the room is my cousin.
④ Susie and I went to the swimming pool.
⑤ Mr. Smith sometimes uses a walking stick.

16. 다음 밑줄 친 부분 중 어법상 어색한 것은?

> I was ① looking for my cell phone, but I couldn't ② find it. I worried about ③ losing my cell phone. At that time, my mom ④ gave me my cell phone. Oh, no! I forgot ⑤ to put it on the sofa.

17. 다음 우리말과 같도록 밑줄 친 부분을 바르게 고치시오.

> 그들은 걷는 것을 멈추고 별을 보았다.
> → They stopped walk and watched the stars.

→ _____

18. 다음 짝지어진 대화 중 어색한 것은?

① A: Could you stop eating here?
　　B: Oh, I'm sorry. I will stop it.

② A: Are you interested in drawing?
　　B: Yes. I enjoy drawing cartoons in my free time.

③ A: Are you going camping this afternoon?
　　B: No. We decided to stay home.

④ A: Do you remember reading this book?
　　B: Yes. I will buy and read the book tomorrow.

⑤ A: How about going shopping?
　　B: That sounds good. I plan to buy some shirts.

19. 다음 우리말을 영어로 바르게 옮긴 것을 모두 고르면?

> 규칙을 따르는 것이 필요하다.

① Follow the rules is necessary.
② To follow the rules is necessary.
③ Following the rules is necessary.
④ Following the rules are necessary.
⑤ To following the rules is necessary.

20. 다음 두 문장의 의미가 다른 것은?

① Telling a lie is a bad habit.
　= To tell a lie is a bad habit.

② Do you mind if I turn on the radio?
　= Do you mind my turning on the radio?

③ The boy stopped jumping on the bed.
　= The boy stopped to jump on the bed.

④ I can speak English very well.
　= I'm good at speaking English.

⑤ Ted loves playing badminton with Jim.
　= Ted loves to play badminton with Jim.

〈서술형 문제〉

[21~22] 다음 우리말과 뜻이 같도록 주어진 단어들을 알맞게 배열하시오.

21.

> 일찍 일어나는 것은 쉽지 않다.
> (not, early, getting up, easy, is)

→ _____

22.

> 외출할 때 너의 우산 가져가는 것을 기억해라.
> (your, umbrella, to, remember, take)

→ _____ when you go out.

23. 다음 우리말과 뜻이 같도록 주어진 단어들을 이용하여 영어 문장을 완성하시오.

> Jay는 자정 전에 설거지를 마쳤다.
> (finish, before, do the dishes)

→ Jay _____
　morning.

24. 다음 대화에서 어법상 어색한 부분을 두 군데 찾아 바르게 고쳐 쓰시오.

> A: You are good at playing the piano.
> B: I enjoy to play the piano after school.
> A: Do you want to be a pianist?
> B: Yes, I hope being a great pianist.

(1) _____ → _____
(2) _____ → _____

25. 다음 대화의 내용과 일치하도록 빈칸에 알맞은 말을 쓰시오.

> Mom: Did you call your dad?
> Fred: Oh, I forgot it. I'll call him now.

→ Fred forgot _____.

현재완료란 무엇인가?
현재완료시제는 과거에 시작된 동작이나 상태가 현재까지 영향을
미치는 경우에 쓰며 「have[has]+과거분사」 형태로 나타낸다.
I **have seen** him before.

현재완료는 어떤 의미를 나타내는가?
현재완료시제는 경험(~한 적이 있다), 계속(계속 ~해 왔다), 결과
(~해 버렸다), 완료(막 ~했다)의 의미를 나타낸다.

Chapter 4. 현재완료

18 현재완료의 쓰임과 형태

- 현재완료는 과거의 한 시점에서 일어난 일이 현재까지 영향을 미칠 때 사용한다. 현재완료는 「have[has]+과거분사」의 형태로 나타낸다.

현재완료
I have lost my cell phone.

과거
I lost my cell phone.

현재
I don't have it now.

- 현재완료는 명백한 과거 시점을 나타내는 부사(구)나 when이 이끄는 부사절과는 함께 쓸 수 **없다**.

  I **have been** to Japan last month. (×) → I **went** to Japan last month. (○) / I **have been** to Japan. (○)

  The store **has closed** yesterday. (×) → The store **closed** yesterday. (○) / The store **has closed**. (○)

Practice

A. 다음 괄호 안에서 알맞은 것을 고르시오.

1. I have (saw / seen) the girl before.

2. Sean has (live / lived) here for two years.

3. He has (lose / lost) his wallet.

4. They have (finish / finished) their work.

B. 다음 주어진 동사를 이용하여 현재완료로 바꿔 쓰시오.

1. I _____ _____ the environment problems. (study)

2. Mike _____ _____ to Nigeria. (be)

3. My uncle _____ _____ to Busan. (go)

4. The children _____ _____ something. (eat)

C. 다음 우리말과 뜻이 같도록 현재완료를 이용하여 문장을 완성하시오.

1. 나는 전에 Julie를 만난 적이 있다. (meet)
   → I _____ _____ Julie before.

2. 그들은 중국어를 10년 동안 배우고 있다. (learn)
   → They _____ _____ Chinese for ten years.

3. Sue는 체중을 줄였다. (lose)
   → Sue _____ _____ her weight.

4. 그녀는 학교에 결석하고 있다. (be)
   → She _____ _____ absent from school.

Grammar Tip

「주어+have[has]+과거분사」는 「주어've[주어's]+과거분사」로 줄여 쓸 수 있다.
I have = I've
He has = He's

A. before 전에
   lose 잃어버리다
   wallet 지갑

B. environment 환경

C. weight 무게, 체중
   be absent from ~에 결석하다

19 현재완료의 용법

· 현재완료는 네 가지 용법이 있다.

	내용	예문
경험	'~한 적이 있다' 과거부터 현재까지의 경험을 말할 때	I **have watched** the movie twice. She **has been** to Canada before.
계속	'~해 오고 있다' 과거에 일어난 일이 현재까지 계속되고 있을 때	I **have known** Jake for three years. Linda **has been** sick since last Friday.
결과	'~해 버렸다' 과거에 일어난 일이 원인이 되어 그 결과가 현재에 영향을 미칠 때	My brother **has lost** his backpack. Emma **has gone** to Paris.
완료	'(벌써, 지금 막) ~했다' 과거에 시작한 일이 현재에 끝났을 때	I **have finished** my homework. We **have arrived** in New York.

Practice

A. 다음 밑줄 친 현재완료의 용법을 쓰시오.

1. I <u>have been</u> to this museum. _____

2. Brad <u>has gone</u> to China. _____

3. My family <u>has stayed</u> in this hotel. _____

4. We <u>have done</u> the work. _____

B. 다음 두 문장의 뜻이 같도록 빈칸에 알맞은 말을 쓰시오.

1. Snow started to fall three days ago. It still falls.
 → Snow _____ for three days.

2. I lost my yellow cap. I don't have it now.
 → I _____ my yellow cap.

3. Emily went to Spain. She is not here now.
 → Emily _____ to Spain.

C. 다음 우리말과 뜻이 같도록 주어진 단어들을 알맞게 배열하시오.

1. 나는 7년 동안 스페인어를 공부해 오고 있다. (studied, have, Spanish)
 → I _____ for seven years.

2. 그는 그의 바이올린을 잃어버렸다. (lost, violin, has, his)
 → He _____.

3. 나는 태국 음식을 먹어 본 적이 있다. (have, Thai food, tried)
 → I _____.

Grammar Tip

have been to:
~에 가 본 적이 있다(경험)

have gone to:
~에 가 버렸다(결과)

A. stay 머물다

B. fall (눈, 비가) 내리다
 still 여전히

결과를 나타내는 현재완료는 '과거에 ~해 버려서 그 결과 지금은 …하다'라는 의미를 가진다.

C. violin 바이올린
 try 먹어 보다

20 현재완료의 부정문과 의문문

· 현재완료 문장을 부정문과 의문문으로 만들 때 have[has]는 조동사처럼 쓰인다.

부정문	주어+have[has]+not[never]+과거분사 ~.	I **have not**[**haven't**] **eaten** coconut. She **has never met** Tim before.
의문문	Have[Has]+주어+과거분사 ~? – Yes, 주어+have[has]. (긍정) – No, 주어+haven't[hasn't]. (부정)	**Have** you **been** to Hong Kong? – Yes, I have. – No, I haven't.

＊have not과 has not은 haven't와 hasn't로 각각 줄여 쓸 수 있다.

· 의문사가 있는 현재완료 의문문은 의문사를 문장 맨 앞에 쓴다.

<u>How long</u> **have** you **been** to Hong Kong?

Practice

A. 다음 괄호 안에서 알맞은 것을 고르시오.

1. They haven't (arrive / arrived) at the airport yet.

2. I've (don't / never) met a ghost.

3. (Do / Have) you ever visited the old palace?

4. (Have / Has) Tom played the piano?

B. 다음 밑줄 친 부분을 바르게 고치시오.

1. I have <u>eaten never</u> Indian food. _____

2. It hasn't <u>stop</u> raining. _____

3. Have you met Emma since last year? _____
   – No, I <u>have</u>.

4. Has Peter <u>move</u> to Japan? _____
   – Yes, he has.

C. 다음 괄호 안의 지시대로 문장을 바꿔 쓰시오.

1. I have finished the report. (부정문으로)
   → _____

2. She has bought a new bracelet. (의문문으로)
   → _____

3. Wendy has watched the Lion King. (부정문으로)
   → _____

Grammar Tip

A. airport 공항
   yet 아직
   ghost 유령
   palace 궁

현재완료의 부정문에서 not이나 never는 have[has] 뒤에 위치한다.

B. Indian 인도의
   move 옮기다, 이사하다

C. report 보고서
   bracelet 팔찌

Unit 21 과거시제와 현재완료의 차이점

- 과거시제 : 과거 특정 시점에 일어났던 일이나 상황만을 나타내어 현재에 영향을 미치지 않는다.
- 현재완료 : 과거에 일어난 일이 현재까지 영향을 미칠 때 쓴다.

현재완료
I have learned English for ten years.

과거(ten years ago)
I began learning English.

현재(now)
I am learning English.

He **went** to Italy. 〈과거〉
→ 과거에 이탈리아에 갔고, 지금은 이탈리아에 있는지 없는지 알 수 없음.

He **has gone** to Italy. 〈현재완료〉
→ 과거에 이탈리아에 갔고, 현재까지도 이탈리아에 있다는 것을 의미함.

Practice

A. 다음 괄호 안에서 알맞은 것을 고르시오.

1. She (had / have had) lunch an hour ago.

2. We (knew / have known) each other for three years.

3. The store (reduced / has reduced) the prices since last week.

4. Mike (ate / have eaten) pizza last night.

B. 다음 두 문장의 뜻이 같도록 알맞은 것을 고르시오.

1. I started to work at this office three months ago. I still work at this office.
   → I (worked / have worked) at this office for three months.

2. She lived in Korea last year. But, she doesn't live in Korea now.
   → She (lived / has lived) in Korea.

3. They began to join the knitting class a week ago. They still join the knitting class.
   → They (joined / have joined) the knitting class for a week.

C. 다음 우리말과 뜻이 같도록 빈칸에 알맞은 말을 쓰시오.

1. 그는 아프리카로 가 버렸다. → He _____ to Africa.

2. 나는 전에 그 소설을 읽어 본 적이 있다.
   → I _____ the novel before.

3. 우리는 어제 그를 방문했다. → We _____ him yesterday.

Grammar Tip

현재완료는 ago, last, yesterday 처럼 과거를 나타내는 표현과 함께 쓸 수 없다.

A. each other 서로
reduce 낮추다
price 가격

B. month 달, 월
join 참가하다
knit 뜨개질하다

C. novel 소설

22 | 과거시제와 현재완료에 쓰이는 표현

- 과거시제는 주로 과거의 특정 시점을 나타내는 표현과 함께 쓰인다.

> yesterday, last(week, month, year ...), ago, in+연도, when

I **was** absent from school <u>yesterday</u>.   It **rained** heavily <u>last night</u>.

He **went** to the concert <u>two weeks ago</u>.   She **moved** to Vietnam <u>in 2010</u>.

- 현재완료는 용법에 따라 주로 쓰이는 표현이 있다.

경험	ever(지금까지), never(전혀 ~한 적이 없다), once(한 번), twice(두 번), ~ times(~ 번), before(전에)
계속	for(~ 동안), since(~ 이후로), how long(얼마나 오랫동안)
완료	already(이미, 벌써), just(지금 막), yet(아직)

I **have** <u>never</u> **seen** a rainbow. 〈경험〉   We **have lived** here <u>since</u> last year. 〈계속〉

He **has** <u>already</u> **done** his homework. 〈완료〉

Practice

A. 다음 빈칸에 알맞은 말을 〈보기〉에서 골라 쓰시오.

> 〈보기〉 since   once   when   three hours ago

1. I have ridden a horse _____.
2. _____ did you meet Brian?
3. The ceremony began _____.
4. We have stayed here _____ this morning.

B. 다음 밑줄 친 부분을 바르게 고치시오.

1. It <u>rained</u> for three days.   _____
2. He <u>has arrived</u> at the station thirty minutes ago. _____
3. Lucy <u>has lost</u> her purse yesterday. _____
4. She <u>learned</u> diving skills for two years. _____

C. 다음 우리말과 뜻이 같도록 빈칸에 알맞은 말을 쓰시오.

1. 그들은 지금 막 교실 청소를 끝냈다.
   → They _____ _____ _____ cleaning the classroom.
2. 나는 전에 그 공연을 본 적이 있다.
   → I _____ _____ the show _____.
3. 그녀는 어제 진주 목걸이를 샀다.
   → She _____ a pearl necklace _____.

A. 다음 괄호 안의 말을 알맞은 형태로 바꿔 쓰시오.

1. I _____ to Taiwan twice. (be)

2. They _____ comic books for two hours. (read)

3. I _____ catching balls for a long time. (practice)

4. Henry _____ about the news last week. (hear)

B. 다음 밑줄 친 부분을 바르게 고치시오.

1. I <u>never have raised</u> a cat. _____

2. They <u>have built</u> this bridge in 2000. _____

3. My sister has played the piano <u>since</u> five hours. _____

4. <u>Do you have ever seen</u> a horror movie? _____

C. 다음 질문에 알맞은 답을 <보기>에서 골라 쓰시오.

> <보기> Yes, I've visited there three times.
> No, I haven't finished it yet.
> I've studied English for six years.

1. A: Have you ever visited Jejudo?
   B: _____

2. A: How long have you studied English?
   B: _____

3. A: Have you finished your exam?
   B: _____

D. 다음 우리말과 뜻이 같도록 주어진 단어들을 알맞게 배열하시오.

1. 그는 얼마나 오랫동안 여기에서 살았니? (lived, he, here, has)
   → How long _____?

2. 우리는 지금 막 여기에 도착했다. (arrived, have, here, just)
   → We _____.

3. Susan은 그녀의 결혼반지를 잃어버렸다. (lost, wedding ring, has, her)
   → Susan _____.

4. 나는 해외에 가 본 적이 없다. (been, have, never, abroad)
   → I _____.

Grammar Tip

A. Taiwan 대만
practice 연습하다
for a long time 오랫동안
catch 잡다

B. raise (동물을) 기르다
build 건설하다
bridge 다리

C. yet 아직
exam 시험

현재완료에서 just와 already는 보통 have와 과거분사 사이에, yet은 문장 끝에 위치한다.

D. wedding ring 결혼반지
abroad 해외로, 해외에

[1-2] 다음 빈칸에 알맞은 것을 고르시오.

1.
> They have studied Spanish culture
> _____.

① yesterday   ② last week
③ in 2015   ④ three months ago
⑤ for two years

2.
> I started fixing my computer this morning, but I _____ fixing it yet.

① don't have finished   ② have finished
③ don't finish   ④ haven't finished
⑤ not have finished

3. 다음 두 문장을 한 문장으로 바꿀 때 빈칸에 알맞은 것은?

> Cindy moved to Canada three years ago.
> + She still lives there.
> → Cindy _____ in Canada for three years.

① lived   ② living
③ have lived   ④ has lived
⑤ to live

4. 다음 중 어법상 어색한 것은?
① Tom has stayed here since 2012.
② The train has already left.
③ He has been to Japan last winter.
④ Emily hasn't been late for school.
⑤ I have never eaten a mango.

5. 다음 대화의 빈칸에 공통으로 알맞은 것은?

> · I _____ seen a koala before.
> · _____ you heard this song?

① has   ② have
③ hasn't   ④ do
⑤ did

6. 다음 밑줄 친 부분을 바르게 고친 것은?

> He is absent from school since last Friday.

① was   ② being
③ been   ④ has been
⑤ haven't been

[7-8] 다음 밑줄 친 부분의 쓰임이 〈보기〉와 같은 것을 고르시오.

7.
> 〈보기〉 We have known each other since last year.

① Eric has finished the project.
② I have never seen a whale.
③ My mom has lost her watch.
④ He has played the cello for an hour.
⑤ They haven't visited the museum before.

8.
> 〈보기〉 Lisa has not arrived at the station.

① Have you ever met the President?
② I have won the prize many times.
③ My sister has gone to India.
④ He has been ill since last night.
⑤ We have done our work for today.

9. 다음 대답에 대한 질문으로 알맞은 것은?

> *A*: _____
> *B*: No, I haven't. I want to be there someday.

① Did you go to Italy?
② Have you ever gone to Italy?
③ Have you ever go to Italy?
④ Have you ever been to Italy?
⑤ Have you ever being to Italy?

10. 다음 문장을 의문문으로 바르게 바꾼 것은?

> Kelly has finished writing a letter.

① Has Kelly finish writing a letter?
② Has Kelly finished writing a letter?
③ Did Kelly finish writing a letter?
④ Have Kelly finished writing a letter?
⑤ Does Kelly has finished writing a letter?

11. 다음 문장의 밑줄 친 부분을 바르게 고치시오.

> I have bought a new dress last summer.

→ _____

12. 다음 대화의 빈칸에 알맞은 것은?

> *A*: Have you ever watched this movie?
> *B*: _____ It was really interesting.

① Yes, I do.   ② No, I don't.
③ Yes, I have.   ④ No, I haven't.
⑤ No, I didn't.

13. 다음 빈칸에 알맞은 말이 순서대로 짝지어진 것은?

> I _____ Mark at first ten years ago.
> I _____ him since then.

① met – knew
② met – have known
③ meet – known
④ have met – knew
⑤ have met – have known

14. 다음 두 문장을 같은 뜻이 되도록 한 문장으로 바꾸시오.

> Jay started to read the book two days ago. + He still reads it.

= Jay _____ the book for two days.

15. 다음 우리말을 바르게 영작한 것은?

> 우리는 그 동물원에 한 번 가 본 적이 있다.

① We went to the zoo once.
② We have been to the zoo once.
③ We have gone to the zoo once.
④ We has been to the zoo once.
⑤ We haven't gone to the zoo once.

16. 다음 밑줄 친 부분 중 어색한 것은?

① We never have been to India.
② I have already finished my homework.
③ She hasn't done the dished yet.
④ They have just finished watering the tree.
⑤ Have you ever met Jake these days?

17. 다음 짝지어진 대화 중 어색한 것은?

① A: How long have you learned French?
　 B: I have learned French for two years.

② A: When did you read the book?
　 B: I have read it twice.

③ A: Has Dora finished writing a diary?
　 B: Yes, she has. She is watching TV now.

④ A: Have you ever been to the island?
　 B: No, not yet. I plan to visit there this weekend.

⑤ A: Did you see Andy this morning?
　 B: No, I haven't seen him these days.

18. 다음 중 빈칸에 have가 들어갈 수 없는 것은?

① I _____ lost my cell phone.
② They _____ studied math since 2010.
③ We _____ visited the museum last week.
④ _____ you watched Spider Man?
⑤ I _____ lived here for three years.

19. 다음 괄호 안의 동사를 알맞은 형태로 바꿔 쓰시오.

We (stay) here since last Friday.

→ _____

20. 다음 두 문장의 뜻이 같도록 빈칸에 알맞은 말을 쓰시오.

Henry went to Japan, so he isn't here now.

= Henry _____ to Japan.

〈서술형 문제〉

21. 다음 두 문장이 같은 뜻이 되도록 현재완료를 이용하여 쓰시오.

She lost her new cap yesterday, so she doesn't have it now.

= _____

22. 다음 대화의 내용과 일치하도록 빈칸에 알맞은 말을 쓰시오.

A: Amy, have you ever played the violin?
B: No, I haven't. I want to learn it someday.

Amy _____ _____ the violin, but she wants to learn it.

23. 다음 주어진 단어를 넣어 부정문으로 바꿔 쓰시오.

I have seen a polar bear. (never)

→ _____

24. 다음 우리말과 뜻이 같도록 주어진 단어들을 알맞게 배열하시오.

우리는 지금 막 쿠키 굽는 것을 마쳤다.
(just, baking, we, cookies, finished, have)

→ _____

25. 다음 중 어법상 어색한 부분을 두 군데 찾아 바르게 고치시오.

A: Jenny, have you ever be to Laos?
B: Yes, I have. I have visited there last year. I had a lot of fun.

(1) _____ → _____
(2) _____ → _____

조동사란 무엇인가?
조동사는 동사의 의미를 보충하는 역할을 하거나 부정문, 진행형, 완료형 등을 만드는 데 쓰인다. 주어의 수와 인칭에 관계없이 항상 같은 형태로 쓰이고 뒤에 동사원형이 온다.
I **can** play the piano.

조동사는 어떤 의미로 쓰이는가?
조동사에는 will, can, must, should 등이 있으며 미래, 가능, 허가, 추측, 의무, 충고 등의 의미를 나타낸다.

Chapter 5. 조동사

23 | can, could

- can: '~할 수 있다, ~해도 좋다'라는 의미로 능력이나 허락, 요청을 나타내는 조동사이다. can은 주어와 상관없이 항상 같은 형태로 쓰며 뒤에는 동사원형이 온다. can의 과거형은 could이다.

능력	~할 수 있다	I **can** speak Japanese very well.
허락	~해도 좋다	You **can** use this computer.
요청	~해 주시겠어요?	**Can** you help me?

* 요청을 할 때 can 대신 could를 쓰면 정중한 표현이 된다.
  Could I borrow your cell phone?

- can이 능력을 나타낼 때는 be able to로 바꿔 쓸 수 있고, 허락을 나타낼 때는 may로 바꿔 쓸 수 있다.

  I **can** ride a bike. = I **am able to** ride a bike. 〈능력〉

  You **can** sit here. = You **may** sit here. 〈허락〉

Practice

A. 다음 괄호 안에서 알맞은 것을 고르시오.

1. I can (solve / solves) that problem.

2. She (can / cans) make sandwiches.

3. They could not (use / used) this machine.

4. (Can / Are) you tell me the truth?

B. 다음 두 문장의 뜻이 같도록 되도록 빈칸에 알맞은 말을 쓰시오.

1. I can read Chinese.
   = I _____ _____ _____ read Chinese.

2. Can I use your pen? = _____ I use your pen?

3. They could pass the exam.
   = They _____ _____ _____ pass the exam.

4. Can he make pizza? = _____ he _____ _____ make pizza?

C. 다음 우리말과 뜻이 같도록 주어진 단어들을 알맞게 배열하시오.

1. 나는 스키를 잘 탈 수 있다. (well / ski / can)
   → I _____.

2. 그는 어젯밤에 잠을 잘 수가 없었다. (not / could / sleep / well)
   → He _____ last night.

3. 제가 TV를 켜도 될까요? (I / on / Could / turn)
   → _____ the TV?

 Grammar Tip

can[could]의 부정문은 cannot [could not]으로 쓰고, can't [couldn't]로 줄여 쓸 수 있다.
He **cannot[can't]** go home early.

A. machine 기계
     truth 진실

can은 be able to로 바꿔 쓸 수 있는데 주어에 따라 be동사의 형태가 달라진다.
could를 be able to로 바꿔 쓸 때는 be동사의 과거형으로 쓴다.

B. pass 통과하다

C. turn on ~을 켜다

24 | will, be going to

- will: '~할 것이다, ~일 것이다'라는 의미로 앞으로 일어날 단순한 미래의 일, 지금 결정한 미래의 일, 주어의 의지가 포함된 막연한 미래를 나타내는 조동사이다. will은 주어와 상관없이 항상 같은 형태로 쓰며 뒤에는 동사원형이 온다. will의 과거형은 would이다.

예정, 의지	~할 것이다	I **will** visit my grandparents. I **will** not[won't] come to the party.
요청	~해 주시겠어요?	**Will** you pass me the salt?

  * 요청을 할 때 will 대신 would를 쓰면 정중한 표현이 된다.
  Would you open the window, please?

- be going to: '~할 것이다'라는 의미로 현재 상황을 근거로 예측한 일, 미리 결정한 미래의 일, 주어의 의지와 무관하게 당연히 올 미래를 나타낼 때 쓴다. be going to 뒤에는 동사원형이 온다.
  I**'m going to** see a movie this weekend.
  Are you **going to** have lunch with Jim?

 ## Practice

A. 다음 괄호 안에서 알맞은 것을 고르시오.

1. I will (go / goes) camping.
2. Will you (help / helping) me?
3. (Are / Will) you going to invite him?
4. I will (study / studied) hard for the exam.

B. 다음 문장에서 <u>어색한 부분</u>을 찾아 동그라미 하고 바르게 고치시오.

1. I will carrying your bag. _____
2. He not will bring the book tomorrow. _____
3. Will you are my partner? _____
4. It is going to rains in the evening. _____

C. 다음 우리말과 뜻이 같도록 빈칸에 알맞은 말을 쓰시오.

1. 그들이 교실을 청소할 것이다.
   → They _____ _____ the classroom.
2. 부탁 좀 들어주시겠어요?
   → _____ you _____ me a favor?
3. 나는 내일 콘서트에 갈 것이다.
   → I _____ _____ _____ _____ to the concert tomorrow.

Grammar Tip

will이 있는 문장의 의문문은 「will+주어+동사」의 어순으로 쓴다.
be going to가 있는 문장의 의문문은 「Be동사+주어+going to ~?」의 형태로 쓴다.

A. go camping 캠핑하러 가다
  invite 초대하다

B. carry 들고 있다. 나르다

will은 주로 주어의 의지나 막연한 미래의 일을 말할 때 쓰고, be going to는 가까운 미래에 계획된 일이나 이미 예정되어 있는 일을 나타낼 때 쓴다.

C. do ~ a favor 부탁을 들어주다

25 | must, have to

- must: '~해야 한다, ~임에 틀림없다'라는 의미로 의무나 강한 추측을 나타내는 조동사이다. must는 주어와 상관없이 항상 같은 형태로 쓰며 뒤에는 동사원형이 온다.

의무	~해야 한다	You **must** keep the promise.
강한 추측	~임에 틀림없다	He **must** be tired.

- have to: '~해야 한다'라는 의미로 의무의 뜻으로 쓰인 must와 바꿔 쓸 수 있다. 주어가 3인칭 단수일 때는 has to를 쓰고 과거일 때는 had to를 쓴다. have[has] to 뒤에는 동사원형이 온다.

의무	~해야 한다	I **have to** go home early today. She **has to** read the book. We **had to** visit Amy yesterday.

- must와 have to: 모두 의무를 나타내지만 부정형은 서로 다른 뜻을 가진다.

must not	~해서는 안 된다(금지)	You **must not** waste time.
don't have to	~할 필요가 없다(불필요)	We **don't have to** hurry.

Practice

A. 다음 괄호 안에서 알맞은 것을 고르시오.

1. She (have to / has to) get up early.

2. I (have to / had to) return the book last week.

3. He stayed up late last night. He (must / has to) be sleepy.

4. You (don't have to / doesn't have to) pay now.

B. 다음 두 문장의 뜻이 같도록 빈칸에 알맞은 말을 쓰시오.

1. 그들은 지루함에 틀림없다.   → They _____ be bored.

2. 너는 과일을 살 필요가 없다.   → You _____ buy fruit.

3. 우리는 밤에 외출해서는 안 된다. → We _____ go out at night.

C. 다음 빈칸에 알맞은 말을 〈보기〉에서 골라 쓰시오.

〈보기〉 must not   must   don't have to   had to

1. It is Sunday today. We _____ go to school.

2. He didn't have breakfast. He _____ be hungry.

3. You _____ make noise during class.

4. She _____ go see a doctor yesterday.

Grammar Tip

'~할 필요가 없다'는 don't have to로 표현하는데, 주어가 3인칭 단수일 때는 doesn't have to로 쓴다.

A. return 되돌려주다
    pay 돈을 내다

B. bored 지루해하는
    go out 외출하다

have[has] to의 과거형은 had to로 표현한다.

C. make noise 떠들다
    during class 수업 중에

Unit 26 | may, should

· may: '~해도 좋다, ~일지도 모른다'라는 의미로 허락이나 추측을 나타내는 조동사이다. may는 주어와 상관없이 항상 같은 형태로 쓰며 뒤에는 동사원형이 온다.

허락	~해도 좋다	You **may** come to my house.
추측	~일지도 모른다	She **may** be a math teacher.

* may가 허락을 나타내는 의미로 쓰일 때는 can과 바꿔 쓸 수 있다.
  You **may** use my computer. = You **can** use my computer. 〈허락〉

· should: '해야 한다, ~하는 게 좋겠다'라는 의미로 의무나 충고를 나타내는 조동사이다. should는 주어와 상관없이 항상 같은 형태로 쓰며 뒤에는 동사원형이 온다.

의무, 충고	~해야 한다, ~하는 게 좋겠다	We **should** wear seat belts. You **should** not[shouldn't] pick flowers. You **should** exercise every day.

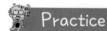 Practice

A. 다음 우리말과 뜻이 같도록 괄호 안에서 알맞은 것을 고르시오.

1. 너는 공공장소에서 조용히 해야 한다.
   → You (may / should) be quiet in public.

2. 우리는 미술관에서 어떤 것도 만져서는 안 된다.
   → We (may not / should not) touch anything in the gallery.

3. 너는 30분 동안 TV를 봐도 좋다.
   → You (may / should) watch TV for 30 minutes.

4. 내일 비가 올지도 모른다.
   → It (may / should) rain tomorrow.

B. 다음 문장에서 어색한 부분을 찾아 동그라미 하고 바르게 고치시오.

1. She not should talk about it. _____

2. Jim should loses his weight. _____

3. You play may computer games. _____

4. The news may not is true. _____

C. 다음 밑줄 친 부분에 유의하여 우리말로 해석하시오.

1. You <u>should listen</u> to others.
   → _____

2. She <u>may be late</u> for school.
   → _____

3. <u>May I borrow</u> your pen?
   → _____

unit 27 | 관용 표현

「would like to+동사원형」 =「want to+동사원형」	'하고 싶다' (소망을 나타냄)	I **would like to** invite you. = I **want to** invite you. *I would like to = I'd like to 〈축약형〉
「Would you like to+동사원형~?」	'하시겠어요?' (정중한 제안)	A: **Would you like to** join us for dinner? B: Yes, I would. / I'd like to, but I can't.
「had better+동사원형」	'~하는 것이 좋다' (충고나 조언)	You **had better** do your homework.
「had better not+동사원형」	'~안하는 것이 좋다' (had better 부정형)	I **had better not** go out now. *I had better = I'd better 〈축약형〉
「used to+동사원형」	'~하곤 했었다' '(전에는) ~이었다' (과거의 습관, 상태)	I **used to** walk to school. She **used to** have curly hair.

Practice

A. 다음 빈칸에 알맞은 말을 〈보기〉에서 골라 기호를 쓰시오.

> 〈보기〉 a. I'd better take a rest.
> b. I'd like to go on a picnic.
> c. I used to live in Seoul.

1. It's sunny today. _____

2. I feel sick. _____

3. _____ I live in Toronto now.

B. 다음 문장에서 <u>어색한</u> 부분을 찾아 동그라미 하고 바르게 고치시오.

1. I'd like to plays ping pong with her. _____

2. There used be a tall tree next to my house. _____

3. You had not better go out. _____

C. 다음 우리말과 뜻이 같도록 주어진 단어들을 알맞게 배열하시오.

1. 나는 아침에 운동을 하곤 했다. (exercise / the / to / used / morning / in)
   → I _____.

2. 우리와 함께 영화 보러 가실래요? (to / like / you / go / would)
   → _____ see a movie with us?

3. 너는 많은 물을 마시는 게 좋겠다. (water / better / had / lots of / drink).
   → You _____.

Grammar Tip

「used to+동사원형」은 과거의 습관이나 상태를 나타내는데 '지금은 ~하지 않고 있다, 지금은 ~이 없다'라는 의미를 가진다.

A. take a rest 쉬다

B. ping pong 탁구
next to ~의 옆에

C. go see a movie 영화 보러 가다
lots of 많은

A. 다음 밑줄 친 부분을 바르게 고쳐 쓰시오.

1. I will <u>visits</u> my aunt next week. ＿＿＿＿＿＿＿

2. <u>Do</u> he able to speak Chinese? ＿＿＿＿＿＿＿

3. Could you <u>turned</u> off the TV? ＿＿＿＿＿＿＿

4. You <u>don't should</u> cross the street here. ＿＿＿＿＿＿＿

B. 다음 두 문장이 같은 뜻이 되도록 빈칸에 알맞은 말을 쓰시오.

1. She can't play the piano.

= She ＿＿＿＿＿ ＿＿＿＿＿ ＿＿＿＿＿ play the piano.

2. You must go see a doctor.

= You ＿＿＿＿＿ ＿＿＿＿＿ go see a doctor.

3. You can have yogurt in the fridge.

= You ＿＿＿＿＿ have yogurt in the fridge.

4. I want to take a walk.

= I ＿＿＿＿＿ ＿＿＿＿＿ ＿＿＿＿＿ take a walk.

C. 다음 빈칸에 알맞은 말을 <보기>에서 골라 쓰시오.

> <보기> You don't have to order anything.
> You had better take an umbrella.
> You must not go to bed late.

1. You're often late for school. ＿＿＿＿＿＿＿＿＿＿＿

2. It's going to rain. ＿＿＿＿＿＿＿＿＿＿＿

3. There is lots of food here. ＿＿＿＿＿＿＿＿＿＿＿

D. 다음 우리말과 뜻이 같도록 빈칸에 알맞은 말을 쓰시오.

1. 그는 정기적으로 그 방을 청소해야만 했다.

→ He ＿＿＿＿＿ ＿＿＿＿＿ ＿＿＿＿＿ the room regularly.

2. Sally는 오늘 바쁠지도 모른다.

→ Sally ＿＿＿＿＿ ＿＿＿＿＿ busy today.

3. 나는 금발 머리를 가졌었다.

→ I ＿＿＿＿＿ ＿＿＿＿＿ ＿＿＿＿＿ blonde hair.

Grammar Tip

be able to가 있는 문장의 의문문은 「Be+주어+able to ～?」의 형태로 쓴다.

A. aunt 숙모
turn off ～을 끄다
cross 건너다

B. go see a doctor 병원에 가다
fridge 냉장고
take a walk 산책하다

C. order 주문하다

D. regularly 정기적으로, 규칙적으로
blonde hair 금발 머리

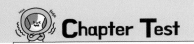

[1-2] 다음 빈칸에 알맞은 것을 고르시오.

1.
> We get up late. We _____ hurry.

① must ② cannot
③ may ④ won't
⑤ going to

2.
> You'd better _____ a scarf.

① wear ② wears
③ wearing ④ to wear
⑤ wore

3. **다음 두 문장의 뜻이 같도록 빈칸에 알맞은 것은?**

> I like to eat cheese, but now I don't eat.
> = I _____ eat cheese.

① had better ② used to
③ could ④ may
⑤ have to

4. **다음 중 어법상 어색한 것은?**
① She is going to swim tomorrow.
② He doesn't have to wash the dishes.
③ You not should run in the classroom.
④ Can I borrow your scissors?
⑤ Will you meet Jenny this weekend?

5. **다음 두 문장이 같은 뜻이 되도록 빈칸에 알맞은 말을 쓰시오.**

> He must do his homework before dinner.

= He _____ _____ do his homework before dinner.

6. **다음 빈칸에 공통으로 알맞은 것은?**

> · I _____ like to have cake for dessert.
> · _____ you close the window, please?

① will ② can
③ should ④ would
⑤ must

[7-8] 다음 밑줄 친 부분의 쓰임이 나머지 넷과 다른 것을 고르시오.

7. ① He <u>must</u> take a taxi.
② We <u>must</u> protect wild animals.
③ She <u>must</u> be a famous singer.
④ You <u>must</u> study hard for the test.
⑤ They <u>must</u> save water for the future.

8. ① <u>Can</u> I sit here?
② They <u>can</u> help you.
③ Susie <u>can</u> skate very well.
④ <u>Can</u> you remember his name?
⑤ She <u>can</u> solve the math problem.

9. 다음 두 문장의 의미가 <u>다른</u> 것은?

① I cannot ride a bike.
  = I'm not able to ride a bike.
② We must keep the rules.
  = We have to keep the rules.
③ May I join your team?
  = Can I join your team?
④ I want to buy new shoes.
  = I'd like to buy new shoes.
⑤ You don't have to go school today.
  = You must not go school today.

[10~11] 다음 대화의 빈칸에 알맞은 것을 고르시오.

10.
A: It's hot here. _____ I turn on the fan?
B: Sure.

① Have   ② May
③ Must   ④ Should
⑤ Am

11.
A: Do I have to take an umbrella?
B: No, you _____. The rain has stopped.

① can't   ② won't
③ shouldn't   ④ must not
⑤ don't have to

12. 다음 빈칸에 들어갈 알맞은 말을 쓰시오.

Julia was very busy all day.
She _____ be tired now.

13. 다음 중 나머지 넷과 의미가 <u>다른</u> 것은?

① You cannot eat in the library.
② You may not eat in the library.
③ You must not eat in the library.
④ You should not eat in the library.
⑤ You don't have to eat in the library.

14. 다음 밑줄 친 부분을 바르게 고친 것은?

A: Where is Henry?
B: I'm not sure. He <u>be</u> at the park.

① must be   ② should be
③ used be   ④ could be
⑤ may be

15. 다음 문장에서 어법상 <u>어색한</u> 부분을 찾아 바르게 고치시오.

You had not better call him.

_____ → _____

16. 다음 문장에 대한 충고로 알맞지 <u>않은</u> 것은?

I want to lose weight.

① You should not eat junk food.
② You should exercise regularly.
③ You should go jogging every day.
④ You should not eat anything at night.
⑤ You should not drink a lot of water.

17. 다음 우리말을 바르게 영작한 것은?

> 우리는 지난주에 그를 방문해야 했다.

① We must visit him last week.
② We used to visit him last week.
③ We had to visit him last week.
④ We had better visit him last week.
⑤ We were able to visit him last week.

18. 다음 빈칸에 들어갈 말이 바르게 짝지어진 것은?

> · You look bored. You _____ go find something exciting.
> · I _____ play the guitar, but I can now.

① used to – can't
② had better – couldn't
③ must – won't
④ should – have to
⑤ may – must

19. 다음 우리말과 뜻이 같도록 빈칸에 알맞은 것을 <u>모두</u> 고르면?

> 너는 지금 집에 가도 좋다.
> = You _____ go home now.

① can   ② will
③ should   ④ may
⑤ must

20. 다음 중 학교에서 지켜야 할 규칙으로 알맞지 <u>않은</u> 것은?

① You have to wear school uniform.
② You should do your homework.
③ You shouldn't run in the hallway.
④ You don't have to be late for school.
⑤ You must not use your cell phone during class.

〈서술형 문제〉

21. 다음 두 문장이 같은 뜻이 되도록 must를 이용하여 문장을 완성하시오.

> Don't talk loudly on the bus.

= You _____ talk loudly on the bus.

[22-23] 다음 우리말과 같도록 괄호 안의 단어들을 이용하여 문장을 완성하시오. (알맞은 조동사를 넣을 것)

22.

> 그는 어제 자전거를 탈 수 없었다.
> (ride / he / yesterday / bike / a)

→ _____

23.

> 나는 방과 후에 축구를 하곤 했다.
> (play / I / soccer / school / after)

→ _____

24. 다음 밑줄 친 부분에 대한 충고의 말을 should를 이용하여 <u>두 개</u> 쓰시오.

> I have some <u>bad habits</u>. I don't eat vegetables. I usually watch TV late at night.
> → You _____.
> → You _____.

25. 다음 상황에서 a girl이 극장에서 지켜야 할 규칙을 괄호 안의 단어들을 이용하여 문장을 완성하시오.

> Eric and his friend went to see a movie. Before the movie, they turned off their cell phones. But a girl behind Eric <u>talked someone on the phone</u>.

→ She _____.
(have to / turn)

분사란 무엇인가?

분사는 동사에 -ing(현재분사)나 -ed(과거분사)를 붙여 만든 형태로 문장에서 형용사로 쓰인다.

Look at the **sleeping** cat.

현재분사와 과거분사는 각각 어떤 역할을 하는가?

현재분사는 be동사와 함께 쓰여 진행형을 만들거나 능동, 진행의 의미로 명사를 수식한다. 과거분사는 be동사와 함께 쓰여 수동태를 만들거나 have 동사와 함께 쓰여 완료형을 만들고 수동, 완료의 의미로 명사를 수식한다.

Chapter 6. 분사

28 현재분사의 쓰임

- 현재분사 : 「동사원형＋-ing」의 형태로 '~하는, ~하고 있는'의 뜻으로 능동과 진행의 의미를 가진다.

명사 수식	명사의 앞이나 뒤에서 명사를 수식	Look at the **running** man. The man **running** at the park is my uncle.
진행형	be동사와 함께 쓰여 진행형을 만듦	We **are watching** the movie. Susie **is baking** bread in the kitchen.

- 현재분사와 동명사는 형태는 같지만 각각 다른 역할을 한다.
  현재분사는 '~하고 있는'의 뜻으로 동작이나 상태를 나타내고, 동명사는 '~하기 위한'의 뜻으로 목적이나 용도를 나타내며 문장에서 주어, 목적어, 보어의 역할을 한다.
  A **sleeping** baby is cute. 〈현재분사 – 진행〉
  This **sleeping** bag is very warm. 〈동명사 – 용도〉

Practice

A. 다음 괄호 안의 말을 알맞은 형태로 바꿔 쓰시오.
1. My aunt is ＿＿＿＿＿＿＿＿＿ pictures. (take)
2. Jenny is ＿＿＿＿＿＿＿＿＿ her dog in the garden. (walk)
3. The boy ＿＿＿＿＿＿＿＿＿ on the stage is my brother. (dance)
4. He looks at the ＿＿＿＿＿＿＿＿＿ kite on the hill. (fly)

B. 다음 밑줄 친 부분이 현재분사인지 동명사인지 쓰시오.
1. My hobby is playing badminton. ＿＿＿＿＿＿＿
2. Eric is reading the novel. ＿＿＿＿＿＿＿
3. The guests are in the waiting room. ＿＿＿＿＿＿＿
4. The woman wearing glasses is Susan. ＿＿＿＿＿＿＿

C. 다음 우리말과 뜻이 같도록 주어진 단어들을 알맞게 배열하시오.
1. Sarah는 일기를 쓰고 있다. (diary / is / a / writing)
   → Sarah ＿＿＿＿＿＿＿＿＿＿＿＿＿＿＿＿＿＿＿.
2. 미소 짓고 있는 여자는 나의 엄마이다. (smiling / is / woman / the)
   → ＿＿＿＿＿＿＿＿＿＿＿＿＿＿＿＿ my mom.
3. 그 강아지는 바닥에서 자고 있다. (floor / sleeping / on / is / the)
   → The puppy ＿＿＿＿＿＿＿＿＿＿＿＿＿＿＿＿.

Grammar Tip
현재분사가 단독으로 명사를 수식할 때는 명사 앞에 위치하고 수식어구와 함께 쓰이면 명사 뒤에 위치한다.

A. kite 연
hill 언덕

B. hobby 취미
waiting room 대기실

C. write a diary 일기를 쓰다
floor 바닥

Unit 29 과거분사의 쓰임

- 과거분사 :「동사원형+-ed」의 형태로 '~된, ~받는'의 뜻을 나타내며 수동과 완료의 의미를 가진다.

명사 수식	명사의 앞이나 뒤에서 명사를 수식	There is a **broken** dish on the floor. She is carrying a box **filled** with flowers.
완료형과 수동태	have 동사와 함께 쓰여 완료형, be동사와 함께 쓰여 수동태를 만듦	I **have known** Brian for ten years. The book **is written** by Carol.

- 과거분사는 보통 「동사원형+-ed」의 형태이지만 불규칙 변화하는 경우도 있다.

  break–broken, write–written, make–made, know–known, send–sent, speak–spoken ...

Practice

A. 다음 괄호 안에서 알맞은 것을 고르시오.

1. (Baking / Baked) onions taste sweet.

2. He bought a (using / used) car.

3. Look at the (breaking / broken) window.

4. They know the (smiling / smiled) boy.

B. 다음 빈칸에 알맞은 말을 〈보기〉에서 골라 알맞은 형태로 쓰시오.

〈보기〉 write	boil	cover	make

1. Julie ate two _____ eggs.

2. I read a book _____ in Chinese.

3. The mountain is _____ with snow.

4. He is looking for a table _____ of wood.

C. 다음 우리말과 뜻이 같도록 빈칸에 알맞은 말을 쓰시오.

1. Cindy에 의해 보내진 선물은 지갑이었다.

   → The gift _____ by Cindy was a purse.

2. 그는 그때 잠긴 문을 열 수 없었다.

   → He couldn't open the _____ door then.

3. 그들은 그들의 아빠가 요리한 음식을 좋아한다.

   → They like food _____ by their dad.

30 분사의 명사 수식

Unit

- 현재분사나 과거분사가 단독으로 쓰여 명사를 수식할 때는 명사 앞에 위치한다.

We look at the **crying** baby.

There are **fallen** leaves on the street.

- 현재분사나 과거분사가 목적어, 부사구, 보어 등의 수식어구와 함께 쓰이면 명사 뒤에 위치한다.

The girl **lying** on the bed is Jenny.

Sally bought a jacket **made** in France.

Practice

A. 다음 괄호 안의 분사가 들어갈 곳을 고르시오.

1. The ① boys ② soccer are ③ my classmates. (playing)

2. This ① is the ② wallet ③. (stolen)

3. I know the ① student ② a yellow ③ skirt. (wearing)

4. The ① fence ② in pink ③ is pretty. (painted)

B. 다음 밑줄 친 부분을 우리말로 해석하시오.

1. Look at the rising sun!　　→ _____

2. Who is the man reading a book?　　→ _____

3. This house built 100 years ago looks great.　→ _____

C. 다음 우리말과 뜻이 같도록 주어진 단어들을 알맞게 배열하시오.

1. 그는 깨진 꽃병을 청소하고 있다.

(the / cleaning / broken / is / vase / up)

→ He _____.

2. 나는 중고 자전거가 필요하다. (bicycle / a / used / need)

→ I _____.

3. 피자를 먹고 있는 소녀는 나의 여동생이다.

(eating / girl / pizza / the / is)

→ _____ my sister.

4. 그녀는 영어로 쓰인 책들을 읽는 것을 좋아한다.

(books / in / written / English)

→ She likes reading _____.

Grammar Tip

A. stolen steal의 과거분사형, 훔친
fence 울타리

현재분사는 능동과 진행의 의미(~한)로 해석하고 과거분사는 수동과 완료의 의미(~된)로 해석한다.

B. rise 뜨다
build 짓다, 건설하다

C. vase 꽃병

31 | 감정을 나타내는 분사

· 사람의 감정을 나타내는 동사의 현재분사와 과거분사는 형용사로 쓰이는 경우가 있다.
주어가 감정을 유발할 때는 현재분사를 쓰고, 주어가 감정을 느낄 때는 과거분사를 쓴다.

현재분사(~하게 하는) – 주어가 감정을 유발할 때	과거분사(~하게 된) – 주어가 감정을 느낄 때
interesting	interested
boring	bored
exciting	excited
surprising	surprised
shocking	shocked
satisfying	satisfied
disappointing	disappointed

The movie was **exciting**.   I was **excited** at the movie.

Practice

A. 다음 괄호 안에서 알맞은 것을 고르시오.

1. He was (surprising / surprised) by the news.

2. Their magic show was (amazing / amazed).

3. I'm (interesting / interested) in cooking.

4. The result was (disappointing / disappointed).

B. 다음 괄호 안에 주어진 말을 빈칸에 알맞은 형태로 쓰시오.

1. His speech was _____ at that time. (bore)

2. She is _____ about the picnic. (excite)

3. I think this story is _____. (interest)

4. Children saw the accident. They were _____. (shock)

C. 다음 문장에서 어색한 부분을 찾아 동그라미 하고 바르게 고치시오.

1. I wasn't satisfying with my grade.   _____

2. She was watching an excited soccer game.   _____

3. Judy met an interested boy yesterday.   _____

4. I couldn't sleep well, so I'm very tiring.   _____

Grammar Tip

A. amaze 놀라게 하다
result 결과

B. speech 연설
accident 사고

현재분사는 감정의 원인이 되는 일이 주어이거나 그 일을 꾸며 줄 때 쓰고 과거분사는 주로 사람을 주어로 하여 느끼는 감정을 표현할 때 쓴다.

C. grade 성적

65

Unit 32 | 분사구문

- 분사구문 : 현재분사를 사용하여 부사절을 간단하게 부사구로 만든 것을 가리킨다.
- 분사구문을 만드는 법 : ① 접속사를 생략한다. ② 주어를 생략한다. ③ 부사절의 동사를 「동사원형＋-ing」의 형태로 바꾼다.

Because Anne was sick, she was absent from school today.
  ↓   ↓   ↓
  ×   ×   Being sick, she was absent from school today.

- 분사구문은 때, 이유, 양보, 조건, 동시동작, 연속동작 등의 다양한 의미를 나타낸다.

때	When I arrived at home, I felt hungry. = **Arriving** at home, I felt hungry.
이유	Because I got up late, I missed the train. = **Getting** up late, I missed the train.
양보	Though he was rich, he was not happy. = **Being** rich, he was not happy.
조건	If you turn right, you'll see the hospital. = **Turning** right, you'll see the hospital.
동시동작	While he was watching TV, he fell asleep. = **Watching** TV, he fell asleep.
연속동작	He left for London at six, and he arrived there at ten. = He left for London at six, **arriving** there at ten.

Practice

A. 다음 밑줄 친 부분을 분사구문으로 바꿔 쓰시오.

1. When she heard the news, she was very suprised.
   = _____, she was very suprised.

2. Because I had a headache, I went see a doctor.
   = _____, I went see a doctor.

3. Though he ate lunch, he still felt hungry.
   = _____, he still felt hungry.

B. 다음 두 문장이 같은 뜻이 되도록 괄호 안의 말을 이용하여 문장을 바꿔 쓰시오.

1. Being busy, Jimmy didn't go camping. (because)
   = _____, he didn't go camping.

2. Reading a comic book, I ate some snacks. (while)
   = _____, I ate some snacks.

3. Studying harder, you'll get good grades. (if)
   = _____, you'll get good grades.

C. 다음 밑줄 친 부분을 우리말로 해석하시오.

1. Feeling tired, I went to bed early. → _____

2. Smiling brightly, she ran to Jim. → _____

3. Turning left, you'll find a drugstore. → _____

Grammar Tip

A. headache 두통

부사절의 동사가 진행형인 문장을 분사구문으로 바꿀 때는 Being을 생략하고 「동사원형＋-ing」를 쓴다.
While he **was drinking** water, he took a walk.
= **Drinking** water, he took a walk.

B. snack 간식

C. drugstore 약국

 **Review Test**

A. 다음 빈칸에 알맞은 말을 <보기>에서 골라 알맞은 형태로 쓰시오.

<보기>	use	throw	bake	swim

1. Look at those _____ kids at the beach.

2. They ate _____ potatoes for breakfast.

3. He bought a _____ camera last month.

4. Do you know the girl _____ a ball?

B. 다음 우리말과 뜻이 같도록 주어진 단어들을 바르게 배열하시오.

1. 저 소파에 앉아 있는 남자는 나의 삼촌이다.
   (sofa / man / that / sitting / on / the)
   → _____ is my uncle.

2. 나는 스페인어로 쓰인 시를 몇 편 읽었다.
   (written / poems / in / some / Spanish)
   → I read _____.

3. 나는 피아노 수업을 듣는 그 소녀를 알고 있다.
   (a / girl / taking / the / lesson / piano)
   → I know _____.

4. 저 깨진 접시들을 조심해. (broken / plates / those)
   → Be careful of _____.

C. 다음 괄호 안에 주어진 말을 빈칸에 알맞은 형태로 쓰시오.

1. The city has an _____ amusement park. (amaze)

2. I think science is an _____ subject. (interest)

3. We were _____ at the baseball game. (excite)

4. Brian is sometimes _____ with his job. (bore)

D. 다음 두 문장이 같은 뜻이 되도록 분사구문으로 바꿔 쓰시오.

1. Because I don't have enough money, I can't go shopping.
   = _____, I can't go shopping.

2. Though I drink cold water, I still feel hot.
   = _____, I still feel hot.

3. While he was cleaning the room, he listened to music.
   = _____, he listened to music.

4. When she came home, she was very sleepy.
   = _____, she was very sleepy.

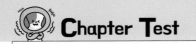

[1-2] 다음 빈칸에 알맞은 것을 고르시오.

1.
> Do you know the woman _____ coffee over there?

① drink   ② drinks
③ drinking   ④ is drinking
⑤ dranks

2.
> Look at the _____ mirror.

① break   ② breaks
③ breaking   ④ broken
⑤ to break

3. 다음 빈칸에 공통으로 알맞은 것은?

> · Students are _____ in the room.
> · The girl _____ on the stage is Judy.

① sing   ② sings
③ singing   ④ sang
⑤ to sing

4. 다음 밑줄 친 부분의 쓰임이 나머지 넷과 다른 것은?
① I know the man selling hot dogs.
② She enjoyed playing badminton.
③ It was a really boring comic book.
④ I saw a swimming boy in the lake.
⑤ The boy holding a ball is my brother.

[5-6] 다음 대화의 빈칸에 들어갈 말이 바르게 짝지어진 것을 고르시오.

5.
> A: Why are the children _____?
> B: The soccer game is really _____.

① exciting − exciting
② exciting − excited
③ excited − exciting
④ excited − excited
⑤ excite − exciting

6.
> A: Are you _____ in history?
> B: No, I'm not. I think math is an _____ subject.

① interesting − interesting
② interested − interested
③ interesting − interested
④ interested − interesting
⑤ to interest − interesting

7. 다음 괄호 안의 단어를 알맞은 형태로 바꿔 쓰시오.

> His performance was very _____. (disappoint)

_____

[8-9] 다음 단어가 들어갈 알맞은 위치를 고르시오.

8.
> playing

The ① girl ② the piano ③ is ④ my friend Lisa ⑤.

9.
> locked

Could ① you ② open ③ this ④ window ⑤?

[10-11] 다음 우리말과 뜻이 같도록 빈칸에 알맞은 것을 고르시오.

10.

> 나는 샌드위치를 만들기 위해 삶은 달걀 몇 개가 필요하다.
> → I need some _____ eggs to make sandwiches.

① boil　　　　② to boil
③ boiling　　　④ boiled
⑤ boils

11.

> 그녀는 그 소식에 놀랐다.
> → She was _____ at the news.

① surprise　　　② surprising
③ surprised　　　④ surprises
⑤ be surprising

12. 다음 중 어법상 어색한 것은?
① The concert was amazing.
② Yesterday was a tired day.
③ We were bored with the movie.
④ The food at the restaurant is satisfying.
⑤ They were excited by the party.

13. 다음 두 문장을 한 문장으로 쓸 때 빈칸에 알맞은 것은?

> This is an interesting book. + It is written by Andrew.
> = This is an interesting book _____ by Andrew.

① write　　　　② writing
③ writes　　　　④ wrote
⑤ written

[14-15] 다음 두 문장의 뜻이 같도록 빈칸에 알맞은 것을 고르시오.

14.

> When he met Jenny, he gave her some flowers.
> = _____ Jenny, he gave her some flowers.

① Meet　　　　② Being meet
③ Meeting　　　④ Met
⑤ To meet

15.

> Taking a walk, I looked up at the stars.
> = _____, I looked up at the stars.

① Because I was taking a walk
② While I was taking a walk
③ Though I was taking a walk
④ If I was taking a walk
⑤ After I was taking a walk

[16-17] 다음 우리말을 바르게 영작한 것을 고르시오.

16.

> 그는 영화를 보면서 팝콘을 먹고 있다.

① Watch a movie, he is eating popcorn.
② Watching a movie, he is eating popcorn.
③ To watch a movie, he is eating popcorn.
④ Watched a movie, he is eating popcorn.
⑤ Being watching a movie, he is eating popcorn.

17.

> 나는 나무로 만든 자동차를 보았다.

① I saw the car made of wood.
② I saw the car making of wood.
③ I saw the made of wood car.
④ I saw the wood car made of.
⑤ I saw made of wood the car.

18. 다음 두 문장이 같은 뜻이 되도록 빈칸에 알맞은 말을 쓰시오.

> Because I was busy, I canceled the picnic.

= _____ busy, I canceled the picnic.

19. 다음 밑줄 친 부분을 바르게 고친 것은?

> His behavior at the party was shock.

① shocked　　　　② shocking
③ shocks　　　　　④ to shock
⑤ have shocked

20. 다음 문장의 밑줄 친 부분을 부사절로 바꿔 쓸 때, 빈칸에 알맞은 것은?

> Being tired, he came home early.
> = _____, he came home early.

① And he was tired
② While he was tired
③ If he was tired
④ Because he was tired
⑤ Though he was tired

〈서술형 문제〉

21. 다음 우리말과 뜻이 같도록 주어진 단어들을 이용하여 문장을 완성하시오. (동사의 형태를 바르게 바꿀 것)

> 축구를 하고 있는 저 남자는 매우 유명한 배우이다.
> (soccer / man / actor / is / the / famous / play / a / .)

→ _____

22. 다음 대화에서 어법상 어색한 부분을 찾아 바르게 고치시오.

> A: How was the concert?
> B: It was very interested. All the people at the concert were very excited.
> A: I'd like to see it some day.

_____ → _____

23. 다음 〈보기〉와 같이 두 문장을 한 문장으로 바꿔 쓰시오.

> 〈보기〉
> I don't know the woman. + The woman is talking to them.
> = I don't know the woman talking to them.

I like this chocolate cake. + This is made by my mom.
= _____

24. 다음 문장과 같은 뜻이 되도록 분사구문을 이용하여 문장을 쓰시오.

> While he was listening to music, he cooked dinner.

= _____

25. 다음 문장과 같은 뜻이 되도록 괄호 안의 단어를 이용하여 바꿔 쓰시오.

> Having a bad cold, she had to get some rest. (because)

= _____

수동태란 무엇인가?
주어가 동작을 행하는 경우를 능동태라 하고 동작의 대상이 주어
가 되어 어떠한 행위를 당하는 경우를 나타낼 때 수동태라 한다.
This novel **was written by** Hemingway.

수동태는 어떻게 나타내는가?
수동태는 「be동사+과거분사(p.p) ~ by+행위자(목적격)」의 형태
로 쓴다.

Chapter 7. 수동태

33 수동태의 쓰임과 형태

· 능동태는 행위자가 주어가 되어 어떠한 동작을 스스로 하는 것을 나타내고, 수동태는 행위의 대상이 주어가 되어 '~되다, ~당하다'의 의미를 나타낸다.

· 수동태 만드는 법
  ① 능동태의 목적어(행위의 대상)를 수동태의 주어로 한다.
  ② 능동태의 동사를 「be동사+과거분사(p.p)」의 형태로 바꾼다.
     be동사의 시제는 능동태의 시제와 일치시킨다.
  ③ 능동태의 주어(행위자)를 「by+행위자(목적격)」의 형태로 문장의 끝에 놓는다.

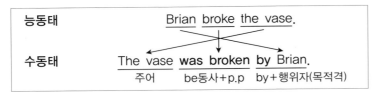

능동태	Brian broke the vase.
수동태	The vase **was broken** by Brian.
	주어 　 be동사+p.p　 by+행위자(목적격)

· 수동태에서 행위자가 일반인이거나 밝힐 필요가 없을 때 「by+행위자(목적격)」는 생략할 수 있다.
English **is spoken** all over the world (by people).

Practice

A. 다음 괄호 안에서 알맞은 것을 고르시오.

1. This book is (loving / loved) by students.
2. The cookies were (making / made) by her.
3. Smart phones are (using / used) by many people.
4. This music was (writing / written) in 2015.

B. 다음 문장에서 어색한 부분을 찾아 바르게 고치시오.

1. This building was built by he. _____
2. The plant is grew by the farmer. _____
3. The car is washing by my dad. _____
4. The guitar was play by Jenny. _____

C. 다음 두 문장이 같은 뜻이 되도록 능동태는 수동태로, 수동태는 능동태로 바꿔 쓰시오.

1. Alex repaired the computer.
   → The computer _____.

2. He cleaned the room.
   → The room _____.

3. The telephone was invented by Bell.
   → Bell _____.

4. Jim's backpack was found by her.
   → She _____.

Grammar Tip

수동태는 행위를 당하는 대상을 강조하거나 행위자를 모르는 경우에 주로 사용하는 문장 형태이다.

B. plant 식물

C. repair 수리하다
invent 발명하다

34 수동태의 시제

- 수동태의 시제는 be동사로 나타낸다.
  ① 수동태의 현재시제 : 「be동사의 현재형(am/are/is)+과거분사」
     The bike **is repaired by** Denis. ← Denis <u>repairs</u> the bike. 〈능동태〉
  ② 수동태의 과거시제 : 「be동사의 과거형(was/were)+과거분사」
     The bike **was repaired by** Denis. ← Denis <u>repaired</u> the bike. 〈능동태〉
  ③ 수동태의 미래시제 : 「will+be+과거분사」
     The bike **will be repaired by** Denis. ← Denis <u>will repair</u> the bike. 〈능동태〉

Practice

A. 다음 괄호 안에서 알맞은 것을 고르시오.

1. The biscuits (are baked / were baked) by Kate yesterday.

2. The movie (is released / will be released) next week.

3. This big tower (is built / was built) last year.

4. The wall (was painted / will be painted) tomorrow.

B. 다음 문장을 수동태로 바꿔 쓰시오.

1. Susan will send the parcel.
   → _____

2. My mom made some sandwiches.
   → _____

3. Many young people love this song.
   → _____

C. 다음 우리말과 뜻이 같도록 주어진 단어를 이용하여 문장을 완성하시오.

1. 그 장소는 매일 많은 관광객들에 의해 방문되고 있다. (visit)
   → The place _____ _____ by many tourists every day.

2. 이 책은 학생들에 의해 출판될 것이다. (publish)
   → This book _____ _____ _____ by students.

3. 그 소녀는 어제 경찰에 의해 발견되었다. (find)
   → The girl _____ _____ by the police yesterday.

4. 두 마리의 개가 자원봉사자들에 의해 구조되었다. (save)
   → Two dogs _____ _____ by volunteers.

Grammar Tip

A. biscuit 비스킷
release 개봉하다, 공개하다

조동사 뒤에는 동사원형이 와야 하므로 미래시제의 수동태에서는 will 뒤에 원형 be를 써야 한다.

B. parcel 소포

C. tourist 관광객
publish 출판하다
save 구하다
volunteer 자원봉사자

35 | 수동태의 부정문과 의문문

- 수동태의 부정문 : 「be동사+not+과거분사~by+목적격」

  This dress **was not designed by** Angela.

  The book **isn't written by** him.

- 의문사가 없는 수동태의 의문문 : 「Be동사+주어+과거분사~by+목적격?」

  Was this picture **taken by** Sue? – Yes, it **was**. / No, it **wasn't**.

  Were the letters **sent** to them? – Yes, they **were**. / No, they **weren't**.

- 의문사가 있는 수동태의 의문문 : 「의문사+be동사+주어+과거분사~by+목적격?」

  When **was** the seed **planted**? – It **was planted** yesterday.

  Where **were** the glasses **found**? – They **were found** under the bed.

Practice

A. 다음 주어진 단어들을 바르게 배열하시오.

1. Bananas _____ in cold areas. (not, grown, are)

2. The problems _____ by Jack. (solved, were, not)

3. Fred _____ at the party. (not, was, invited)

4. The cat _____ care of by Henry. (taken, not, is)

B. 다음 대화의 빈칸에 알맞은 말을 쓰시오.

1. *A*: _____ some bread _____ by Kate?

   B: Yes, it was. She ate it well.

2. *A*: _____ the bike _____ by Jane?

   B: No, it _____. It was fixed by Jason.

3. *A*: _____ _____ the email _____?

   B: It was sent last night.

C. 다음 문장을 괄호 안의 지시대로 바꿔 쓰시오.

1. The drama was written by Shakespeare. (부정문으로)

   → _____

2. The light bulb was invented by Edison. (의문문으로)

   → _____

3. Was the mushroom soup made by Lisa? (When을 넣어서)

   → _____

Grammar Tip

A. area 지역

problem 문제

solve 풀다, 해결하다

invite 초대하다

의문사가 없는 수동태의 의문문에 대한 대답은 긍정일 때는 「Yes, 주어+be동사」, 부정일 때는 「No, 주어+be동사+not」으로 답한다.

B. fix 고치다, 수리하다

C. light bulb 전구

mushroom 버섯

36 | 조동사가 있는 수동태

· 조동사가 있는 수동태 : 「조동사+be+과거분사~by+목적격」

조동사 뒤에는 동사원형이 와야 하므로 be동사는 주어의 인칭과 수에 상관없이 항상 원형 be로 쓴다.

The nature **should be protected by** us. ← We should protect the nature. 〈능동태〉

This math problem **can be solved by** Wendy. ← Wendy can solve this math problem. 〈능동태〉

The magic show **may be seen by** them today. ← They may see the magic show today. 〈능동태〉

· 조동사가 있는 수동태의 부정은 조동사 뒤에 not을 쓴다. 「조동사+not+be+과거분사~by+목적격」

The trash **should not be thrown** on the street.

Practice

A. 다음 우리말과 뜻이 같도록 괄호 안에서 알맞은 것을 고르시오.

1. 이 방은 Mike에 의해 청소되어야 한다.
   → This room (is / should be) cleaned by Mike.

2. 많은 악기들이 그녀에 의해 연주될 수 있다.
   → Many musical instruments can (play / be played) by her.

3. 너의 개는 여기 데려와서는 안 된다.
   → Your dog (should not / not should) be brought here.

B. 다음 문장에서 <u>어색한</u> 부분을 찾아 동그라미 하고 바르게 고치시오.

1. The promise should is kept. _____

2. His secret must be not told. _____

3. Your money can be save. _____

4. A new house is will built by Carol. _____

5. The party can is held by them. _____

C. 다음 괄호 안에 주어진 조동사를 넣어 문장을 다시 쓰시오.

1. A lot of flowers are used for the wedding. (will)
   → _____.

2. The truck is sold by an old man. (may)
   → _____.

3. The task is finished by her. (should)
   → _____.

4. The rules are followed by students. (must)
   → _____.

Grammar Tip

A. musical instrument 악기
bring 데려오다

조동사의 부정문을 수동태로 만들 때는 조동사 뒤에 not을 쓰면 된다.

B. promise 약속
secret 비밀

C. wedding 결혼식
task 업무, 일

A. 다음 빈칸에 알맞은 것을 <보기>에서 골라 알맞은 형태로 쓰시오.

<보기>	use	tell	build	play

1. This bridge was _____ by Mr. Green.
2. The piano is _____ by my sister.
3. Sugar is _____ in many kinds of food.
4. His story was _____ by the reporters.

B. 다음 문장에서 어색한 부분을 바르게 고치시오.
1. Young people is loved her design.   _____ → _____
2. The letter was sent by his.   _____ → _____
3. The festival was hold yesterday.   _____ → _____
4. Wild animals should be protect by us.   _____ → _____

C. 다음 우리말과 뜻이 같도록 괄호 안의 단어들을 바르게 배열하시오.
1. 영어가 전 세계에서 말해지고 있니? (spoken / is / English)
   → _____ all over the world?
2. 나의 휴대 전화가 어디서 발견되었니?
   (was / my / found / cell phone / where)
   → _____?
3. 이 소설은 Charles에 의해 쓰이지 않았다.
   (by / not / written / Charles / was)
   → This novel _____.
4. 많은 사진이 외국인들에 의해 찍힐 수 있다.
   (can / taken / by / foreigners / be)
   → Many pictures _____.

D. 다음 두 문장이 같은 뜻이 되도록 수동태로 바꿔 쓰시오.
1. Koreans make these cars.
   = _____ Koreans.
2. Children should not touch this machine.
   = _____ by children.
3. He caught the rabbit yesterday.
   = _____ yesterday.
4. The young man will finish the project.
   = _____ the young man.

Unit 37 4형식 문장의 수동태

· 4형식 문장은 직접목적어와 간접목적어를 주어로 하여 두 개의 수동태 문장으로 만들 수 있다. 직접목적어를 주어로 하는 경우에는 간접목적어 앞에 전치사 to, for, of를 쓴다.

My mom gave <u>me</u> <u>a skirt</u>.
            간접목적어 직접목적어

→ I **was given** a skirt by my mom. 〈간접목적어 주어〉

→ A skirt **was given to** me by my mom. 〈직접목적어 주어〉

· send, buy, make, get, cook 등의 동사는 직접목적어를 주어로 하는 수동태만 만들 수 있다.

Henry bought me a pen.

→ I was bought a pen by Henry. (×) 〈간접목적어 주어〉

→ A pen **was bought for** me by Henry. (○) 〈직접목적어 주어〉

Practice

A. 다음 괄호 안에서 알맞은 것을 고르시오.

1. A new backpack was bought (to me / for me) by Tony.

2. He (gave / was given) a camera by his sister.

3. A beautiful dress was (making / made) for Ann by her mom.

4. Some flowers were sent (to her / for her) by Peter.

B. 다음 빈칸에 알맞은 것을 〈보기〉에서 골라 알맞은 형태로 쓰시오.

〈보기〉 ask	cook	show	teach

1. English is _____ to children by Sue.

2. Soup was _____ for us by my aunt.

3. Some questions were _____ of me by him.

4. We were _____ an envelope by David.

C. 다음 문장을 두 가지 형태의 수동태로 바꿔 쓰시오.

1. She told us an interesting story.
   → We _____.
   → An interesting story _____.

2. Robert gave me a nice gift.
   → I _____.
   → A nice gift _____.

Grammar Tip

4형식 문장을 직접목적어를 주어로 하는 수동태로 바꿀 때 간접목적어 앞에 쓰는 전치사는 동사에 따라 달라진다.
to를 쓰는 동사 :
give, send, teach, tell ...
for를 쓰는 동사 :
make, cook, buy, get ...
of를 쓰는 동사 : ask

A. backpack 가방

B. envelope 봉투

give, show, tell, ask, tell, teach 등의 수여동사는 2가지 형태의 수동태를 만들 수 있다.

C. gift 선물

38 | 5형식 문장의 수동태

- 목적격 보어가 명사, 형용사, to부정사인 5형식 문장은 목적어를 주어로 바꾸고, 목적격 보어를 「be동사+과거분사」 뒤에 그대로 써주어 수동태 문장으로 바꿀 수 있다.

  They call the baby Luna. 〈능동태〉 → The baby **is called** Luna by them. 〈수동태〉
  　　　　　목적어　　목적격보어

  I asked him to open the window. 〈능동태〉 → He **was asked** to open the window **by** me. 〈수동태〉

- 목적격 보어가 동사원형인 지각동사나 사역동사가 쓰인 5형식 문장은 목적어를 주어로 바꾸고, 목적격 보어인 동사원형을 to부정사의 형태로 바꾸어 「be동사+과거분사」 뒤에 써주면 수동태 문장으로 바꿀 수 있다.

  I saw him play the baseball. 〈능동태〉 → He **was seen** to play the baseball **by** me. 〈수동태〉
  지각동사 목적어 목적격보어

  My mom made me clean the room. 〈능동태〉 → I **was made** to clean the room **by** my mom. 〈수동태〉
  　　　　사역동사

Practice

A. 다음 문장을 수동태로 바꿔 쓰시오.

1. The people believe Ken honest.
   → _____

2. My parents called him a genius.
   → _____

3. We helped Amy carry the desk.
   → _____

B. 다음 우리말 뜻과 같도록 주어진 단어들을 알맞게 배열하시오.

1. 그녀의 아들은 그녀에 의해 그 책을 복사하게 되었다.
   (made / was / to / the book / copy)
   → Her son _____ by her.

2. 그들은 나에 의해 그 문제를 풀 것을 요청받았다.
   (solve / problem / asked / by / to / me / the / were)
   → They _____.

3. 그가 우는 것이 내게 보였다. (cry / was / to / by / seen / me)
   → He _____.

C. 다음 우리말 뜻과 같도록 주어진 단어들을 이용하여 문장을 완성하시오.

1. 그 코트는 나를 따뜻하게 해 주었다. (keep, warm)
   → I _____ _____ _____ by the coat.

2. 그는 그녀로부터 운동을 하라는 충고를 들었다. (advise, exercise)
   → He _____ _____ _____ _____ by her.

3. 그녀는 수영하는 것이 우리에게 목격되었다. (see, swim)
   → She _____ _____ to _____ by us.

39 동사구의 수동태

- 동사구가 있는 문장을 수동태로 바꿀 때는 동사구를 하나의 동사로 취급하므로 동사구의 전치사를 빠뜨리지 않도록 주의해야 한다.

Jenny <u>takes care of</u> the dog. → The dog **is taken** care of **by** Jenny.

My brother <u>gave up</u> the race. → The race **was given up by** my brother.

- 자주 쓰는 동사구

turn on ~을 켜다	laugh at ~을 비웃다	run over (차가) ~을 치다
turn off ~을 끄다	look for ~을 찾다	give up ~을 포기하다
take care of ~을 돌보다	look after ~을 돌보다	put off ~을 연기하다
ask for ~을 요청하다	look up to ~을 존경하다	bring up ~을 양육하다

Practice

A. 다음 괄호 안에서 알맞은 것을 고르시오.

1. My cell phone was turned (off by / of by) me.

2. The children are (looked for / looked after) by the woman.

3. His concert will be put (off by / on by) them.

4. The players were laughed (at by / of by) him.

B. 다음 우리말 뜻과 같도록 주어진 단어들을 알맞게 배열하시오.

1. Sam에 의해 전등이 켜졌다. (on / was / by / Sam / turned)

   → The light _____.

2. 젊은 남자가 차에 치었다. (car / over / by / run / was / a)

   → A young man _____.

3. 그 선생님은 학생들에게 존경을 받는다.

   (looked / by / up / is / students / to)

   → The teacher _____.

C. 다음 문장을 수동태로 바꿔 쓰시오.

1. She brought up her nephew.

   → _____

2. Our team gave up the game.

   → _____

3. I take care of my little brother.

   → _____

4. We looked for a new house.

   → _____

Grammar Tip

A. player 선수

길이가 긴 동사구도 하나의 단어로 취급하므로 자주 쓰는 동사구는 외워두는 것이 좋다.

B. light 전등

C. nephew 남자 조카

unit 40 | by+행위자 생략

· 「by+행위자」를 생략하는 수동태 : 수동태에서 행동의 주체인 행위자가 일반인이거나 중요하지 않은 경우, 또는 행위자를 알 수 없는 경우에는 「by+행위자」를 생략할 수 있다.

The Internet **is used** all over the world.   My purse **was stolen** on the subway.
These cookies **are sold** at the bakery.

· by 이외에 다른 전치사를 쓰는 수동태 : 수동태 문장에서 일반적으로 「by+행위자」로 나타내는데 by 대신에 다른 전치사를 쓰는 경우가 있다.

She **is satisfied with** the result.

be covered with ~으로 덮여 있다	be worried about ~을 걱정하다
be interested in ~에 관심 있다	be crowded with ~로 붐비다
be surprised at ~에 놀라다	be known to ~에게 알려져 있다
be filled with ~로 가득 차다	be known for ~로 유명하다
be satisfied with ~에 만족하다	be made of ~로 만들어지다
be disappointed with ~에 실망하다	be made from ~로 만들어지다

Practice

A. 다음 문장에서 생략할 수 있는 부분에 밑줄을 그으시오.

1. English is spoken in many countries by people.
2. This castle was built in 1890 by someone.
3. The pretty girl was called Emma by us.

B. 다음 빈칸에 알맞은 것을 〈보기〉에서 골라 쓰시오.

〈보기〉 at   of   with   about   for

1. The mountain is covered _____ snow.
2. Many people were surprised _____ the news.
3. The chef is known _____ steak.
4. This table is made _____ wood.
5. My mom worried _____ my health.

C. 다음 우리말 뜻과 같도록 주어진 단어들을 이용하여 문장을 완성하시오.

1. 그 방은 풍선으로 가득 찼다. (fill)
   → The room is _____ _____ balloons.
2. 치즈는 우유로 만들어진다. (make)
   → Cheese is _____ _____ milk.
3. 나는 그의 태도에 실망했다. (disappoint)
   → I _____ _____ _____ his behavior.

A. 다음 문장에서 <u>어색한</u> 부분을 바르게 고치시오.

1. A red dress was given for her by Mike. _____

2. The kids were made doing their homework by her. _____

3. Wendy was seen run at the park. _____

4. This blouse is made from silk. _____

B. 다음 우리말과 뜻이 같도록 괄호 안의 단어들을 바르게 배열하시오.

1. 그 소년은 우리들에게 영웅이라 불렸다. (a / called / hero / was)
→ The boy _____ by us.

2. 그들이 노래를 부르는 소리가 내게 들렸다. (to / heard / sing / were)
→ They _____ a song by me.

3. 그가 우리에게 맛있는 음식을 요리해 주었다.
(for / cooked / by / him / was / us)
→ Delicious food _____.

4. Cindy는 그녀의 이모에 의해 돌봐 진다.
(taken / her / is / aunt / by / of / care)
→ Cindy _____.

C. 다음 빈칸에 알맞은 것을 <보기>에서 골라 알맞은 형태로 쓰시오.

<보기>	satisfy	crowd	know	surprise

1. Paris _____ _____ _____ the Eiffel Tower.

2. It's Saturday. The street _____ _____ _____ cars.

3. We won the first prize. We _____ _____ _____ the result.

4. Mike saw the accident. He _____ _____ _____ it.

D. 다음 문장을 수동태로 바꿔 쓰시오.

1. Some people laughed at the actor.
→ _____

2. My uncle bought me a bike.
→ _____

3. His song makes us happy.
→ _____

4. His parents watched him play the piano.
→ _____

[1-2] 다음 빈칸에 알맞은 것을 고르시오.

1.
America _____ by Columbus in 1492.

① discovers ② discovered
③ is discovered ④ was discovered
⑤ was discovering

2.
The window _____ by Jim.

① not broken ② was not broken
③ not was broken ④ didn't broken
⑤ was broken not

3. 다음 대화의 빈칸에 알맞은 것은?

· The bottle is filled _____ water.
· The table was covered _____ dust.

① of ② at
③ to ④ for
⑤ with

4. 다음 대화의 밑줄 친 부분 중 어법상 어색한 것은?

A: ①Where ②were these pictures
③taken?
B: They ④took in Jejudo. I ⑤went there
last weekend.

5. 다음 밑줄 친 부분 중 생략할 수 있는 것은?
① The book was found by Maria.
② This bag was designed by my sister.
③ The house was built by his uncle.
④ Her song is loved by old people.
⑤ French is spoken in Canada by people.

[6-7] 다음 괄호 안의 단어의 알맞은 형태를 고르시오.

6.
The room (clean) by Lucy tomorrow.

① is cleaned ② was cleaned
③ will clean ④ will be cleaned
⑤ will to clean

7.
Water (save) by us.

① should save ② should saved
③ should be saving ④ should be saved
⑤ should is saved

[8-9] 다음 우리말과 뜻이 같도록 빈칸에 알맞은 것을
고르시오.

8.
나는 그에게서 체중을 줄이라는 충고를 들었다.
→ I was advised _____ weight by him.

① lose ② losing
③ to lose ④ lost
⑤ be lose

9.
그 시계는 아버지가 나에게 주신 것이다.
→ The watch _____ me by my dad.

① give ② gave
③ given to ④ was given to
⑤ was given for

10. 다음 중 어법상 <u>어색한</u> 것은?

① Was this book written by Clara?
② The party will be held this weekend.
③ Polar bears should be protected by people.
④ He was named "Spider Man" by Susie.
⑤ She was made learn English by her mom.

11. 다음 빈칸에 들어갈 말이 바르게 짝지어진 것은?

· The ring is made _____ gold.
· I'm not interested _____ rap music.

① of – in   ② of – at
③ from – in   ④ from – of
⑤ from – with

[12-13] 다음 문장을 수동태로 바꿀 때 빈칸에 알맞은 것을 고르시오.

12.
Did Korean make these cars?
→ _____ by Korean?

① Did these cars made
② Are these cars made
③ Was these cars made
④ Were these cars made
⑤ Were these cars to make

13.
Chris looks up to his parents.
→ His parents _____ by Chris.

① is looked up
② are looked up
③ are looked up to
④ looked up to
⑤ were looked up to

14. 다음 문장을 수동태로 바르게 바꾼 것은?

Kate made him a toy car.

① He was made a toy car by Kate.
② A toy car was made to him by Kate.
③ A toy car was to made him by Kate.
④ A toy car was made for him by Kate.
⑤ He was made a toy car for me by Kate.

15. 다음 괄호 안의 단어를 알맞은 형태로 바꿔 쓰시오.

A: When was Tony (bear)?
B: He was (bear) in 2010.

_____

[16-17] 다음 우리말을 바르게 영작한 것을 고르시오.

16.
시간은 낭비되어서는 안 된다.

① Time should be wasted.
② Time should not wasted.
③ Time should not be waste.
④ Time should be not wasted.
⑤ Time should not be wasted.

17.
그가 길을 건너는 것이 내게 목격되었다.

① He was seen to cross the street by me.
② He was seen cross the street by me.
③ He was seen crossed the street by me.
④ He was seen crosses the street by me.
⑤ He was seen to crossing the street by me.

18. 다음 중 나머지 넷과 의미가 다른 것은?

① Sarah taught me English.

② I was taught English by Sarah.

③ Sarah taught English to me.

④ English was taught to me by Sarah.

⑤ I taught Sarah English.

19. 다음 중 문장의 전환이 바르지 <u>못한</u> 것은?

① They didn't eat pizza.

　→ Pizza was not eaten by them.

② She will visit the center.

　→ The center will be visited by her.

③ Where did you find your dog?

　→ Where is your dog found by you?

④ When did he paint the Mona Lisa?

　→ When was the Mona Lisa painted by him?

⑤ He made me clean the room.

　→ I was made to clean the room by him.

20. 다음 두 문장의 의미가 같도록 빈칸에 알맞은 말을 써서 능동태를 완성하시오.

> Eric was believed honest by me.

= I believed _____.

〈서술형 문제〉

21. 다음 우리말 뜻과 같도록 괄호 안에 주어진 단어를 이용하여 바르게 영작하시오.

> 이 도시는 딸기들로 유명하다. (know)

→ _____

22. 다음 문장을 지시대로 바꿔 쓰시오.

> I use a smartphone.

(1) _____
　(수동태 긍정문)

(2) _____
　(수동태 부정문)

(3) _____
　(수동태 의문문)

23. 다음 문장을 두 개의 수동태로 바꿔 쓰시오.

> Lisa gave Tony the comic book.

→ Tony _____.

→ The comic book _____.

24. 다음 대화의 빈칸에 알맞은 말을 쓰시오.

> A: _____ this chair moved by Sam?
>
> B: No, it _____. It was moved _____ Daniel.

25. 다음 문장을 수동태로 바꿔 쓸 때 어법상 어색한 곳을 찾아 고치시오.

> They saw the leaves fall.
> → The leaves were seen fall by them.

_____ → _____

대명사란 무엇인가?
대명사는 명사를 대신해서 쓰는 말로, 앞에 나온 명사의 반복을
피해 대명사로 간결하게 나타낸다.

대명사의 종류에는 무엇이 있는가?
대명사에는 인칭대명사(I, my, me ...), 지시대명사(this, that ...),
부정대명사(one, some ...), 재귀대명사(myself, yourself ...) 등
이 있다.
There are two balls. **One** is big, and **the other** is small.
I made this cake **myself**.

Chapter 8. 대명사

41 | one, some, any

- 부정대명사 : 정해지지 않은 사람이나 사물을 나타낼 때 쓰는 대명사이다.

  ① one: 앞에 나온 명사의 반복을 피하기 위해 쓰며 똑같은 것이 아니라 같은 종류의 대상을 나타낸다. 단수명사
    는 one으로 대신하고, 복수명사는 ones로 대신한다.

    I lost <u>my cell phone</u>. I have to buy **one**. 〈one = 같은 종류의 cell phone〉

    I bought <u>a new bike</u>. I really like **it**. 〈it = the new bike〉

  ② some: '약간, 몇몇, 어떤 사람들'의 뜻으로 긍정문이나 권유문에 쓰인다.

    Some of my friends like pizza.   Would you like **some** juice?

  ③ any: '어느 ~도 (…않다)'라는 뜻으로 부정문이나 '약간'의 뜻으로 의문문에 쓰인다.

    I don't have **any** money.   Do you have **any** plans for weekend?

Practice

A. 다음 괄호 안에서 알맞은 것을 고르시오.

1. He lost his mug. He will order a new (one / it).

2. I need a pen. Please lend me (one / it).

3. These boots are too big for me. Do you have small (ones / them)?

4. Alice doesn't like the blue bag. She wants the red (one / it).

5. Is this your laptop? May I use (one / it)?

B. 다음 빈칸에 some과 any 중 알맞은 것을 쓰시오.

1. _____ of the students go to the concert.

2. I don't want _____ sweets now.

3. Can I get _____ water?

4. I need _____ paper. Do you have _____?

C. 다음 밑줄 친 부분을 바르게 고치시오.

1. Do you have <u>some</u> pets?   _____

2. She bought a black dress. She likes <u>one</u>.   _____

3. Would you like <u>any</u> tea?   _____

4. He has an old wallet, but his brother has a new <u>it</u>.

    _____

5. We made three balls: a red one and two blue <u>them</u>.

    _____

Grammar Tip

one은 같은 종류의 사물을 대신하고, it은 앞에 나온 똑같은 사물을 대신할 때 쓴다.

A. mug 머그컵
order 주문하다
laptop 노트북

B. concert 공연
sweets (사탕 등) 단 것

C. pet 애완동물
tea 차

42 | all, both, each, every

④ all: '모두, 모든'의 뜻으로 뒤에 나오는 명사에 따라 단수 또는 복수 취급한다.

All <u>the people</u> in this town <u>are</u> kind. (all+복수명사 → 복수 취급)

All <u>the money</u> <u>was</u> used for food. (all+단수명사 → 단수 취급)

⑤ both: '둘 다, 양쪽의'라는 뜻으로 항상 복수 취급한다.

Both of the women <u>play</u> the flute well.   **Both** of my brothers <u>are</u> students.

⑥ each: '각각, 각각의'라는 뜻으로 항상 단수 취급한다.

Each country <u>has</u> its own history.

⑦ every: '모든'이라는 뜻으로 명사의 단수형과 함께 쓰여 단수 취급한다.

Every girl <u>likes</u> the actor. (every+단수명사 → 단수 취급)

 ## Practice

A. 다음 괄호 안에서 알맞은 것을 고르시오.

1. (All / Every) morning, I take a walk.

2. (Each / Both) of the men are married.

3. (All / Each) my friends like meat.

4. (Each / All) season has its own beauty.

5. Every room (is / are) very clean.

B. 다음 밑줄 친 부분을 바르게 고치시오.

1. All <u>member</u> can use this machine. _____

2. Each group <u>have</u> a good idea for event. _____

3. Every <u>rabbits</u> has long ears. _____

4. Both of them <u>is</u> interested in music. _____

5. I bought two hats. Each one <u>were</u> very cheap. _____

C. 다음 우리말과 뜻이 같도록 빈칸에 알맞은 말을 쓰시오.

1. 그 반의 모든 학생들이 그 축제를 즐긴다.

→ _____ _____ in the class enjoys the festival.

2. 나의 언니 둘 다 요리사이다.

→ _____ of my sisters _____ chefs.

3. 우리들 각각은 규칙들을 가지고 있다.

→ _____ of us _____ rules.

4. 모든 병들이 물로 가득 차 있다.

→ _____ the bottles _____ filled with water.

Grammar Tip

all과 every는 둘 다 '모두'의 의미를 가지지만 every는 뒤에 「단수명사+단수동사」의 형태를 가진다.

A. take a walk 산책하다
marry 결혼하다
meat 고기
beauty 아름다움

B. member 회원
cheap 값이 싼

C. festival 축제
chef 요리사
rule 규칙

Unit

43 | 부정대명사의 표현

one ~, the other ...: (둘 중) 하나는 ~, 또 하나는 …	I have two skirts. **One** is blue, and **the other** is red.
one ~, the others ...: (많은 것 중) 하나는 ~, 나머지 전부는 …	She has four children. **One** is a boy, and **the others** are girls.
one ~, another ...., the other –: (셋 중) 하나는 ~, 또 하나는 …, 나머지 하나는 –	There are three cats. **One** is white, **another** is black, and **the other** is brown.
some ~, others ...: 일부는 ~, 또 다른 일부는 …	There are lots of fruits on the table. **Some** are apples, and **others** are oranges.
some ~, the others ...: 일부는 ~, 나머지 전부는 …	**Some** of my family like spring, **the others** like fall.
each other: 서로 (둘 사이)	The boy and the girl looked at **each other**.
one another: 서로 (셋 이상일 때)	The three students respect **one another**.

Practice

A. 다음 빈칸에 알맞은 말을 〈보기〉에서 골라 문장을 완성하시오.

〈보기〉 one   another   the other   the others

1. Two girls are in the room. _____ has curly hair, and the other has straight hair.

2. He has three cars. One is white, and _____ are black.

3. There are three flowers in the vase: one is rose, _____ is lily, and the other is tulip.

4. Brian bought two backpacks. One is small, and _____ is big.

B. 다음 우리말과 뜻이 같도록 빈칸에 알맞은 말을 쓰시오.

1. 일부는 축구를 좋아하고, 또 다른 일부는 야구를 좋아한다.
   → _____ like soccer, and _____ like baseball.

2. 농장에 많은 동물들이 있다. 일부는 개이고, 나머지 전부는 양이다.
   → There are many animals in the farm. _____ are dogs, and _____ are sheep.

3. 그 두 친구는 서로 이해하려고 노력한다.
   → The two friends try to understand _____.

C. 다음 문장에서 틀린 부분을 찾아 동그라미 하고 바르게 고치시오.

1. I will visit two countries this summer. One is China, and another is Japan.

2. My sister has three umbrellas. One is green, the others is yellow, the other is pink.

Grammar Tip

A. curly 곱슬곱슬한
straight 곧은
vase 꽃병
lily 백합

구어체에서는 셋 이상에서 one another 대신 each other를 구분 없이 쓰기도 한다.

B. try to ~하기 위해 노력하다
understand 이해하다

C. umbrella 우산

44 재귀대명사의 용법

· 재귀대명사 : 인칭대명사의 소유격이나 목적격에 -self(-selves)를 붙여서 만드는데, '~ 자신'이라는 뜻을 나타낸다.

	단수	복수
1인칭	myself 나 자신	ourselves 우리들 자신
2인칭	yourself 너 자신	yourselves 너희들 자신
3인칭	himself 그 자신 herself 그녀 자신 itself 그것 자신	themselves 그들 자신

① 재귀 용법 : 재귀대명사가 목적어로 쓰여 주어 자신을 가리키는 것을 재귀 용법이라고 한다. 이때 재귀대명사는 생략할 수 없다.
Can you introduce **yourself** to them? (동사의 목적어)
I looked at **myself** in the mirror. (전치사의 목적어)

② 강조 용법 : 주어, 목적어, 보어 등을 강조할 때 그 뒤나 문장의 끝에 쓰이는 것을 강조 용법이라고 한다. 이때 재귀대명사는 생략할 수 있다.
Sally can ride the bike (**herself**). (주어 강조)
They like Mike (**himself**). (목적어 강조)

Practice

A. 다음 괄호 안에서 알맞은 것을 고르시오.

1. Henry said to (him / himself), "I'm happy."
2. She (her / herself) decorated the room.
3. I'm proud of (my / myself).
4. The boys built the ship (himself / themselves).

B. 다음 괄호 안의 말을 알맞은 형태로 바꿔 쓰시오.

1. The kids _____ cleaned the room. (they)
2. This party _____ was really fun. (it)
3. She said to _____, "It will be okay." (she)
4. I'll introduce _____ to you. (I)

C. 다음 밑줄 친 재귀대명사의 용법을 쓰시오.

1. We decided to enter the contest <u>ourselves</u>. _____
2. I sometimes talk to <u>myself</u> in the mirror. _____
3. You have to take care of <u>yourselves</u>. _____
4. Mike <u>himself</u> finished his homework. _____

Grammar Tip

A. decorate 장식하다
be proud of ~을 자랑스러워하다

B. fun 재미있는
introduce 소개하다

강조 용법의 재귀대명사는 뜻을 강조하기 때문에 생략해도 문법이 성립한다.

C. decide 결정하다
enter 참가하다
take care of 돌보다

Unit 45 재귀대명사의 관용 표현

· 재귀대명사 : 동사나 전치사의 목적어로 쓰여 숙어처럼 사용된다.

by oneself (= alone)	혼자서	beside oneself	제정신이 아닌
for oneself	혼자 힘으로	enjoy oneself	즐겁게 보내다
of oneself	저절로	help oneself (to)	(~을) 마음껏 먹다

She traveled to Europe **by herself**.   I repaired the machine **for myself**.

The door was closed **of itself**.   The man was **beside himself** with anger.

We **enjoyed ourselves** on the stage.   **Help yourself to** the pizza.

Practice

A. 다음 우리말과 뜻이 같도록 빈칸에 알맞은 말을 쓰시오.

1. 초콜릿을 마음껏 먹어.

   → _____ _____ to the chocolate.

2. 그들은 축제에서 즐겁게 보냈다.

   → They _____ _____ at the festival.

3. 그 TV는 저절로 꺼졌다.

   → The TV was turn off _____ _____ .

4. 우리는 그 소식에 제정신이 아니었다.

   → We were _____ _____ with that news.

B. 다음 문장을 우리말로 해석하시오.

1. He lives in this house by himself.

   → _____

2. The baby opened the box for himself.

   → _____

3. The light fell down of itself.

   → _____

C. 다음 우리말과 뜻이 같도록 주어진 단어들을 알맞게 배열하시오.

1. Chris는 주로 아침을 혼자 먹는다.

   (has / himself / breakfast / usually / by)

   → Chris _____ .

2. 나는 혼자 힘으로 그 그림을 걸어야만 한다.

   (the / for / picture / hang / myself / must)

   → I _____ .

3. 케이크를 마음껏 먹어. (the / help / to / yourself / cake)

   → _____ .

Grammar Tip

A. festival 축제

turn off 끄다

B. fall down 떨어지다

그 외 재귀대명사의 관용 표현:
between ourselves
우리끼리 얘기인데
of itself 본래

C. have breakfast 아침 식사를 하다
hang 걸다

A. 다음 빈칸에 알맞은 말을 <보기>에서 골라 문장을 완성하시오.

<보기>	one	ones	any	every	all

1. _____ my classmates were invited at the party.

2. These pants are small. Do you have bigger _____?

3. _____ student here is going to join the game.

4. I need a brush. Can you lend me _____?

5. I don't have _____ coins now.

B. 다음 문장에서 <u>어색한</u> 부분을 찾아 동그라미 하고 바르게 고치시오.

1. Jim has three shirts. It is black, and the others are blue.

2. Julia has two sons. One is a teacher, and another is an actor.

3. There are many students in the gym. Some are playing basketball, and the other are playing badminton.

4. The two man talked to one another.

C. 다음 괄호 안의 단어를 알맞은 재귀대명사의 형태로 바꿔 쓰시오.

1. Emma thought about _____. (she)

2. We _____ helped the animals in need. (we)

3. Mike introduced _____ to his classmates. (he)

4. The people decided to clean the beach _____. (they)

D. 다음 우리말과 뜻이 같도록 재귀대명사를 이용하여 문장을 완성하시오.

1. 네 혼자 힘으로 이 문제를 풀어 봐.
   → Please solve this problem _____ _____.

2. Henry는 콘서트에서 즐겁게 보냈다.
   → Henry _____ _____ at the concert.

3. 이 쿠키들을 마음껏 먹어.
   → _____ _____ to these cookies.

4. 나는 혼자 영화 보러 가는 것을 좋아하지 않는다.
   → I don't like to go to the movies _____ _____.

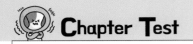

[1-2] 다음 빈칸에 알맞은 것을 고르시오.

1.
> My computer is broken. I will buy a new _____.

① it   ② one
③ ones   ④ some
⑤ any

2.
> Five girls are playing basketball. I know _____ of them.

① every   ② both
③ all   ④ any
⑤ another

3. 다음 빈칸에 들어갈 말이 바르게 짝지어진 것은?
> There are many bottles on the table. _____ are empty, and _____ are filled with water.

① One – another   ② Some – the other
③ Some – the others   ④ Some – other
⑤ Some – any

4. 다음 밑줄 친 부분이 가리키는 것을 영어로 쓰시오.
> These sandals are too expensive. Do you have any cheaper ones?

5. 다음 밑줄 친 부분의 쓰임이 나머지와 다른 것은?
① I can do it myself.
② Brian introduced himself to them.
③ Some boys fell down and hurt themselves.
④ Kate always feels proud of herself.
⑤ We looked at ourselves in the mirror.

6. 다음 중 어법상 어색한 것은?
① Alice bought some flowers.
② They don't have any money.
③ Every student should keep the rules.
④ Each of us have a nickname.
⑤ Both of them were wrong.

7. 다음 밑줄 친 부분과 바꿔 쓸 수 있는 것은?
> Julia sometimes goes swimming alone.

① by herself   ② for herself
③ of herself   ④ of her
⑤ by oneself

8. 다음 빈칸에 공통으로 알맞은 것은?
> · Would you like _____ milk?
> · _____ people like pizza, and others like spaghetti.

① any   ② some
③ one   ④ another
⑤ the other

9. 다음 밑줄 친 부분 중 생략할 수 없는 것은?

① The man <u>himself</u> answered the question.
② His song became famous <u>itself</u>.
③ I don't like talking about <u>myself</u>.
④ Julie wrote this book <u>herself</u>.
⑤ We designed that building <u>ourselves</u>.

10. 다음 우리말을 바르게 영작한 것은?

> 소녀 둘 다 K-pop에 관심이 있다.

① Each of the girls is interested in K-pop.
② All the girls are interested in K-pop.
③ Every girl is interested in K-pop.
④ Both of the girls are interested in K-pop.
⑤ Both of the girls is interested in K-pop.

11. 다음 우리말과 뜻이 같도록 빈칸에 알맞은 것은?

> David와 그의 친구들은 직접 초대장을 만들 것이다.
> = David and his friends will make the invitation cards _____.

① them   ② yourself
③ ourselves   ④ himself
⑤ themselves

12. 다음 밑줄 친 부분 중 어법상 어색한 것은?

> A: Do you have ①<u>any</u> pets?
> B: Yes, I ②<u>have</u> three. ③<u>One</u> is a dog, ④<u>another</u> is a cat, and ⑤<u>the others</u> is an iguana.

[13-14] 다음 두 문장의 뜻이 같도록 빈칸에 알맞은 말을 쓰시오.

13.
> Sarah's family had fun on the beach.

= Sarah's family _____ _____ on the beach.

14.
> All countries have their own tradition.

= Every _____ _____ its own tradition.

15. 다음 빈칸에 알맞은 말을 쓰시오.

> Sam has four caps: a white _____ and three black _____.

16. 다음 빈칸에 yourself가 들어갈 수 <u>없는</u> 것은?

① Help _____ to this bread.
② You should take care of _____.
③ Can you go there for _____?
④ Did you enjoy _____ at the party?
⑤ You and I were beside _____ at that time.

17. 다음 문장에서 어법상 어색한 부분을 찾아 바르게 고치시오.

> Each of the members of the club play musical instruments.

_____ → _____

18. 다음 우리말과 뜻이 같도록 빈칸에 알맞은 말을 쓰시오.

> 그녀의 세 아들은 서로 믿는다.

→ Her three sons trust ＿＿＿＿＿ ＿＿＿＿＿.

19. 다음 밑줄 친 부분의 해석이 잘못된 것은?

① The window opened of itself. (저절로)

② We were beside ourselves when we heard the news. (제정신이 아닌)

③ Linda sometimes travels by herself. (그녀의 가족과 함께)

④ The guests enjoyed themselves at this city. (즐겁게 보내다)

⑤ Help yourself to these macaroons. (마음껏 먹다)

20. 다음 괄호 안의 단어를 알맞은 형태로 바꿔 쓴 것은?

> All of my money (be) used for snacks yesterday.

① be ② was
③ were ④ to be
⑤ will be

〈서술형 문제〉

21. 다음 빈칸에 알맞은 말을 쓰시오.

> I bought three candles for my family.
> One is white, ＿＿＿＿＿ is pink, and ＿＿＿＿＿ is purple.

[22-23] 다음 우리말과 뜻이 같도록 주어진 단어들을 이용하여 문장을 바르게 영작하시오.

22.

> 모든 학생들은 학교 규칙을 따라야 한다.
> (every, have to, follow, the school rules)

→ ＿＿＿＿＿＿＿＿＿＿＿＿＿＿＿

23.

> Monica는 혼자 힘으로 한국어를 배웠다.
> (learn, Korean, for oneself)

→ ＿＿＿＿＿＿＿＿＿＿＿＿＿＿＿

24. 다음 글에서 어법상 어색한 곳을 두 군데 찾아 바르게 고치시오.

> Eric has classes from Monday to Friday. He doesn't have some classes during weekend. Each class is about 45 minutes themselves. Every day, he has five or six classes. All his classes are in different rooms.

(1) ＿＿＿＿＿＿＿ → ＿＿＿＿＿＿＿

(2) ＿＿＿＿＿＿＿ → ＿＿＿＿＿＿＿

25. 다음 표를 보고 빈칸에 알맞은 부정대명사를 쓰시오.

	5 boys	
like	baseball	soccer
	3	2
have	dog	cat
	1	4

(1) There are five boys. ＿＿＿＿ like baseball, and ＿＿＿＿ ＿＿＿＿ like soccer.

(2) ＿＿＿＿ the boys have a pet. ＿＿＿＿ has a dog, and ＿＿＿＿ ＿＿＿＿ have a cat.

형용사란 무엇인가?

형용사는 명사나 대명사를 앞이나 뒤에서 수식하거나 주어나 목적
어를 보충 설명해 주는 보어 역할을 한다.

These are **beautiful** flowers.
The party was **fun**.

부사란 무엇인가?

부사는 문장 내에서 동사, 형용사, 부사 또는 문장 전체를 수식하
는 역할을 한다. 시간, 장소, 횟수, 정도 등을 나타낸다.

She eats lunch **quickly**.
I **usually** watch TV at night.

Chapter 9. 형용사와 부사

46 | 형용사와 부사의 쓰임

- 형용사 : 명사를 수식하거나 주어나 목적어를 보충 설명해주는 역할을 한다.

  We went to the **famous** restaurant. 〈명사 수식〉

  Alan's performance was **wonderful**. 〈주어 보충 설명〉

- 부사 : 문장 내에서 동사, 형용사, 부사, 문장 전체를 수식하는 역할을 한다.

  The girl smiled **warmly**. 〈동사 수식〉　　This cake is **really** sweet. 〈형용사 수식〉

  Sam likes baseball **very** much. 〈부사 수식〉

  Suddenly, the driver stopped his car. 〈문장 전체 수식〉

- 빈도부사 : 빈도나 횟수를 나타내는 부사로 대부분 일반동사 앞이나 be동사 또는 조동사 뒤에 위치한다.

  never ⟶ sometimes ⟶ often ⟶ usually ⟶ always
  (결코 ～않다)　(때때로, 가끔)　(자주, 종종)　(보통, 대개)　(항상, 늘)

  I **always** take a walk after breakfast.　　Do you **often** eat out?

  They will **never** visit the amusement park.

Practice

A. 다음 두 문장이 같은 뜻이 되도록 빈칸에 알맞은 말을 쓰시오.

1. Kelly is tall. = Kelly is a _____ girl.

2. The movie was exciting. = It was an _____ movie.

3. These earrings are expensive. = These are _____ earrings.

B. 다음 빈칸에 알맞은 말을 〈보기〉에서 골라 문장을 완성하시오.

〈보기〉 hot　　　sour　　　luckily　　　slowly

1. My grandma walked around the garden _____.

2. This summer is really _____.

3. _____, Jamie and I passed the test.

4. Lemons taste _____.

C. 다음 주어진 단어를 넣어 문장을 다시 쓰시오.

1. I wake up early in the morning. (never)
   → _____

2. Kate goes swimming in her free time. (usually)
   → _____

3. Fred is tired on Mondays. (always)
   → _____

Grammar Tip

형용사는 명사를 수식하는 한정적 용법과 주어나 목적어의 보어로 쓰이는 서술적 용법이 있다.

A. earring 귀걸이
expensive 비싼

형용사는 be, become, look, smell 등과 같은 동사의 보어로 쓰여 주어의 상태나 성질을 설명한다.

B. walk around 돌아다니다
luckily 운 좋게도
taste ～한 맛이 나다
sour (맛이) 신

C. wake up (잠에서) 깨다
free time 여가 시간
tired 피곤한

Unit 47 | 수량형용사

• 수량형용사 : 명사 앞에 쓰여 명사의 수와 양을 나타내는 형용사로 many, much, few, little 등이 있다.

	약간 있는(긍정)	거의 없는(부정)	많은	
셀 수 있는 명사 앞	a few	few	many	a lot of
셀 수 없는 명사 앞	a little	little	much	lots of

*a lot of, lots of는 셀 수 있는 명사와 셀 수 없는 명사 앞에 모두 쓸 수 있다.

A **few** letters were sent to Jay. (몇 통의 편지들)　　There is **a little** milk in the bottle. (약간 있는 우유)

There are **few** seats in the stadium. (거의 없는 좌석들)　　We had **little** snow this winter. (거의 안내린 눈)

Many people watch baseball games. (많은 사람들)　　I don't have **much** time. (많은 시간)

Practice

A. 다음 괄호 안에서 알맞은 것을 고르시오.

1. There was too (many / much) traffic.

2. Can I ask you a few (question / questions)?

3. There is (few / little) money in his wallet.

4. Jake made (much / lots of) mistakes.

5. She has (a few / a little) jam in her jar.

B. 다음 밑줄 친 부분을 바르게 고치시오.

1. There is a few food in the fridge. _____

2. Little people agreed with me. _____

3. My brother has much bad habits. _____

4. I have lots of book to read. _____

5. There is few rain in the desert. _____

C. 다음 문장을 바르게 해석하시오.

1. (1) She saves a little money.

→ _____

(2) She saves little money.

→ _____

2. (1) There were a few students in the classroom.

→ _____

(2) There were few students in the classroom.

→ _____

Grammar Tip

수량형용사 뒤에 셀 수 있는 명사가
오면 반드시 복수형으로 쓴다.

A. traffic 교통량
mistake 실수
jar (잼 등을 담는) 병

B. fridge 냉장고
agree 동의하다
habit 습관
desert 사막

C. save 모으다, 저축하다

unit 48 -thing+형용사/the+형용사

- 형용사가 일반적으로 명사를 수식할 때는 앞에서 수식하는데, -thing, -body, -one으로 끝나는 대명사를 수식할 때는 반드시 뒤에 위치한다.

  I'm making <u>something</u> **special** for my friends.

  He met <u>someone</u> **interesting** in the park.

- 「the+형용사」: '~한 사람들'이라는 뜻으로 「형용사+복수 보통명사」로 바꿔 쓸 수 있다.

  The rich are not always happy. = **Rich people** are not always happy.

  She helped a lot of **the poor**. = She helped a lot of **poor people**.

Practice

Grammar Tip

-body, -thing, -one으로 끝나는 대명사는 형용사가 뒤에서 수식한다.

A. cold 차가운
   soft 부드러운
   towel 수건
   wrong 잘못된

B. popular 인기 있는
   homeless 집이 없는

C. strange 이상한
   elderly 연세가 드신

A. 우리말과 같은 뜻이 되도록 빈칸에 알맞은 말을 쓰시오.

1. 나는 어제 새로운 신발을 샀다.
   → I bought _____ _____ yesterday.

2. 저에게 시원한 마실 것을 좀 주세요.
   → Please give me _____ _____ to drink.

3. Mike는 그녀에게 부드러운 수건을 주었다.
   → Mike gave her a _____ _____.

4. 뭔가 잘못된 게 있니?
   → Is there _____ _____?

B. 다음 문장을 바르게 해석하시오.

1. She helped the sick in the hospital.
   → _____

2. This food is popular with the young.
   → _____

3. He built the house for the homeless.
   → _____

C. 우리말과 같은 뜻이 되도록 주어진 단어들을 알맞게 배열하시오.

1. 너는 어떤 이상한 것을 찾았니? (anything, find, did, strange, you)
   → _____

2. 나는 어제 유명한 누군가를 만났다. (met, yesterday, someone, famous, I)
   → _____

3. 그것은 노인들을 위해 도움이 된다. (helpful, the, it, for, elderly, is)
   → _____

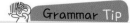

A. 다음 빈칸에 알맞은 말을 <보기>에서 골라 문장을 완성하시오.

> <보기>   few   a few   little   a little

1. There are _____ books about history. Let's read them.

2. Jenny doesn't like sugar. She adds _____ sugar to her coffee.

3. I need _____ cheese to make hamburgers.

4. The singer isn't popular. He has _____ fans.

B. 다음 문장에서 밑줄 친 부분을 바르게 고치시오.

1. I don't have <u>many</u> time to stay here. _____

2. They <u>eat always</u> breakfast. _____

3. I want to be <u>special someone</u>. _____

4. The performance was <u>perfectly</u>. _____

C. 다음 밑줄 친 부분에 유의하여 문장을 해석하시오.

1. He planted <u>a few</u> flowers in the garden.
   → _____

2. She is <u>never</u> late for school.
   → _____

3. My mom helped <u>the sick</u>.
   → _____

4. At that time, Eva had <u>little</u> food.
   → _____

D. 다음 우리말과 같은 뜻이 되도록 괄호 안의 단어들을 알맞게 배열하시오.

1. 이 스테이크는 좋은 냄새가 난다. (good, steak, this, smells)
   → _____

2. 나는 책상 위에서 중요한 것을 찾았다.
   (found, important, desk, I, on, something, the)
   → _____

3. 그릇에 많은 소금이 있다. (in, is, a lot of, bowl, the, there, salt)
   → _____

4. 젊은이들은 미래의 희망이다.
   (future, the, young, are, the, of, the, hope)
   → _____

Grammar Tip

A. add 넣다

빈도부사는 일반동사 앞이나 be동사, 조동사의 뒤에 위치한다.

B. stay 머무르다
   special 특별한
   performance 공연

「the+형용사」는 「형용사+people」로 바꿔 쓸 수 있다.

C. plant 심다
   garden 정원
   at that time 그 당시에, 그때에

D. smell 냄새가 나다
   bowl 그릇

[1-2] 다음 빈칸에 알맞은 것을 고르시오.

1.
> Do you have _____ time? I have something to tell you.

① few　　　　② a few
③ many　　　④ little
⑤ a little

2.
> Jane has _____ skirts because she doesn't like them.

① little　　　② a little
③ few　　　　④ a lot of
⑤ much

3. 다음 빈칸에 들어갈 말이 바르게 짝지어진 것은?

> · Sally is busy today. She has _____ work to do.
> · How _____ eggs do you need?

① many – many　　② many – much
③ a little – much　④ a lot of – many
⑤ lots of – few

4. 다음 빈칸에 알맞지 않은 것은?

> We had _____ snow last year.

① little　　　② a little
③ much　　　④ few
⑤ lots of

5. 다음 중 어법상 어색한 것은?

① I know something fun about him.
② Is there anything wrong?
③ I need someone helpful.
④ Do you know special anyone?
⑤ Brian will meet somebody new.

6. 다음 우리말을 바르게 영작한 것은?

> 그는 종종 점심으로 피자와 샐러드를 먹는다.

① He often eat pizza and salad for lunch.
② He often eats pizza and salad for lunch.
③ He eats often pizza and salad for lunch.
④ He eats pizza and often salad for lunch.
⑤ He eats pizza and salad for lunch often.

7. 다음 괄호 안의 단어를 알맞은 형태로 바꾼 것은?

> The rich (be) not always happy.

① is　　　　② are
③ am　　　　④ being
⑤ to be

8. 다음 중 밑줄 친 부분이 어법상 어색한 것은?

① He eats food very <u>slowly</u>.
② She is very honest. She <u>never</u> tells a lie.
③ The picture looks <u>interesting</u>.
④ You can make soup <u>easy</u>.
⑤ My sister is young, but she always acts <u>wisely</u>.

9. 다음 우리말과 뜻이 같도록 빈칸에 알맞은 말을 쓰시오.

> 밖에 폭우가 내렸다. 거리에 사람들이 거의 없었다.

→ It rained heavily outside. There were _____ people on the street.

10. 다음 밑줄 친 부분 중 어법상 어색한 것은?

> Peter is a very ①famous baseball player. ②Many people came to watch his game. There ③were ④little empty ⑤seats in the stadium.

[11-12] 다음 두 문장의 뜻이 같도록 빈칸에 알맞은 말을 쓰시오.

11.
> He drinks milk every morning.

= He _____ _____ milk in the morning.

12.
> Lots of people enjoyed themselves at the concert.

= _____ _____ enjoyed themselves at the concert.

13. 다음 중 helpful이 들어갈 알맞은 위치는?

> You ①have ②to ③do ④something ⑤.

[14-15] 다음 우리말과 뜻이 같도록 배열할 때 네 번째로 오는 것을 고르시오.

14.
> 나는 너를 위해 달콤한 뭔가를 가져왔다.
> (for, something, I, you, got, sweet)

① for
② something
③ you
④ got
⑤ sweet

15.
> 가난한 사람들을 돕는 것은 어렵지 않다.
> (help, not, is difficult, the, to, poor)

① is
② help
③ poor
④ the
⑤ not

16. 다음 빈칸에 a little이 들어갈 수 없는 것은?

① I have _____ money in my pocket.
② Brian adds _____ flour in the bowl.
③ Kate needs _____ salt to make bread.
④ Some people have _____ trouble using this machine.
⑤ There are _____ houses near the lake.

17. 다음 밑줄 친 부분과 바꿔 쓸 수 있는 말을 두 단어로 쓰시오.

> We should respect old people.

→ _____ _____

18. 다음 문장에서 어법상 어색한 부분을 찾아 바르게 고치시오.

> I can speak Japanese a few.

_____ → _____

19. 다음 문장을 괄호 안의 지시대로 바꿀 때 빈칸에 알맞은 말을 쓰시오.

> I want to eat spicy things.
> (things를 something으로)

= I want to eat _____ _____.

20. 다음 밑줄 친 부분의 해석이 잘못된 것은?

① The homeless need some places to live.
(집 없는 사람들)
② The sick need special care. (병)
③ You must be polite to the elderly.
(나이 든 사람들)
④ There are a few interesting photos on the wall. (약간 있는)
⑤ Is there anything wrong with the car?
(잘못된 것)

〈서술형 문제〉

21. 다음 두 문장이 같은 뜻이 되도록 주어진 말을 이용하여 쓰시오.

> Sam is a careful driver. (carefully)

= Sam _____ _____.

[22-23] 다음 우리말과 뜻이 같도록 주어진 단어들을 바르게 배열하시오.

22.
> 우리는 토요일에 자주 캠핑하러 간다.
> (go, we, Saturday, camping, often, on)

→ _____

23.
> 나는 공원에서 낯선 누군가를 보았다.
> (at, someone, I, park, strange, the, saw)

→ _____

24. 다음 글에서 어법상 어색한 곳을 찾아 바르게 고치시오.

> Linda's parents often give her an allowance. It is not small, but Linda always complains. She spends many money on snacks. She saves little money.

_____ → _____

25. 다음 대화의 내용과 일치하도록 the를 넣어 문장을 완성하시오.

> A: Who are those kind men?
> B: Both are my teachers, Mike and Robert. They sometimes make food for poor people and give it to them.

→ Mike and Robert sometimes make food and give it _____ _____.

Go! Go!

비교란 무엇인가?
둘 이상의 대상을 서로 비교하여 무엇이 더 ~한지, 가장 ~한지
나타낸다.

비교의 방법에는 무엇이 있는가?
비교하는 방법에는 형용사나 부사의 형태를 그대로 사용하는 원급
비교(as+원급+as)와 비교급(비교급+than), 최상급 비교(the+최
상급)가 있다.
He is **as tall as** his dad.
A train is **longer than** a bus.
She runs **the fastest** in her class.

Chapter 10. 형용사와 부사의 비교

49 | 비교급, 최상급의 규칙 변화

· 형용사, 부사의 비교급과 최상급 만들기

	비교급	최상급	예
대부분의 형용사, 부사	원급+er	원급+est	tall-taller-tallest, long-longer-longest
-e로 끝날 때	원급+r	원급+st	large-larger-largest, nice-nicer-nicest
「자음+y」로 끝날 때	y→i+er	y→i+est	happy-happier-happiest, easy-easier-easiest
「단모음+단자음」으로 끝날 때	자음 추가+er	자음 추가+est	big-bigger-biggest, hot-hotter-hottest
3음절 이상 또는 -ful, -ing, -less, -ous, -ly 등으로 끝날 때	more+원급	most+원급	beautiful-more beautiful-most beautiful, famous-more famous-most famous

Practice

A. 다음 빈칸에 알맞은 비교급과 최상급을 쓰시오.

1. small – _____ – _____

2. fat – _____ – _____

3. slowly – _____ – _____

4. busy – _____ – _____

B. 다음 괄호 안에서 알맞은 것을 고르시오.

1. Rabbits are (faster / more fast) than turtles.

2. Math is (difficulter / more difficult) than science.

3. An elephant is the (bigest / biggest) of all animals.

4. He is the (famousest / most famous) in Korea.

C. 다음 우리말과 뜻이 같도록 주어진 단어를 알맞은 형태로 바꿔 쓰시오.

1. 이번 여름은 작년보다 더 덥다. (hot)
   → This summer is _____ than last year.

2. 축구가 배구보다 더 인기 있다. (popular)
   → Soccer is _____ _____ than volleyball.

3. Sally는 학교에서 가장 키가 큰 소녀이다. (tall)
   → Sally is the _____ girl in her school.

4. 나의 가방은 셋 중에서 가장 무겁다. (heavy)
   → My bag is the _____ of three.

50 비교급, 최상급의 불규칙 변화

· good, bad, many, little의 비교급과 최상급은 불규칙하게 변한다.

원급	비교급	최상급	예
good / well	better	best	Tony feels **better** than yesterday.
bad / ill	worse	worst	It was the **worst** movie.
many / much	more	most	I read **more** books than Jenny.
little	less	least	She usually sleeps **less** than 6 hours a day.

Practice

A. 다음 빈칸에 알맞은 비교급과 최상급을 쓰시오.

1. well – ＿＿＿＿＿＿ – ＿＿＿＿＿＿

2. little – ＿＿＿＿＿＿ – ＿＿＿＿＿＿

3. many – ＿＿＿＿＿＿ – ＿＿＿＿＿＿

4. ill – ＿＿＿＿＿＿ – ＿＿＿＿＿＿

B. 다음 우리말과 뜻이 같도록 주어진 단어를 알맞은 형태로 바꿔 쓰시오.

1. Eden은 그의 팀에서 최고의 선수이다. (good)
   → Eden is the ＿＿＿＿＿＿ player in his team.

2. 그는 우리가 생각했던 것보다 더 나빠 보인다. (bad)
   → He looks ＿＿＿＿＿＿ than we thought.

3. 나는 너보다 더 적은 돈을 썼다. (little)
   → I spent ＿＿＿＿＿＿ money than you.

4. 너는 어떤 운동을 가장 좋아하니? (much)
   → Which sport do you like the ＿＿＿＿＿＿?

C. 다음 문장을 바르게 해석하시오.

1. I have more books than Jenny.
   → ＿＿＿＿＿＿＿＿＿＿＿＿＿＿＿＿

2. Your cell phone is better than mine.
   → ＿＿＿＿＿＿＿＿＿＿＿＿＿＿＿＿

3. He was the worst singer.
   → ＿＿＿＿＿＿＿＿＿＿＿＿＿＿＿＿

Grammar Tip

A. ill 아픈

good/well, bad/ill, many/much 는 비교급과 최상급의 형태가 같으므로 의미를 잘 구분하도록 한다.

B. spend (시간, 돈을) 쓰다

C. mine 나의 것

51 | as + 원급 + as

- 원급 비교 :「as+형용사[부사]의 원급+as」의 형태로 '~만큼 …한[하게]'의 뜻을 나타낸다. 비교하는 대상의 정도가 같음을 나타낸다.

  Chris is **as tall as** Henry.

  Science is **as interesting as** math.

- 원급 비교의 부정 :「not as[so]+형용사[부사]의 원급+as」의 형태로 '~만큼 …하지 않은[않게]'의 뜻을 나타낸다.

  My hair is not **as[so] long as** yours.

  I don't watch the news **as[so] often as** my dad.

 Practice

A. 다음 괄호 안에서 알맞은 것을 고르시오.

1. Peter runs as (fast / faster) as David.

2. Kate is not as (old / older) as Tim.

3. Pizza is not so delicious (as / so) spaghetti.

4. I'm as (smart / smarter) as my sister.

B. 다음 문장에서 어법상 틀린 부분을 찾아 동그라미 하고 바르게 고쳐 쓰시오.

1. This bag is as bigger as mine. _____

2. I read as more books as Amy. _____

3. A pig's tail is as not long as a horse's. _____

4. She is not as beautiful so her sister. _____

C. 다음 우리말과 같은 뜻이 되도록 빈칸에 알맞은 말을 쓰시오.

1. 나는 Mike만큼 천천히 먹는다.
   → I eat _____ _____ _____ Mike.

2. 나에게 중국어는 영어만큼 쉽다.
   → Chinese is _____ _____ _____ English for me.

3. 오늘은 어제만큼 춥지 않다.
   → Today is _____ _____ _____ _____ yesterday.

4. 이 의자는 저 의자만큼 무겁지 않다.
   → This chair is _____ _____ _____ _____ that one.

Unit 52 | 비교급 + than

- 비교급 비교 : 「비교급+than」의 형태로 '~보다 더 …한[하게]'의 뜻을 나타낸다. 비교하는 두 대상 중 한쪽의 정도가 높음을 나타낸다.

  China is **bigger than** Korea.   I know him **better than** you.

- 「less+원급+than」은 '~보다 덜 …한[하게]'의 뜻을 나타낸다.

  This building is **less tall than** that tower.

  = This building is <u>not as[so] tall as</u> that tower. = That tower is <u>taller than</u> this building.

- 비교급 강조 : 비교급 앞에 much, far, even, still, a lot 등을 써서 '훨씬, 더욱 더'의 의미로 비교급을 강조한다.

  This computer works **much** <u>better</u> than that one.

Practice

A. 다음 우리말과 같은 뜻이 되도록 빈칸에 알맞은 말을 쓰시오.

1. 한라산은 지리산보다 높다.
   → Halla Mountain is _____ _____ Jiri Mountain.
2. 나의 가방은 네 것보다 가볍다.
   → My bag is _____ _____ yours.
3. 그녀는 그녀의 여동생보다 아름답다.
   → She is _____ _____ her sister.
4. 소년들은 보통 소녀들보다 덜 조심스럽다.
   → Boys are commonly _____ _____ _____ girls.

B. 다음 두 문장이 같은 뜻이 되도록 빈칸에 알맞은 말을 쓰시오.

1. Math is not as interesting as music.
   = Math is _____ _____ than music.
2. June is not as hot as July. = June is _____ _____ than July.
3. Jane is not as tall as Sally. = Sally is _____ _____ Jane.

C. 다음 우리말과 뜻이 같도록 주어진 단어들을 알맞게 배열하시오.

1. 건강이 돈보다 훨씬 더 중요하다.
   (important, health, even, money, more, than, is)
   → _____
2. 비행기는 자동차보다 훨씬 더 빠르다.
   (a car, is, faster, a plane, than, much)
   → _____
3. 이 자전거는 저것보다 훨씬 더 가격이 싸다.
   (that one, a lot, cheaper, this bike, than, is)
   → _____

Grammar Tip

A. light 가벼운
commonly 흔히, 보통
careful 조심하는, 주의 깊은

B. June 6월
July 7월

비교급을 강조하는 말은 much, far, even, still, a lot 등이 있으며, very는 비교급 앞에 쓸 수 없다.

C. important 중요한

53 | the+최상급

- 최상급 비교 : 「the+최상급」의 형태로 '~에서 가장 …한[하게]'의 뜻을 나타낸다. 최상급 비교는 세 개 이상의 대상을 비교하며 그 정도가 가장 높음을 나타낸다.
  February is **the shortest** month.
  Alice is **the tallest** girl in her class.
- 「the+최상급」 뒤에는 대개 비교하는 범위나 대상을 나타내는 말이 온다.
  「the+최상급+in+비교 범위[장소, 집단]」: '~에서 가장 …한[하게]'
  「the+최상급+of+비교 대상[기간]」: '~ 중에서 가장 …한[하게]'
  Jejudo is the **largest** island **in** Korea.
  She is the **most famous** actress **of** the three.

 ## Practice

Grammar Tip

A. 다음 괄호 안에서 알맞은 것을 고르시오.

1. The Nile is (longest / the longest) river.

2. Brian is the (more popular / most popular) player in his team.

3. August is the hottest month (in / of) the year.

4. It is the smallest country (in / of) the world.

A. popular 인기 있는
player 운동선수

B. 다음 빈칸에 알맞은 말을 〈보기〉에서 골라 알맞은 형태로 바꿔 쓰시오.

〈보기〉 delicious	strong	difficult	pretty

1. Pizza is _____ _____ _____ food.

2. The elephant is _____ _____ animal in this zoo.

3. Math is _____ _____ _____ subject for me.

4. Jennifer is _____ _____ girl in her group.

B. delicious 맛있는
subject 과목

C. 다음 주어진 단어를 이용하여 문장을 완성하시오.

1. Tony는 다섯 중에서 가장 돈이 많다. (rich)
   → Tony is _____ _____ _____ the five.

2. 이 식당은 마을에서 가장 오래되었다. (old)
   → This restaurant is _____ _____ _____ the town.

3. 이 영화는 모든 것 중에서 가장 흥미롭다. (exciting)
   → This movie is _____ _____ _____ all.

보통 최상급 뒤에 in이 오는 경우에는 장소나 범위를 나타내는 단수명사를, of가 오는 경우에는 비교 대상을 나타내는 복수명사를 쓴다.

C. rich 부유한, 부자인

54 비교 구문 1

「as+형용사[부사] 원급+as+주어+can[could]」 = 「as+형용사[부사] 원급+as+possible」	'가능한 ~한[하게]'	I'll be there **as soon as** I can. = I'll be there **as soon as** possible. *동사가 현재형이면 can, 과거형이면 could를 쓴다.
「배수사+as+형용사[부사] 원급+as」 = 「배수사+비교급+than」	'~보다 …배 더 –한'	This box is **twice as heavy as** that one. = This box is **twice heavier than** that one.
「the+비교급, the+비교급」	'~하면 할수록 더욱 …한'	**The warmer** it is, **the better** I feel.
「비교급+and+비교급」 *get, become, grow 등의 동사 뒤에 쓰임	'점점 더 ~한[하게]'	Everything will get **better and better**.

Practice

A. 우리말과 같은 뜻이 되도록 주어진 단어를 이용하여 문장을 완성하시오.

1. 그는 그의 팔을 가능한 높이 뻗었다. (high)
   → He stretched his arms as _____ as he could.

2. 이 다리는 저것보다 세 배 더 길다. (long)
   → This bridge is three times as _____ as that one.

3. 나이가 들면 들수록 더 약해진다. (old, weak)
   → The _____ you get, the _____ you become.

4. 겨울에는 날씨가 점점 더 추워진다. (cold)
   → In winter, it is getting _____ and _____.

B. 다음 문장을 바르게 해석하시오.

1. I have twice as many books as she has.
   → _____

2. Ben became smarter and smarter.
   → _____

3. The harder you study, the better grades you'll get.
   → _____

C. 다음 두 문장이 같은 뜻이 되도록 빈칸에 알맞은 말을 쓰시오.

1. I spoke as loudly as I could.
   = I spoke _____ _____ _____ _____.

2. This red shirt is twice as big as that blue one.
   = This red shirt is twice _____ _____ that blue one.

3. They ran to the station as fast as possible.
   = They ran to the station as fast _____ _____ _____.

Grammar Tip

「as+형용사나 부사의 원급+as+주어+can[could]」에서 시제에 따라 can과 could를 구분해서 쓴다.

A. stretch 뻗다

배수사를 나타낼 때 '두 배'는 twice로 나타내고 '세 배' 이상은 「해당 숫자+times」로 나타낸다.
twice, three times, four times, five times …

B. grade 성적

more and more는 '점점 더 많은'의 뜻이다.
More and more people are interested in their free time.

C. loudly 크게
station 역

unit 55 | 비교 구문 2

- 「one of the＋최상급＋복수명사」: '가장 ~한 것들 중 하나'라는 뜻으로 단수 취급한다.

  Mozart is **one of the greatest musicians** in the world.

  One of the best soccer players is Heung-Min Son.

- 원급이나 비교급을 사용하여 최상급의 의미를 나타낼 수 있다.

  ① 「부정 주어＋as[so]＋원급＋as A」: '어떤 것도 A만큼 ~하지 못한'

  No (other) student is **as[so] tall as** Mike.

  ② 「부정 주어＋비교급＋than A」: '어떤 것도 A보다 더 ~하지 못한'

  No (other) student is **taller than** Mike.

  ③ 「A＋비교급＋than any other 단수명사」: 'A가 다른 ~보다 더 …한'

  Mike is **taller than any other** student.

Practice

Grammar Tip

A. 다음 우리말과 같은 뜻이 되도록 주어진 단어를 이용하여 문장을 완성하시오.

1. Einstein은 세계에서 가장 위대한 과학자들 중 한 명이다. (great)

   → Einstein is _____ _____ _____ _____ scientists in the world.

2. 가장 바쁜 도시들 중 한 곳은 New York이다. (busy)

   → _____ _____ _____ _____ cities is New York.

3. 그것은 한국에서 가장 오래된 집들 중 하나이다. (old)

   → It is _____ _____ _____ _____ houses in Korea.

B. 다음 밑줄 친 부분을 어법상 바르게 고쳐 쓰시오.

1. Jenny is one of the smartest <u>student</u> in her school. _____

2. One of the most popular sports <u>are</u> soccer. _____

3. No other man is <u>strong</u> than Tim. _____

4. It is richer than any other <u>countries</u> in the world. _____

C. 다음 문장이 같은 뜻이 되도록 빈칸에 알맞은 말을 쓰시오.

Helen is the youngest girl in this group.

= No other _____ in this group is as _____ _____ Helen.

= _____ _____ girl in this group is _____ than Helen.

= Helen is younger _____ _____ _____ girl in this group.

> **A.** scientist 과학자
>
> 「one of the＋최상급」 뒤에는 복수 명사가 온다.
>
> **B.** country 나라
>
> **C.** group 그룹, 모임

A. 다음 빈칸에 알맞은 말을 <보기>에서 골라 알맞은 형태로 바꿔 쓰시오.

> <보기>　warm　　high　　big　　cold

1. A tiger is ＿＿＿＿＿＿＿ than a cat.
2. Seoul is not so ＿＿＿＿＿＿＿ as Jeju in winter.
3. Baekdu Mountain is ＿＿＿＿＿＿＿ mountain in Korea.
4. January is the ＿＿＿＿＿＿＿ month of the year.

B. 다음 문장에서 밑줄 친 부분을 바르게 고치시오.

1. Brian can run the fastest <u>in</u> the three. ＿＿＿＿＿＿＿
2. Poems are not as interesting <u>so</u> cartoons. ＿＿＿＿＿＿＿
3. The sooner we leave, <u>early</u> we will arrive. ＿＿＿＿＿＿＿
4. No animal in the world is as <u>bigger</u> as an elephant.

＿＿＿＿＿＿＿

C. 다음 우리말과 같은 뜻이 되도록 빈칸에 알맞은 말을 쓰시오.

1. 그녀는 반에서 가장 빠른 소녀들 중 한 명이다.
   → She is ＿＿＿＿ ＿＿＿＿ the ＿＿＿＿ ＿＿＿＿ in her class.
2. 점점 더 많은 사람들이 영어를 배우고 있다.
   → ＿＿＿＿ ＿＿＿＿ ＿＿＿＿ people are learning English.
3. 이 컴퓨터는 저것보다 세 배 더 비싸다.
   → This computer is three times ＿＿＿＿ ＿＿＿＿ ＿＿＿＿ that one.
4. 어떤 후식도 이 케이크보다 달콤하지 않다.
   → No dessert is ＿＿＿＿ ＿＿＿＿ this cake.

D. 다음 문장과 뜻이 같도록 빈칸에 알맞은 말을 쓰시오.

1. Jenny is not as heavy as Monica.
   = Jenny is ＿＿＿＿ ＿＿＿＿ than Monica.
2. This room is twice as large as that one.
   = This room is ＿＿＿＿ ＿＿＿＿ than that one.
3. Peter practices the piano as hard as possible.
   = Peter practices the piano as hard as ＿＿＿＿ ＿＿＿＿.
4. This is the longest bridge in the world.
   = This is longer than ＿＿＿＿ ＿＿＿＿ ＿＿＿＿ in the world.

Grammar Tip

A. January 1월

「the+비교급, the+비교급」은 '~하면 할수록 더욱 …한'의 뜻이다.

B. leave 떠나다
　cartoon 만화

'가장 ~한 것 중 하나'는 「one of the+최상급+복수명사」로 표현한다.

C. dessert 후식

D. practice 연습하다
　bridge 다리

1. 다음 중 비교급, 최상급의 연결이 바르지 <u>못한</u> 것은?

   ① busy – busier – busiest
   ② thin – thiner – thinest
   ③ nice – nicer – nicest
   ④ little – less – least
   ⑤ useful – more useful – most useful

[2-3] 다음 빈칸에 알맞은 것을 고르시오.

2.
   This cell phone is _____ than mine.

   ① good   ② better
   ③ best   ④ more good
   ⑤ the best

3.
   Kate is as _____ as Susan.

   ① pretty   ② prettier
   ③ more pretty   ④ prettiest
   ⑤ the prettiest

4. 다음 우리말과 뜻이 같도록 할 때 빈칸에 알맞은 것은?

   그는 가능한 빨리 저녁을 먹었다.
   → He had dinner _____.

   ① as fast as possible
   ② as fast as he can
   ③ as fast as could
   ④ as fast as he possible
   ⑤ as fast as could he

[5-6] 다음 빈칸에 알맞지 <u>않은</u> 것을 고르시오.

5.
   This is more _____ than that.

   ① popular   ② famous
   ③ interesting   ④ boring
   ⑤ heavy

6.
   Jake swims _____ better than Tony.

   ① much   ② a lot
   ③ very   ④ even
   ⑤ still

7. 다음 빈칸에 공통으로 알맞은 것은?

   · She is _____ most beautiful actress.
   · _____ longer I waited, _____ more
   bored I felt.

   ① as   ② so
   ③ the   ④ than
   ⑤ no

8. 다음 빈칸에 들어갈 말이 바르게 짝지어진 것은?

   · Sally is not _____ tall as her sister.
   · These shoes are less heavy _____
   those ones.

   ① as – as   ② as – than
   ③ so – as   ④ so – so
   ⑤ than – so

9. 다음 우리말을 바르게 영작한 것은?

> 에베레스트 산은 세계의 다른 어떤 산보다 높다.

① Mount Everest is higher than any other mountains in the world.
② Mount Everest is higher than any other mountain in the world.
③ Mount Everest is high any other mountain in the world.
④ Mount Everest is higher any other mountain in the world.
⑤ Mount Everest is one of the highest mountain in the world.

10. 다음 빈칸에 들어갈 말이 나머지와 다른 하나는?
① Edison is the greatest inventor _____ the world.
② Soccer is one of the most popular sports _____ Korea.
③ This is the best restaurant _____ our town.
④ August is the hottest month _____ the year.
⑤ Sally is the tallest student _____ her class.

11. 다음 중 어법상 어색한 것은?
① She is as busy as a bee.
② This book is thicker than that one.
③ He gets up much earlier than his dad.
④ Jenny is most famous artist in her country.
⑤ Today is the coldest day of this month.

12. 다음 두 문장을 한 문장으로 바꿔 쓸 때 빈칸에 알맞은 말을 쓰시오.

> This blue backpack is 15 dollars.
> That red backpack is 30 dollars.

→ That red backpack is _____ _____ expensive as this blue backpack.

[13-14] 다음 문장에서 어법상 어색한 부분을 찾아 바르게 고쳐 쓰시오.

13.
> In winter it is getting cold and cold.

_____ → _____

14.
> One of the most difficult subjects are math.

_____ → _____

15. 다음 중 문장의 의미가 나머지 넷과 다른 것은?
① Sam is the best baseball player in our team.
② No other baseball player in our team is as good as Sam.
③ No other baseball player in our team is better than Sam.
④ Sam is one of the best baseball players in our team.
⑤ Sam is better than any other baseball player in our team.

16. 다음 대화의 밑줄 친 부분 중 어법상 어색한 것은?

> A: Who runs ①the fastest ②in your school?
> B: Peter. He can run ③faster than ④any other ⑤boys.

17. 다음 두 문장이 같은 뜻이 되도록 빈칸에 알맞은 말을 쓰시오.

> She called me back as soon as possible.

= She called me back as soon as _____ _____ .

18. 다음 중 어법상 옳은 것은?

① The older she got, wiser she became.
② No cities in Korea is not as big so Seoul.
③ No other singer is better than Jim.
④ This room is twice as large that room.
⑤ Susie is one of the tallest model in the U.S.

19. 다음 <보기>의 문장과 뜻이 같은 것은?

<보기> Bikes are cheaper than cars.

① Cars are cheaper than bikes.
② Bikes are as cheap as cars.
③ Cars are not so cheap as bikes.
④ Bikes are more expensive than cars.
⑤ Bikes are less cheap than cars.

20. 다음 표의 내용과 일치하지 <u>않는</u> 것은?

Subjects	English	Math	Science	History
Scores	90	95	85	90

① The English score is higher than the science score.
② The math score is the highest of the four.
③ The science score is lower than the history score.
④ The history score is the lowest of all.
⑤ The English score is not as high as the math score.

<서술형 문제>

21. 다음 괄호 안의 단어를 알맞은 형태로 바꿔 쓰시오.

A: How was the movie?
B: It was _____ movie of all. The story was very boring and I fell asleep. (bad)

22. 다음 세 문장이 같은 뜻이 되도록 빈칸에 알맞은 말을 쓰시오.

Picasso is the greatest artist in the world.

= _____ other artist in the world is as _____ _____ Picasso.

= Picasso is greater _____ _____ _____ _____ _____ in the world.

[23-24] 다음 우리말과 뜻이 같도록 괄호 안의 단어들을 바르게 배열하시오.

23.
지구는 달보다 네 배 크다. (than, four, the earth, bigger, the moon, is, times)

→ _____

24.
건강은 우리의 인생에서 가장 중요한 것 중의 하나이다. (the, health, one of, of, is, most, things, life, our, important)

→ _____

25. 다음 Lisa와 친구들의 일주일 동안의 기록표를 보고 빈칸에 알맞은 말을 쓰시오.

	Lisa	Kate	Paul
Spend money	25 dollars	15 dollars	25 dollars
Read books	3 books	5 books	1 book

(1) Paul spent as _____ money _____ Lisa.
(2) Kate spent _____ _____ money of the three.
(3) Kate read _____ _____ books of the three.
(4) Lisa read _____ books _____ Kate.

접속사란 무엇인가?
접속사는 단어와 단어, 구와 구, 절과 절을 연결하는 말로 등위 접속사, 종속접속사, 상관접속사 등이 있다.

접속사의 종류에는 무엇이 있는가?
문법적 역할이 대등한 것을 연결하는 등위접속사(and, but, or), 명사절이나 시간, 이유, 조건 등의 부사절을 이끄는 종속접속사 (that, when, because, if), 짝을 이루어 사용하는 상관접속사 (both A and B, either A or B) 등이 있다.
She is a great singer **and** composer.
We're late **because** we missed the bus.
Both Jenny **and** I are interested in taking pictures.

Chapter 11. 접속사

Unit 56 | and, but, or

- and: '그리고, ~와'라는 뜻으로 서로 대등한 내용을 연결한다.
  I met Peter **and** we went out for a walk.
- but: '그러나, 하지만'의 뜻으로 서로 반대되는 내용을 연결한다.
  Penguins can swim, **but** they can't fly.
- or: '또는'이라는 뜻으로 둘 중 선택하여 말할 때 쓴다.
  I will be there on Monday **or** Tuesday.
- 「명령문, and ...」: '~해라, 그러면 … 할 것이다'의 뜻으로 if를 사용하여 바꿔 쓸 수 있다.
  Exercise regularly, **and** you'll be healthy.
  = **If** you exercise regularly, you'll be healthy.
- 「명령문, or ...」: '~해라, 그렇지 않으면 … 할 것이다'의 뜻으로 if ~ not 또는 unless를 사용하여 바꿔 쓸 수 있다.
  Hurry up, or you'll miss the train.
  = If you **don't** hurry up, you'll miss the train. = **Unless** you hurry up, you'll miss the train.

Practice

Grammar Tip

and를 사용하여 세 개 이상의 것을 연결할 때는 마지막에 and를 쓴다.

A. 다음 괄호 안에서 알맞은 것을 고르시오.

1. He knocked the door (and / but) went in.
2. We can go on a picnic (but / or) stay at home.
3. My grandma is over 80, (and / but) she still goes to work.
4. Fred can speak Korean, Japanese, (and / but) English.

A. knock 두드리다

B. 다음 우리말과 뜻이 같도록 주어진 단어들을 알맞게 배열하시오.

1. 그녀는 예쁘지는 않지만 매우 인기 있다.
   (very, not, is, popular, she, pretty, but)
   → _____

2. 현금이나 신용카드로 계산할 수 있습니다.
   (credit card, can, or, you, by, pay, cash)
   → _____

3. 지금 출발해라, 그러면 너는 버스를 탈 수 있다.
   (can, and, now, the, you, leave, catch, bus)
   → _____

B. pay by ~으로 지불하다
catch (버스 등을 시간 맞춰) 타다

C. 다음 두 문장이 같은 뜻이 되도록 빈칸에 알맞은 말을 쓰시오.

1. If you read many books, you will be wiser.
   = _____ _____ _____, _____ you will be wiser.

2. If you don't take a break, you will get tired.
   = _____ _____ _____, _____ you will get tired.

C. wise 현명한

57 | 접속사 that

- 접속사 that이 이끄는 명사절은 '~이라는 것, ~한다는 것'이라는 뜻으로 문장에서 주어나 보어 역할을 한다. that 이 주어로 쓰일 때는 가주어 it을 사용하여 바꿔 쓸 수 있다.

  That your parents love you is true. 〈주어 역할〉

  = It is true that your parents love you.

  The bad news is **that** Jake can't go to the party. 〈보어 역할〉

- that이 이끄는 명사절이 think, know, believe, say, hope 등의 목적어 역할을 할 때 that은 생략할 수 있다.

  I believe (**that**) my dream will come true. 〈목적어 역할〉

  I hope (**that**) she gets better soon. 〈목적어 역할〉

Practice

A. 다음 밑줄 친 that을 생략할 수 있으면 ○, 생략할 수 없으면 ×를 쓰시오.

1. <u>That</u> you can go there is the good news. (   )

2. Susie said <u>that</u> she got an A on the math exam. (   )

3. The problem is <u>that</u> my brother doesn't study at all. (   )

4. I think <u>that</u> he is the best singer in Korea. (   )

B. 다음 우리말 뜻과 같도록 빈칸에 알맞은 말을 쓰시오.

1. 그가 우리에게 거짓말을 한 것은 사실이다.

   → _____ he told us a lie is the truth.

2. 우리는 네가 경기에서 이길 수 있다고 믿는다.

   → We believe _____ you can win the game.

3. 중요한 것은 우리가 최선을 다해야 한다는 것이다.

   → The important thing is _____ we should do our best.

4. 나는 그가 자동차 사고가 났다는 것을 들었다.

   → I heard _____ he had a car accident.

C. 다음 두 문장을 접속사 that을 이용하여 한 문장으로 바꿔 쓰시오.

1. I hope. + You will pass the exam.

   → _____

2. Sally speaks Japanese well. + It's true.

   → _____

3. I think. + We should protect the earth.

   → _____

58 | 시간 접속사 1

- when: '～할 때'라는 뜻으로 시간을 나타내는 부사절을 이끈다.
  I learned French **when** I was young.
- while: '～하는 동안'이라는 뜻으로 시간을 나타내는 부사절을 이끈다.
  Jenny was reading a book **while** I was cooking.
- as: '～할 때'라는 뜻으로 시간을 나타내는 부사절을 이끈다.
  As I heard the news, I was very shocked.
- 시간을 나타내는 부사절에서는 미래의 의미를 나타내더라도 현재 시제를 쓴다.
  I'll tell you **when** Brian is here. (O)
  I'll tell you **when** Brian will be here. (×)

 Practice

A. 다음 우리말과 같은 뜻이 되도록 괄호 안에서 알맞은 것을 고르시오.

1. 그녀는 버스를 기다리는 동안 음악을 들었다.
   → She listened to music (while / when) she was waiting for the bus.

2. 나의 엄마는 피곤하실 때 차 한 잔을 드신다.
   → My mom drinks a cup of tea (and / when) she is tired.

3. 오늘 아침에 일어났을 때 나는 기분이 좋았다.
   → (As / While) I got up this morning, I felt good.

4. 그들은 TV를 보는 동안 간식을 먹었다.
   → They ate some snacks (but / while) they were watching TV.

B. 다음 문장을 우리말로 해석하시오.

1. I'll go out when I'm ready.
   → _____

2. The phone rang while I was taking a shower.
   → _____

3. As I arrived at home, it started raining.
   → _____

C. 다음 두 문장을 괄호 안의 말을 이용하여 한 문장으로 바꿔 쓰시오.

1. He will come to the party. + He finishes his work. (when)
   → _____

2. They were playing soccer. + Someone called them. (while)
   → _____

3. I opened the door. + I dropped my mug. (as)
   → _____

Grammar Tip

while은 동시 동작의 의미가 강하므로 주로 진행형과 함께 쓰인다.

A. wait for ～을 기다리다
   snack 간식

B. ready 준비가 된

C. call 부르다
   drop 떨어뜨리다

59 시간 접속사 2

- before: '~하기 전에'라는 뜻이고, after는 '~한 후에'라는 뜻의 시간을 나타내는 접속사이다.

  You should wash your hands **before** you eat.

  My dad got better **after** he took some medicine.

- until: '~할 때까지'의 뜻으로 계속의 의미를 나타낸다.

  We had to wait **until** it stopped raining.

- since: '~한 이래로'라는 뜻으로 과거부터 현재까지 계속되는 의미를 나타낸다. 주로 현재완료와 함께 쓰인다.

  She <u>has worn</u> glasses **since** she was nine years old.

Practice

A. 다음 괄호 안에서 알맞은 것을 고르시오.

1. Brush your teeth (before / after) you go to bed.

2. I have played the piano (until / since) I was young.

3. Stay in your seat (before / until) we arrive at the gate.

4. She watched a movie (until / after) she finished the work.

B. 다음 빈칸에 알맞은 것을 〈보기〉에서 골라 문장을 완성하시오.

| 〈보기〉 until I lose weight |
| before the movie started |
| after I come back home |

1. I always wash my hands _____.

2. I turned off my cell phone _____.

3. I will exercise _____.

C. 다음 우리말과 뜻이 같도록 주어진 단어들을 알맞게 배열하시오.

1. 나가기 전에 우산을 챙겨라. (go, before, you, out)

   → Take your umbrella _____.

2. Tim은 잠들 때까지 TV를 봤다. (he, asleep, until, fell)

   → Tim watched TV _____.

3. 나는 여기 이사 온 이후로 수영을 배우고 있다. (here, since, moved, I)

   → I have learned to swim _____.

Grammar Tip

A. seat 좌석
    gate 출입구

B. turn off ~을 끄다

before, after, until, since는 전치사로도 쓰이는데 전치사로 쓰일 때는 뒤에 명사나 동명사가 온다.
We sit down **before** reading a book.
My dad gets up **before** 6 a.m.

C. fall asleep 잠들다
    move 이사하다

60 이유 접속사

- **because**: '～때문에'라는 뜻으로 이유를 나타내는 부사절을 이끈다. because of도 '～때문에'라는 뜻으로 이유를 나타내지만, 뒤에는 명사나 동명사가 온다.

  We couldn't play baseball **because** it rained.

  = We couldn't play baseball **because of** rain.

- **as**와 **since**: '～때문에'라는 뜻으로 이유를 나타낸다.

  I went to bed early **as** I was so tired.

  We decided to go to the beach **since** it was a nice day.

 Practice

A. 다음 빈칸에 알맞은 말을 〈보기〉에서 골라 쓰시오.

> 〈보기〉 because of a cold
> because I felt hungry
> as the traffic was bad
> since it was so noisy

1. I made sandwiches _____.
2. I was late _____.
3. I couldn't sleep well _____.
4. Jenny was absent for school _____.

B. 다음 밑줄 친 부분을 우리말로 해석하시오.

1. I'm studying because of the math test.

   → _____

2. Since he lost his cell phone, he couldn't call me.

   → _____

3. As the movie is interesting, many people want to see it.

   → _____

C. 다음 괄호 안의 말을 이용하여 한 문장으로 바꿔 쓰시오.

1. We couldn't arrive on time. + We missed the train. (since)

   → _____

2. He was weak. + He decided to exercise. (as)

   → _____

3. The bank was closed. + It was Sunday. (because)

   → _____

 Grammar Tip

because 뒤에는 절(주어+동사)이 오고 because of 뒤에는 명사나 동명사가 나온다.

A. cold 감기
traffic 교통량

접속사 as의 여러 가지 의미
(1) ～ 때문에
  I was late **as** I got up late.
(2) ～할 때
  I was sleeping **as** I got a call.
(3) ～대로
  Do **as** I say!

B. call 전화하다

C. on time 시간에 딱 맞춰
  miss 놓치다
  weak 약한

61 | 결과 접속사

- so: '그래서'의 뜻으로 결과를 나타낸다. so가 있는 문장은 이유를 나타내는 접속사를 사용하여 바꿔 쓸 수 있다.
  The room was dark, **so** I turned on the light.
  = I turned on the light **because[as, since]** the room was dark.
- 「so+형용사[부사]+that」: '너무 ~해서 …하다'의 뜻으로 결과를 나타낸다.
  The table was **so** heavy **that** I couldn't carry it.
  I got up **so** late **that** I missed the school bus.

Practice

A. 다음 두 문장을 접속사 so를 이용하여 한 문장으로 바꿔 쓰시오.

1. Jake felt tired. + He came back early.
   → _____ .

2. I was very busy. + I couldn't go see a movie.
   → _____ .

3. We won the first prize. + We are all happy.
   → _____ .

B. 다음 우리말과 같은 뜻이 되도록 빈칸에 알맞은 말을 쓰시오.

1. 나의 남동생은 너무 아파서 병원에 가야 했다.
   → My brother was _____ _____ _____ he had to go to the hospital.

2. 너무 더워서 나는 선풍기를 틀었다.
   → It was _____ _____ _____ I turned on the fan.

3. 그 책은 너무 지루해서 Lisa는 잠이 들었다.
   → The book was _____ _____ _____ Lisa fell asleep.

C. 다음 두 문장이 같은 뜻이 되도록 문장을 완성하시오.

1. I need to ask you something, so I'll visit you.
   = _____ , I'll visit you.

2. He didn't wear a coat, so he got a cold.
   = He got a cold _____ .

3. Because it snowed heavily, the bus couldn't arrive in time.
   = It snowed heavily, _____ .

Grammar Tip

A. prize 상

B. fan 선풍기
fall asleep 잠들다

because, as, since 뒤에는 원인이나 이유를 나타내는 내용이 오고, so 뒤에는 결과를 나타내는 내용이 온다.

C. get a cold 감기에 걸리다
heavily 심하게
in time 제시간 안에

62 조건 접속사

- if: '만약 ~라면'의 뜻으로 조건을 나타내는 부사절을 이끈다. 조건을 나타내는 부사절에서는 미래의 의미를 나타내더라도 현재 시제를 쓴다.

  Let's go hiking **if** you <u>are</u> free tomorrow. (○)

  Let's go hiking **if** you <u>will be</u> free tomorrow. (×)

- unless: '만약 ~하지 않는다면'의 뜻으로 「if ~ not」으로 바꿔 쓸 수 있다.

  Turn off the computer **unless** you use it.

  = Turn off the computer **if** you **don't** use it.

  Unless the weather is good, we will cancel the party.

  = **If** the weather is **not** good, we will cancel the party.

Practice

A. 다음 빈칸에 알맞은 말을 〈보기〉에서 골라 쓰시오.

> 〈보기〉 you hurry
>
> you eat too much sweets
>
> you want to read it

1. You may have a toothache if _____.

2. You will miss the train unless _____.

3. I will lend you this book if _____.

B. 다음 두 문장이 같은 뜻이 되도록 빈칸에 알맞은 말을 쓰시오.

1. If you don't have breakfast, you will be hungry.

   = _____, you will be hungry.

2. You will get wet unless you wear the raincoat.

   = You will get wet _____.

3. You can get hurt if you aren't careful.

   = You can get hurt _____.

C. 다음 우리말과 같은 뜻이 되도록 주어진 단어들을 알맞게 배열하시오.

1. 만약 질문이 있다면 손을 드세요. (have, questions, if, any, you)

   → Raise your hand _____.

2. 만약 네가 바쁘지 않다면, 나를 도와주겠니? (are, unless, busy, you)

   → Will you help me _____?

3. 만약 날씨가 흐리다면 우리는 오늘밤에 별을 볼 수 없다. (if, cloudy, is it)

   → We can't see stars tonight _____.

63 양보 접속사

· though와 although: '비록 ~이지만'의 뜻으로 양보를 나타내는 부사절을 이끈다.

Though the room was old, it was comfortable to stay.

She walked home by herself **although** it was dark.

· even if와 even though: 역시 '비록 ~일지라도, ~임에도 불구하고'의 뜻으로 양보를 나타내는 부사절을 이끈다.

Chris is going to buy the car **even if** it's very expensive.

Even though we took a taxi, we were late for the meeting.

Practice

A. 다음 괄호 안의 말을 이용하여 두 문장을 한 문장으로 바꿔 쓰시오.

1. She is over 50 years old. + She doesn't look old. (though)

   → _____.

2. I don't speak English well. + I will travel to Canada. (although)

   → _____.

3. Andy is young. + He is very brave. (even though)

   → _____.

4. You have lots of money. + You should not waste it. (even if)

   → _____.

B. 다음 우리말과 같은 뜻이 되도록 빈칸에 알맞은 말을 쓰시오.

1. Eric은 비록 키가 작았지만 최고의 선수였다. (although)

   → _____ _____ _____ _____, he was the best player.

2. 비록 그녀가 거짓말을 했지만 나는 그녀를 용서할 것이다. (though)

   → I will forgive her _____ _____ _____ _____ _____.

3. 비록 날씨가 추울지라도 우리는 캠핑을 갈 것이다. (even if)

   → We will go camping _____ _____ _____ _____ _____.

C. 다음 주어진 단어들을 알맞게 배열하여 문장을 완성하시오.

1. (this, old, though, is, car, an)

   → _____, it runs well.

2. (is, holiday, even if, a, tomorrow)

   → _____, my dad has to go to work.

3. (bad, health, even though, is, it, for)

   → My brother likes to eat fast food _____.

Grammar Tip

though, although, even if, even though는 모두 양보의 뜻을 나타내는 부사절을 이끈다.

A. waste 낭비하다

B. tell a lie 거짓말하다

C. fast food 패스트푸드
bad for ~에 나쁜

64 상관 접속사

- both A and B: 'A와 B 둘 다'의 뜻으로 주어로 쓰일 때 복수 취급하여 복수형의 동사를 쓴다.
  Both Sally **and** Tim <u>like</u> baseball.
- either A or B: 'A 또는 B 둘 중 하나'의 뜻으로 주어로 쓰일 때 B에 맞춰 동사의 형태를 결정한다.
  Either you **or** <u>he is</u> going to join us.
- not only A but also B: 'A뿐만 아니라 B도'의 뜻으로 주어로 쓰일 때 B에 맞춰 동사의 형태를 결정한다.
  Not only you **but also** <u>she is</u> very wise.

Practice

A. 다음 괄호 안에서 알맞은 것을 고르시오.

1. She can speak both English (and / or) Japanese.

2. Either you (and / or) Brian has to clean the room.

3. You can call me (both / either) on Saturday or Sunday.

4. Fred is not only a teacher (and / but) also a poet.

B. 다음 우리말과 같은 뜻이 되도록 주어진 단어들을 이용하여 문장을 완성하시오.

1. 너는 그 책을 사거나 빌릴 수 있다.
   → You can _____.
   (book / or / buy / either / the / borrow)

2. 그녀와 나 둘 다 피자를 매우 좋아한다.
   → _____ pizza very much.
   (and / she / I / like / both)

3. 너뿐만 아니라 Alice도 그 영화를 보고 싶어 한다.
   → _____ wants to see the movie.
   (but also / Alice / you / not only)

4. Emma는 배고플 뿐만 아니라 피곤하기도 하다.
   → Emma _____.
   (tired / is / not only / but also / hungry)

C. 다음 문장에서 어법상 어색한 부분을 찾아 동그라미 하고 바르게 고치시오.

1. Both math and science is my favorite subject. _____

2. Either Sam or I has to leave now. _____

3. Not only you but also Jay don't know the answer. _____

4. Both my dad and my mom enjoys cooking. _____

 **Review Test**

 56~64

A. 다음 빈칸에 알맞은 말을 <보기>에서 골라 쓰시오.

> <보기>   that   since   while   or

1. Jennifer has learned Korean _____ she was ten.
2. I washed the dishes _____ my mom was cleaning.
3. I think _____ Nick wants to go shopping.
4. Walk faster, _____ you'll miss the bus.

B. 다음 문장에서 밑줄 친 부분을 바르게 고치시오.

1. <u>Because</u> Maria is young, she is wiser than any other girl.
   _____
2. <u>While</u> I was a child, I wanted to be a soccer player.
   _____
3. Both Jenny <u>or</u> Paul enjoy skating.   _____
4. We had to cancel the picnic <u>because</u> the bad weather.
   _____

C. 다음 우리말과 같은 뜻이 되도록 괄호 안의 단어들을 바르게 배열하시오.

1. Amy는 그녀의 어머니가 돌아오실 때까지 잠자리에 들지 않았다.
   (came, mother, until, her, back)
   → Amy didn't go to bed _____.
2. 나는 치즈 케이크나 아이스크림 둘 중 하나를 먹고 싶다.
   (cheese cake, or, either, ice cream)
   → I'd like to have _____.
3. 너무 추워서 많은 사람들이 코트를 입고 있다.
   (many, so, that, are, wearing, cold, people)
   → It is _____ a coat.
4. 나뿐만 아니라 그녀도 역시 수영을 잘한다.
   (I, but also, she, not only, is)
   → _____ good at swimming.

D. 다음 두 문장이 같은 뜻이 되도록 빈칸에 알맞은 말을 쓰시오.

1. As he got the flu, he was absent from school.
   = He got the flu, _____ he was absent from school.
2. Eat less at night if you don't want to gain weight.
   = Eat less at night _____ you want to gain weight.
3. My dad watches the news after he has dinner.
   = My dad has dinner _____ he watches the news.

Grammar Tip

A. go shopping 쇼핑하러 가다

because 뒤에는 [주어+동사]로 이루어진 절이 오고, because of 뒤에는 명사(구)가 온다.

B. wise 현명한
   cancel 취소하다

C. be good at ~을 잘하다

D. flu 독감
   absent 결석한

125

[1-2] 다음 빈칸에 알맞은 것을 고르시오.

1.
> I lost my cell phone, _____ I have to buy a new one.

① as   ② because
③ so   ④ though
⑤ when

2.
> Exercise regularly, _____ you'll be healthy.

① and   ② but
③ or   ④ until
⑤ that

3. 다음 빈칸에 공통으로 알맞은 것은?
> · Either Brian _____ Max is wrong.
> · Be careful, _____ you'll get hurt.

① and   ② or
③ but   ④ if
⑤ unless

4. 다음 중 밑줄 친 접속사의 쓰임이 어색한 것은?
① Do not speak <u>while</u> you are eating.
② This book is expensive <u>but</u> very useful.
③ <u>Even though</u> it was hot, Henry didn't stop running.
④ <u>When</u> you cross the street, you should watch your step.
⑤ <u>Because</u> the traffic jam, we can't go there in time.

5. 다음 밑줄 친 ①~⑤ 중 생략할 수 있는 것은?
> We ①<u>found</u> ②<u>that</u> ③<u>the movie</u> ④<u>was</u> very ⑤<u>boring</u>.

6. 다음 우리말과 뜻이 같도록 빈칸에 알맞은 것을 모두 고르면?
> 그는 바빴기 때문에 아침 식사를 할 수 없었다.
> → He couldn't have breakfast _____ he was busy.

① as   ② unless
③ because   ④ although
⑤ since

7. 다음 빈칸에 들어갈 말이 바르게 짝지어진 것은?
> · _____ the food was expensive, it tasted good.
> · Wash your face _____ you go to bed.

① Although – before   ② If – while
③ Unless – after   ④ Even – though
⑤ Both – until

8. 다음 우리말을 바르게 영작한 것은?
> 버스가 올 때까지 여기서 기다리자.

① Let's wait until the bus comes.
② Let's wait until the bus will come.
③ Let's wait when the bus comes.
④ Let's wait since the bus comes.
⑤ Let's wait after the bus comes.

9. 다음 빈칸에 공통으로 알맞은 말을 쓰시오.

> · I think _____ she is a good singer.
> · The movie was so scary _____
>   I was shocked.

10. 다음 밑줄 친 that의 쓰임이 나머지 넷과 다른 것은?

① I hope that Fred will get better soon.
② That Susie won the race is true.
③ They believe that Lisa doesn't tell a lie.
④ The good news is that the festival will be held next week.
⑤ I haven't seen that movie before.

11. 다음 중 밑줄 친 부분이 어법상 어색한 것은?

① I'll be happy if he comes with me.
② Both Paul and I don't like sports.
③ Either you or Sam know the answer.
④ Not only she but also he is tall.
⑤ Eric will wait until they visit him.

12. 다음 빈칸에 이어질 말로 알맞은 것은?

> Do your best, _____.

① and you'll be happy with the result
② or you'll be happy with the result
③ after you'll be happy with the result
④ that you'll be happy with the result
⑤ but you'll be happy with the result

13. 다음 우리말과 같은 뜻이 되도록 빈칸에 알맞은 것은?

> 휴식을 취한 후에 나는 훨씬 더 좋아졌다.

→ I felt much better _____ I got some rest.

14. 다음 두 문장을 한 문장으로 바꿔 쓸 때 빈칸에 알맞은 말을 쓰시오.

> Ben is taking swimming lessons.
> + I'm taking swimming lessons, too.

→ _____ Ben _____ I are taking swimming lessons.

15. 다음 밑줄 친 as의 의미가 <보기>와 같은 것은?

> <보기> As the movie was boring,
>   I didn't watch it any more.

① I'll keep the promise as I said.
② I closed the window as it was too noisy.
③ As we heard the news, we couldn't believe it.
④ He was reading as I entered the room.
⑤ I saw Daniel as I was getting off the bus.

[16-17] 다음 문장에서 어법상 어색한 부분을 찾아 바르게 고쳐 쓰시오.

16.
> Not only I but also my sister are interested in baking.

_____ → _____

17.
> I'm going to see a movie when I will meet Mike this evening.

_____ → _____

[18-19] 다음 두 문장이 같은 뜻이 되도록 빈칸에 알맞은 말을 고르시오.

18.

> It was very cold, but many people enjoyed skiing.
> = _____ it was very cold, many people enjoyed skiing.

① Unless   ② If
③ Though   ④ So
⑤ Because

19.

> I was busy, so I couldn't go to the concert.
> = I was so busy _____ I couldn't go to the concert.

① as   ② until
③ that   ④ or
⑤ after

20. 다음 빈칸에 공통으로 알맞은 접속사를 쓰시오.

> · We have studied English _____ we were ten years old.
> · I'll go to the park _____ it is Sunny today.

〈서술형 문제〉

21. 다음 문장들이 같은 뜻이 되도록 빈칸에 알맞은 말을 쓰시오.

> If you don't wear a coat, you'll catch a cold.

= _____ you _____ _____ _____, you'll catch a cold.

= Wear a coat, _____ _____ _____ _____ _____.

22. 다음 우리말과 같도록 괄호 안의 단어들을 바르게 배열하시오.

> Brad나 Sam 둘 중 한 명은 달리기를 잘한다.
> (at, or, Brad, good, either, running, Sam, is)

→ _____

23. 다음 두 문장을 괄호 안의 접속사를 이용하여 한 문장으로 바꿔 쓰시오.

> His computer is in good condition.
> + He wants to buy a new one.
>   (even though)

→ _____

24. 다음 대화의 내용과 일치하도록 문장을 완성하시오.

> *Andy*: Call me when you arrive at home.
> *Jenny*: Sorry, I can't. My cell phone is broken.

→ Jenny can't call Andy
_____.

25. 다음 대화의 빈칸에 알맞은 접속사를 〈보기〉에서 골라 쓰시오.

> 〈보기〉 although if that since when

> A: These cookies are very delicious!
> B: I bought them (1) _____ I went to Japan. These are one of the most popular cookies in Japan.
> A: I heard (2) _____ many people like them.
> B: Have some more (3) _____ you want.

관계사란 무엇인가?
관계사는 두 문장을 연결할 때 같은 말의 반복을 피하기 위해 쓰는 것으로 접속사와 대명사 또는 접속사와 부사의 역할을 한다. 관계사에는 관계대명사와 관계부사가 있다.

관계사는 어떤 역할을 하는가?
관계대명사는 두 문장을 연결하는 「접속사+대명사」의 역할을 하는 것으로 who, which, that 등이 있다.
관계부사는 두 문장을 연결하는 「접속사+부사」의 역할을 하는 것으로 where, when, why, how 등이 있다.
I know the man **who** is sitting on the bench.
This is the town **where** I was born.

Chapter 12. 관계사

Unit 65 관계대명사 who

- 관계대명사 : 두 문장을 연결하는 「접속사+대명사」의 역할을 하며 앞에 나온 명사(선행사)를 수식한다.
- 선행사가 사람이면 관계대명사 who를 쓴다. 이때, 선행사는 관계대명사절에서의 역할에 따라 who, whose, whom을 쓴다.

주격	who	I met the boy. + He is from Italy. → I met the boy **who** is from Italy. 선행사　주격 관계대명사
소유격	whose	I know a girl. + Her father is a math teacher. → I know a girl **whose** father is a math teacher. 선행사　소유격 관계대명사
목적격	whom[who]	He is a singer. + I like him. → He is a singer **whom[who]** I like. 선행사　목적격 관계대명사 * 구어체에서는 목적격 관계대명사 whom 대신 who를 쓰기도 한다.

Practice

A. 다음 괄호 안에서 알맞은 것을 고르시오.

1. The woman (who / whose) lives next door is a doctor.

2. Look at the girl (whose / whom) hair is very long.

3. The boy (whose / whom) you met yesterday was my classmate.

4. I have a friend (who / whom) is good at playing soccer.

B. 다음 빈칸에 알맞은 관계대명사를 쓰시오.

1. Do you know that boy _____ is eating ice cream?

2. The man is my uncle _____ hobby is taking pictures.

3. She is the staff member _____ I called yesterday.

4. The girl _____ we saw this morning was Wendy.

C. 다음 두 문장을 관계대명사를 이용하여 한 문장으로 바꿔 쓰시오.

1. There are many girls. + They are playing badminton.
   → _____

2. He is the boy. + His mother is a famous actress.
   → _____

3. Ms. Green is a teacher. + Everyone respects her.
   → _____

Grammar Tip

주격 관계대명사 다음에는 동사가 바로 오고 목적격 관계대명사 다음에는 「주어+동사」가 온다.

A. next door 옆집

B. hobby 취미
staff member 직원

C. actress 여배우
respect 존경하다

66 관계대명사 which

· 선행사가 사물 또는 동물이면 관계대명사 which를 쓴다. 이때, 선행사는 관계대명사절에서의 역할에 따라 which 또는 whose를 쓴다.

주격	which	I don't like the movie. It has a sad ending. → I don't like the movie which has a sad ending. 　　　　　　　선행사　　주격 관계대명사
소유격	whose	Look at the dog. Its legs are very short. → Look at the dog whose legs are very short. 　　　　　　선행사　　소유격 관계대명사
목적격	which	I'm looking for the cap. My mom bought it for me. → I'm looking for the cap which my mom bought for me. 　　　　　　　선행사　목적격 관계대명사

Practice

A. 다음 두 문장을 관계대명사를 이용하여 한 문장으로 바꿔 쓰시오.

1. Fred has a dog. + Its name is Molly.

→ _____

2. They climbed the mountain. + Its top is covered with snow.

→ _____

3. This is the song. + Many people like it.

→ _____

4. We need a house. + It has a beautiful garden.

→ _____

B. 다음 문장에서 어법상 어색한 부분을 찾아 동그라미 하고 바르게 고쳐 쓰시오.

1. Look at the car which window is broken. _____

2. I bought a book whose is useful for children. _____

3. I'm wearing the dress whose Anne made for me. _____

4. Tony lives in the house who window is always open. _____

C. 다음을 두 개의 문장으로 나눠 쓸 때 빈칸에 알맞은 말을 쓰시오.

1. A giraffe is an animal which has a long neck.

→ A giraffe is an animal. + _____

2. This is the movie which they watched yesterday.

→ This is the movie. + _____

3. Did you see the cap whose color is pink?

→ Did you see the cap? + _____

Grammar Tip

A. top 꼭대기, 정상
be covered with ~로 덮여 있다

B. useful 유용한

목적격 관계대명사가 있는 절은 목적어를 가지고 있지 않지만 두 개의 문장으로 나눠 쓸 때는 목적어를 찾아서 써야 하는 것에 유의한다.

C. neck 목

67 관계대명사의 수 일치

- 관계대명사절의 수식을 받아 주어 부분이 길어지는 경우에 문장의 동사를 잘 찾아서 주어와 수 일치를 한다.

① 주격 관계대명사가 쓰인 절이 주어를 수식할 때

주격 관계대명사절의 수식을 받아 주어 부분이 길어지는 경우에 주어와 동사를 잘 구별해야 한다. 이때, 동사의 수는 관계대명사절과 상관없이 항상 주어의 수에 일치한다.

The boy who is talking on the phone / **is** my brother.

    주어   관계대명사절   동사

② 목적격 관계대명사가 쓰인 절이 주어를 수식할 때

목적격 관계대명사절의 수식을 받아 주어 부분이 길어지는 경우에 주어와 동사를 잘 구별해야 한다. 이때도 동사의 수는 관계대명사절과 상관없이 주어의 수에 일치한다.

The pictures which Sally took yesterday / **are** very nice.

    주어   관계대명사절   동사

Practice

A. 다음 괄호 안에서 알맞은 것을 고르시오.

1. The tree which I planted last year (is / are) growing well.
2. The woman who is playing with kids (is / are) my teacher.
3. The dress which I bought (fit / fits) me.
4. The boy whom I helped (don't / doesn't) speak English.

B. 다음 빈칸에 be동사 현재형의 알맞은 형태를 쓰시오.

1. The school which is at the corner _____ very small.
2. The man whom I saw on the bus _____ a soccer player.
3. The grapes which I bought _____ sour.
4. The girl who is from Mexico _____ very pretty.

C. 다음 우리말과 같은 뜻이 되도록 주어진 단어들을 알맞게 배열하시오.

1. Sam이 좋아하는 소녀는 Jennifer이다. (is, Sam, likes, whom, Jennifer)
   → The girl _____.

2. 내가 읽고 싶어했던 책은 다 팔렸다.
   (was, wanted, sold, read, I, to, out, which)
   → The book _____.

3. 그 사무실에 있는 사람들은 친절하다.
   (are, office, who, work, at, kind, the)
   → The people _____.

Grammar Tip

관계대명사절을 포함한 문장에서는 주어와 동사를 잘 구별해야 한다.

A. plant 심다
fit 맞다

B. corner 모퉁이
sour 맛이 신

C. sold out 다 팔린

68 | 관계대명사 that

- 관계대명사 that은 선행사의 종류와 상관없이 who, whom, which를 대신해 쓸 수 있다. that은 주격과 목적격의 형태가 같다.

  Kate is the girl **that[who]** won the first prize.

  This is the cell phone **that[which]** I want to buy.

- 최상급, 서수, the only, the very, the same, all 등이 선행사를 수식하거나 -thing으로 끝나는 명사 또는 '사람+사물'이 선행사인 경우에는 관계대명사 that을 주로 쓴다.

  This is the <u>funniest movie</u> **that** I've ever seen.

  I gave her <u>all the money</u> **that** I had.

Practice

A. 다음 괄호 안에서 알맞은 것을 <u>모두</u> 고르시오.

1. I met a man (who / whose / that) sister knows you.

2. An architect is someone (who / whom / that) designs buildings.

3. The news (which / whose / that) I heard this morning is true.

4. Look at the girl and the dog (which / that) are running in the park.

B. 다음 밑줄 친 부분과 바꿔 쓸 수 있는 말을 쓰시오.

1. I know the woman <u>that</u> is sitting over there. → _____

2. This is the food <u>that</u> comes from Spain. → _____

3. She is the president <u>that</u> a lot of people like. → _____

4. The box <u>that</u> Jake is holding is very heavy. → _____

C. 다음 주어진 단어들을 알맞게 배열하여 문장을 완성하시오.

1. Columbus was the man _____.
   (discovered, that, in, America, 1492)

2. This is the most delicious cake _____.
   (I've, eaten, ever, that)

3. A car hit a boy and his dog _____.
   (were, street, crossing, that, the)

4. Are there any pants _____?
   (this, that, matches, blouse)

Grammar Tip

소유격 관계대명사 whose는 that으로 바꿔 쓸 수 없다.

A. architect 건축가

B. president 대통령
   hold 들고 있다

C. discover 발견하다
   hit 치다
   cross 건너다
   match 어울리다

A. 다음 빈칸에 알맞은 말을 <보기>에서 골라 쓰시오.

<보기> who   whose   whom   which

1. Look at the bird _____ is flying in the sky.

2. This is my friend _____ has two brothers.

3. They live in the house _____ fence is very high.

4. Do you know the boy _____ I talked with yesterday?

B. 다음 밑줄 친 부분과 바꿔 쓸 수 있는 말을 쓰시오.

1. The singer <u>that</u> is on the stage is my aunt.   _____

2. The game <u>that</u> I wanted to watch was over.   _____

3. Jenny is the girl <u>that</u> I visited this morning.   _____

4. Many animals <u>that</u> live in the forest are in danger.   _____

C. 다음 문장에서 밑줄 친 부분을 바르게 고치시오.

1. I know the cute boy <u>that</u> father is a famous chef.   _____

2. The lady who takes a walk every morning <u>are</u> my grandmother.

_____

3. The house whose roof is red <u>were</u> built last year.   _____

4. This is the saddest movie <u>who</u> I've ever watched.   _____

D. 다음 두 문장을 관계대명사를 이용하여 한 문장으로 바꿔 쓰시오.

1. Look at the cute boy. + He is playing in the garden.

→ Look at the cute boy _____.

2. The shirt looks nice. + Henry is wearing it.

→ The shirt _____ looks nice.

3. I don't know the girl. + Jim likes her.

→ I don't know the girl _____.

4. The students come from Japan. + They live next door.

→ The students _____ live next door.

69 | 관계대명사 what

- what: 선행사를 포함하는 관계대명사로 '~하는 것'이라는 뜻이다. what은 명사절을 이끌며 문장에서 주어, 목적어, 보어의 역할을 한다.

  What Dennis said surprised us. 〈주어〉

  Tell me **what** you want to do. 〈목적어〉

  This book is **what** I wrote last year. 〈보어〉

- what은 the thing(s) that 또는 the thing(s) which로 바꿔 쓸 수 있다.

  Did you hear **what** they said?

  = Did you hear **the thing that[which]** they said?

Practice

A. 다음 괄호 안에서 알맞은 것을 고르시오.

1. (That / What) Anderson needs is love.
2. Sarah is the girl (who / what) made this cake.
3. This movie is (that / what) I watched yesterday.
4. The Louvre Museum (which / what) we wanted to visit was closed.

B. 다음 빈칸에 알맞은 말을 〈보기〉에서 골라 관계대명사 what과 함께 쓰시오.

> 〈보기〉 I really want to have
> I ate for dinner
> I heard from Susie

1. This computer is _____.
2. I can't believe _____.
3. _____ is Italian food.

C. 다음 우리말과 같은 뜻이 되도록 빈칸에 알맞은 말을 쓰시오.

1. Tim이 내게 보여 준 것은 그의 사진이었다.
   → _____ Tim showed me was a picture of him.
   = _____ Tim showed me was a picture of him.

2. 이 책은 내가 지난주에 읽은 것이다.
   → This book is _____ I read last week.
   = This book is _____ I read last week.

3. Jane은 그녀가 거리에서 본 것들을 그렸다.
   → Jane drew _____ she saw in the street.
   = Jane drew _____ she saw in the street.

Grammar Tip

what은 선행사를 포함하는 관계대명사이므로 문장에 선행사가 따로 나와 있지 않다.

A. Louvre Museum 루브르 박물관

B. Italian 이탈리아의

C. picture 사진
   draw 그리다

70 관계대명사의 생략

- 목적격 관계대명사 whom, which, that은 생략할 수 있다.

  This is the bag (which[that]) I'm looking for.

  Sophie is the girl (whom[that]) Henry really wants to meet.

- 주격 관계대명사 뒤에 be동사가 있고 뒤에 현재분사나 과거분사가 올 때 「주격 관계대명사+be동사」는 함께 생략할 수 있다.

  Look at the boys (who are) <u>playing</u> baseball.

  The house (which was) <u>built</u> by Fred was great.

Practice

A. 다음 문장에서 생략할 수 있는 부분에 밑줄을 그으시오.

1. The man that you met at the bus stop is my uncle.

2. This is the song which Ben likes best.

3. We saw the ball which is made of recycled paper.

4. Do you know the girls who are playing tennis over there?

B. 다음 문장에서 생략된 부분을 찾아 넣어 문장을 다시 쓰시오.

1. This is the portrait I drew for myself.

   → _____

2. I know the boy taking a nap on the bench.

   → _____

3. She is the hair designer Ann wants to work with.

   → _____

4. He read the book written in Korean.

   → _____

C. 다음 주어진 단어를 이용하여 관계대명사를 포함하는 문장으로 쓰시오.

1. Look at the boys (swim) in the pool.

   → _____

2. This is the chair (make) of glass.

   → _____

3. Can you see the woman (eat) sandwich?

   → _____

Grammar Tip

A. bus stop 버스 정류장
recycled paper 재활용 종이

B. portrait 초상화
take a nap 낮잠 자다
hair designer 미용사

'~하고 있는'이라는 뜻의 능동의 의미에는 현재분사가, '~된'이라는 뜻의 수동의 의미에는 과거분사가 쓰여 선행사를 수식한다. 이때 분사 앞에는 「주격관계대명사+be동사」가 생략될 수 있다.

C. chair 의자
glass 유리

71 관계부사 1

- 관계부사 : 두 문장을 연결하는 접속사와 부사의 역할을 동시에 하며, 관계부사가 이끄는 절도 문장에서 선행사를 꾸며 주는 형용사적 역할을 한다.

- 선행사가 the time, the day, the year 등 '시간, 때'를 나타낼 때는 when을 쓴다. 관계부사는 「전치사+관계대명사」로 바꿔 쓸 수 있다.

  Do you remember the time? + We went to the zoo then.

  → Do you remember the time when we went to the zoo.
                        선행사   관계부사(= at which)

- 선행사가 the place, the house, the city 등 '장소'를 나타낼 때는 where를 쓴다.

  This is the place. + I grew up there.

  → This is the place where I grew up.
             선행사   관계부사(= in which)

Practice

A. 다음 괄호 안에서 알맞은 것을 고르시오.

1. I can't forget the day (when / where) the accident happened.

2. This is the bank (when / where) my mom works.

3. Do you know the year (when / where) Peter was born?

4. We visited the house (when / where) my mom lived.

B. 다음 두 문장을 관계부사를 이용하여 한 문장으로 쓰시오.

1. The room was very dirty. + We stayed there.
   → The room _____.

2. I don't know the time. + The train arrived then.
   → I don't know _____.

3. Do you know the bakery? + We can buy some pies there.
   → Do you know _____?

C. 우리말과 같은 뜻이 되도록 주어진 단어들을 알맞게 배열하시오.

1. 내일은 그가 돌아오는 날이다. (he, day, back, when, comes, the)
   → Tomorrow is _____.

2. 이 마을은 우리가 휴가를 보냈던 곳이다.
   (we, our, the, where, vacation, spent, place)
   → This town is _____.

3. 그들은 기후가 좀 더 따뜻한 지역으로 이동할 것이다.
   (where, is, the, warmer, climate, area, the)
   → They will move to _____.

Grammar Tip

A. forget 잊다
   happen (어떤 일이) 발생하다
   be born 태어나다

관계부사 when, where가 이끄는 절은 시간이나 장소를 나타내는 선행사를 수식한다.

B. dirty 더러운
   bakery 제과점, 빵집

C. spend (시간을) 보내다
   vacation 휴가
   climate 기후

72 관계부사 2

- 선행사가 the reason으로 '이유'를 나타낼 때는 why를 쓴다. 이때, the reason은 생략하고 쓰는 경우가 많다.

  Tell me the reason. + You were absent for that reason.

  → Tell me (the reason) **why** you were absent.
  　　　　　선행사　　　관계부사(= for which)

- 선행사가 the way로 '방법'을 나타낼 때는 how를 쓰는데 the way와 how는 함께 쓸 수 없으며 둘 중 하나만 쓴다.

  Can you show me the way? + You made this sandwich in that way.

  → Can you show me the way you made this sandwich?

  → Can you show me **how** you made this sandwich?
  　　　　　　　　　관계부사(= in which)

- 선행사가 the time, the place, the reason처럼 특정 정보가 없는 일반적인 경우에는 생략할 수 있다.

  That's (the reason) **why** I was angry.

- 관계부사 앞에 선행사가 있을 때는 관계부사를 생략할 수 있다. 단, where는 생략하더라도 전치사를 써야 한다.

  The time (**when**) the show started was 7 p.m.

Practice

A. 다음 괄호 안에서 알맞은 것을 고르시오.

1. I don't know the reason (why / how) you are sad.

2. Can you tell me (why / how) you found the way?

3. This is (the way / the way how) I solved the problem.

4. That's the reason (where / why) I was late for school.

B. 다음 두 문장을 관계부사를 이용하여 한 문장으로 바꿔 쓰시오.

1. This is the way. + I can stay healthy in that way.

   → _____

2. He explained the reason. + He stopped smoking.

   → _____

3. I am learning the way. + I knit a sweater.

   → _____

C. 다음 문장에서 생략된 부분을 찾아 넣어 문장을 다시 쓰시오.

1. Can you tell me why you don't like Sally?

   → _____

2. This is the town I want to visit someday.

   → _____

3. I'll never forget the day we first met.

   → _____

Grammar Tip

A. find the way 길을 찾다
　　 be late for ~에 늦다

B. stay healthy 건강을 유지하다

특정한 정보를 가지고 있지 않은 일반적인 선행사 the time, the place, the reason 등은 생략할 수 있다.

C. someday 언젠가

A. 다음 빈칸에 알맞은 말을 <보기>에서 골라 쓰시오.

> <보기>   what   when   where   why   how

1. This table is _____ I want to have.

2. I don't know the reason _____ she is angry at me.

3. Do you remember the restaurant _____ we had dinner last weekend?

4. Fred didn't forget the day _____ his daughter won the race.

B. 다음 문장에서 밑줄 친 부분을 바르게 고치시오.

1. That I like most is riding a bike in the park. _____

2. She told me the way how she can swim well. _____

3. The palace when we visited yesterday is beautiful. _____

4. Do you know the time why the museum was closed. _____

C. 다음 문장에서 생략할 수 있는 부분을 찾아 동그라미 하시오.

1. He is wearing shoes which he bought yesterday.

2. Do you know the boy who is playing with Lego blocks?

3. This is the store where I lost my bag.

4. We're looking for straws which are made of paper.

D. 다음 우리말과 같은 뜻이 되도록 빈칸에 알맞은 말을 쓰시오.

1. 이 책은 내가 가장 좋아하는 것이다.
   → This book is _____ _____ _____ best.

2. Tony는 런던에서 산 것을 내게 주었다.
   → Tony gave me _____ _____ _____ in London.

3. 네가 그 수학 문제를 푼 방법을 설명해 주겠니?
   → Can you explain _____ _____ _____ the math problem?

4. 네가 운 이유를 말해 줘.
   → Please tell me the _____ _____ _____ _____.

Grammar Tip

A. race 경주

선행사 the way와 관계부사 how는 함께 쓸 수 없으므로 둘 중 하나만 쓴다.

B. palace 궁전

C. Lego block 레고 블럭
   straw 빨대

D. explain 설명하다

[1-2] 다음 빈칸에 알맞은 것을 고르시오.

1.

> Look at the girl _____ mother is a dentist.

① who   ② whom
③ whose   ④ which
⑤ that

2.

> Do you know the time _____ the bus left?

① when   ② where
③ why   ④ how
⑤ what

3. **다음 빈칸에 공통으로 알맞은 것은?**

> · Look at the dog _____ is barking at them.
> · He read a book _____ is very popular to students.

① who   ② whose
③ whom   ④ which
⑤ what

[4-5] 다음 밑줄 친 부분과 바꿔 쓸 수 있는 것을 고르시오.

4.

> I met the people that came from India.

① who   ② whose
③ whom   ④ which
⑤ what

5.

> He told me the way he repaired the machine.

① why   ② when
③ where   ④ what
⑤ how

6. **다음 중 밑줄 친 관계대명사의 쓰임이 어색한 것은?**

① Do you know the woman who is drinking water?
② Paul is the man whom I interviewed.
③ She ate some cake which is made by Sam.
④ Look at the mountain which top is covered with snow.
⑤ He is the best soccer player that I've ever seen.

7. **다음 빈칸에 들어갈 말이 바르게 짝지어진 것은?**

> · Jenny is the girl _____ Robert fell in love love with.
> · This is _____ I want to have.

① who – which   ② whom – what
③ which – what   ④ that – that
⑤ what – what

8. **다음 우리말을 바르게 영작한 것을 모두 고르면?**

> 이것이 내가 먹고 싶어 했던 것이다.

① This is that I wanted to eat.
② This is what I wanted to eat.
③ This is the thing that I wanted to eat.
④ This is the thing who I wanted to eat.
⑤ This is the thing what I wanted to eat.

9. **다음 밑줄 친 ①~⑤ 중 생략할 수 있는 것은?**

> This is ① the place ② where we ③ stayed ④ during our ⑤ summer vacation.

10. 다음 빈칸에 공통으로 알맞은 말을 쓰시오.

> · The boys _____ are ready for the game are my cousins.
> · That's the backpack _____ Daniel lost.

11. 다음 중 밑줄 친 부분을 생략할 수 <u>없는</u> 것은?

① The news <u>that</u> I heard from Kate was shocking.
② The man <u>who is</u> selling ice cream is my uncle.
③ I'm looking for a house <u>which</u> has many rooms.
④ Is he a doctor <u>whom</u> many people respect?
⑤ This is the bridge <u>which was</u> built 50 years ago.

12. 다음 중 빈칸에 이어질 말로 알맞은 것은?

> Do you remember the country _____?

① where the Olympics were held last year
② when the Olympics were held last year
③ why the Olympics were held last year
④ how the Olympics were held last year
⑤ what the Olympics were held lastyear

13. 다음 밑줄 친 ①~⑤ 중 어법상 <u>어색한</u> 것은?

> A: Do you remember the movie ①<u>which</u> we watched ②<u>it</u> last week?
> B: Yes. It is the ③<u>funniest</u> movie ④<u>that</u> I've ever ⑤<u>watched</u>.

14. 다음 두 문장을 한 문장으로 바르게 연결한 것은?

> The pictures were great. + Wendy took them at the beach.

① The pictures which Wendy took at the beach were great.
② The pictures which Wendy took them at the beach were great.
③ The pictures who Wendy took at the beach were great.
④ The pictures what Wendy took at the beach were great.
⑤ The pictures whose Wendy took at the beach were great.

15. 다음 빈칸에 들어갈 말이 나머지 넷과 <u>다른</u> 것은?

① That is the cell phone _____ my sister designed.
② Can you see the dog _____ ears are very big?
③ I have a doll _____ is made by Jenny.
④ We ate steak _____ the famous chef cooked.
⑤ He gave a book _____ is good for children.

[16-17] 다음 문장에서 어법상 <u>어색한</u> 부분을 찾아 바르게 고쳐 쓰시오.

16.
> The flowers that my dad planted is growing well.

_____ → _____

17.
> Do you believe that Mike said?

_____ → _____

141

18. 다음 두 문장이 같은 뜻이 되도록 빈칸에 알맞은 말을 쓰시오.

> This is the place in which I was born.

= This is the place _____ I was born.

19. 다음 밑줄 친 that의 쓰임이 나머지 넷과 다른 것은?

① I hope that Susan will get better soon.
② She is the girl that helped me in the street.
③ Roy got a letter that is written in French.
④ I'm wearing a coat that my mom bought for me.
⑤ Is there anything that you want to see?

20. 다음 중 어법상 어색한 것은?

① This is how I fixed the computer.
② New York is the city when Jimmy spent his childhood.
③ I don't know the day when we visited Henry.
④ Can you tell me the reason why you were absent from school?
⑤ This is the way he draws circles.

〈서술형 문제〉

21. 다음 두 문장을 관계부사를 이용하여 한 문장으로 연결하고 생략할 수 있는 곳에 괄호 표시하시오.

> I saw old ladies. + They were talking together in the park.

→ _____

22. 다음 두 문장을 관계부사를 이용하여 한 문장으로 연결하시오.

> I don't know the time. + The airplane arrived at that time.

→ _____

[23-24] 다음 우리말과 같은 뜻이 되도록 괄호 안의 단어들을 바르게 배열하시오. (단, 관계대명사를 추가할 것)

23.
> 내가 가장 좋아하는 것은 바이올린을 연주하는 것이다.
> (most, playing, like, I, is, violin, the)

→ _____

24.
> 이것은 Joe가 내게 사 준 시계이다.
> (the, bought, is, Joe, me, watch, for, this)

→ _____

25. 다음 대화에서 어법상 어색한 곳 두 군데를 찾아 바르게 고쳐 쓰시오.

> A: Do you know the artist whose drew this painting?
> B: Yes. His name is Eric. He is the youngest artist that won the first prize in the contest.
> A: How great he is!
> B: His paintings are very colorful and unique. That's the reason when I like them.

(1) _____ → _____
(2) _____ → _____

시제일치란 무엇인가?

주절의 시제에 따라 종속절의 시제를 일치시키는 것을 말한다. 주절의 시제가 현재일 때는 종속절의 시제는 모든 시제가 가능하고, 주절의 시제가 과거일 때는 종속절의 시제는 과거 또는 과거완료가 되어야 한다.

I **think** that Jay **is[will be/was]** a good student.

화법이란 무엇인가?

화법은 누군가가 한 말을 다른 사람에게 전달하는 방법으로 직접화법과 간접화법이 있다. 직접화법은 했던 말을 그대로 인용 부호(" ")에 넣어서 전달하는 방법이고, 간접화법은 접속사를 사용해서 그 말의 내용만 전달하는 방법이다.

He says, "I want to have a new cell phone." (직접화법)
He says **that** he wants to have a new cell phone. (간접화법)

Chapter 13. 일치와 화법

73 시제일치

- 주절의 시제가 현재일 때 종속절의 시제는 모든 시제가 가능하다.
  Fred **thinks** that Cindy likes[will like/liked] him.
- 주절의 시제가 과거일 때 종속절의 시제는 과거나 과거완료가 되어야 한다.
  Carol **said** that she felt[had felt] sleepy.
- 종속절의 내용에 따라 시제일치에 예외가 되는 경우가 있다.
  ① 일반적인 사실을 말할 때는 항상 현재시제를 쓴다.
    He taught us that the earth **goes** around the sun.
  ② 현재 계속되는 습관이나 사실은 항상 현재시제를 쓴다.
    She said that she **takes** a walk every morning.
  ③ 역사적 사실은 항상 과거시제를 쓴다.
    I know that King Sejong **created** Hangeul in 1443.

 Practice

A. 다음 괄호 안에서 알맞은 것을 고르시오.

1. I thought that she (is / was) a famous painter.

2. Eden said that he usually (goes / went) to school by bike.

3. We learned that Edison (invents / invented) the light bulb.

4. I know that Seoul (is / was) the capital of Korea.

B. 다음 주어진 단어를 알맞은 형태로 바꿔 빈칸에 쓰시오.

1. We learned that the earth _____ round. (be)

2. He said that the Korean War _____ out in 1950. (break)

3. We know the sun _____ in the east. (rise)

4. Lydia said that she _____ two brothers. (have)

C. 다음 문장의 동사를 바꿔 쓸 때 빈칸에 알맞은 말을 쓰시오.

1. I think that they will agree with my opinion.
   → I thought that _____.

2. He knows that light travels faster than sound.
   → He knew that _____.

3. He teaches us that Leonardo Da Vinci painted the *Mona Lisa*.
   → He taught us that _____.

74 평서문의 간접화법

· 다른 사람의 말을 그대로 전달하는 직접화법은 전달자의 입장에서 전하는 간접화법으로 바꿔 쓸 수 있다.

· 피전달문이 평서문일 때 간접화법으로 바꾸는 방법

> ① 전달동사 say → say, say to → tell로 바꾼다.
> ② 콤마(,)와 인용 부호("")를 없애고 that을 쓴다. 이때 that은 생략할 수 있다.
> ③ 직접화법의 주어, 목적어, 부사(구)등은 전달자의 입장에서 알맞게 고친다.
> ④ 전달동사의 시제가 현재일 때는 피전달문의 시제는 변화가 없으나, 과거일 때는 현재는 과거로,
>   현재완료와 과거는 과거완료로 바꾼다.

Amy said, "I'm very tired." (직접화법)
→ Amy said **that she was very tired.** (간접화법)

Practice

A. 다음 괄호 안에서 알맞은 것을 고르시오.

1. Susie (said / told) that she felt sick.

2. He (said / told) me that he wanted to be a pilot.

3. Jenny said (that / which) her parents were fine.

4. My brother said that he (doesn't / didn't) have much time.

B. 다음 문장을 간접화법으로 바꿀 때 빈칸에 알맞은 말을 쓰시오.

1. Wendy says, "I'm going home."
   = Wendy _____ that _____ _____ _____ home.

2. He said to me, "I can't swim."
   = He _____ me that _____ _____ swim.

3. Eric said, "I like Ann."
   = Eric _____ that _____ _____ Ann.

4. Tony said, "I saw Emily at the theater."
   = Tony _____ that _____ _____ _____ Emily at the
     theater.

C. 다음 문장을 직접화법으로 바꿀 때 빈칸에 알맞은 말을 쓰시오.

1. Paul said that he could speak French.
   = Paul said, "_____ _____ speak French."

2. Michelle told me that she was in the hospital.
   = Michelle _____ _____ me, "_____ _____ in the
     hospital."

3. She says that it's raining outside.
   = She says, "_____ _____ outside."

Grammar Tip

직접화법을 간접화법으로 전환할 때 쓰는 접속사 that은 목적어 역할을 하는 명사절을 이끌며 생략이 가능하다.

A. pilot (비행기 등의) 조종사
    fine 좋은

B. theater 극장

C. French 프랑스어

unit 75 | 의문사가 없는 의문문의 간접화법

• 피전달문이 의문사가 없는 의문문일 때 간접화법으로 바꾸는 방법

> ① 전달동사 say to → ask로 바꾼다.
> ② 콤마(,)와 인용 부호(" ")를 없애고 피전달문을 「if[whether]+주어+동사」의 순으로 바꾼다.

Sam said to me, "**Do you enjoy soccer?**"
→ Sam asked me **if[whether] I enjoyed soccer.**

Eric said to us, "**Is it cold outside?**"
→ Eric asked us **if[whether] it was cold outside.**

Practice

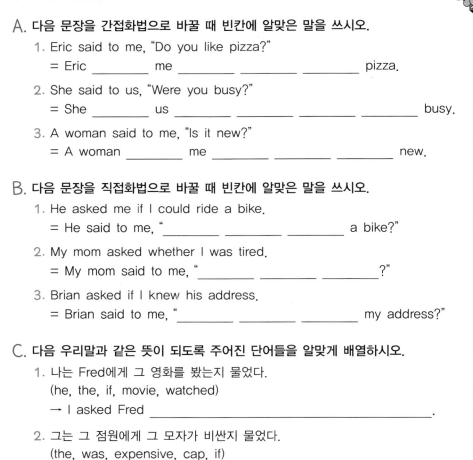

A. 다음 문장을 간접화법으로 바꿀 때 빈칸에 알맞은 말을 쓰시오.

1. Eric said to me, "Do you like pizza?"
   = Eric _____ me _____ _____ _____ pizza.

2. She said to us, "Were you busy?"
   = She _____ us _____ _____ _____ _____ busy.

3. A woman said to me, "Is it new?"
   = A woman _____ me _____ _____ _____ new.

B. 다음 문장을 직접화법으로 바꿀 때 빈칸에 알맞은 말을 쓰시오.

1. He asked me if I could ride a bike.
   = He said to me, "_____ _____ _____ a bike?"

2. My mom asked whether I was tired.
   = My mom said to me, "_____ _____ _____ ?"

3. Brian asked if I knew his address.
   = Brian said to me, "_____ _____ _____ my address?"

C. 다음 우리말과 같은 뜻이 되도록 주어진 단어들을 알맞게 배열하시오.

1. 나는 Fred에게 그 영화를 봤는지 물었다.
   (he, the, if, movie, watched)
   → I asked Fred _____.

2. 그는 그 점원에게 그 모자가 비싼지 물었다.
   (the, was, expensive, cap, if)
   → He asked the clerk _____.

3. 그들은 내게 그들과 함께 할 것인지 물었다.
   (I, them, join, would, whether)
   → They asked me _____.

Grammar Tip

의문사가 없는 의문문의 간접화법에서 피전달문 「if[whether]+주어+동사」의 어순에 유의한다.

A. busy 바쁜
　　 new 새것

B. address 주소

C. clerk 점원
　　 join 함께하다

76 의문사가 있는 의문문의 간접화법

· 피전달문이 의문사가 있는 의문문일 때 간접화법으로 바꾸는 방법

> ① 전달동사 say to → ask로 바꾼다.
> ② 콤마(,)와 인용 부호(" ")를 없애고 피전달문을 「의문사＋주어＋동사」의 순으로 바꾼다.

Robert said to me, "**Where are you going?**"
→ Robert asked me **where I was going**.

Sophie said to Ken, "**What time does the bank close?**"
→ Sophie asked Ken **what time the bank closed**.

Practice

A. 다음 문장을 간접화법으로 바꿀 때 빈칸에 알맞은 말을 쓰시오.

1. Daniel said to me, "Where do you live?"

    = Daniel _____ me _____ _____ _____.

2. I said to my sister, "Who told you about it?"

    = I _____ my sister _____ _____ _____ her about it."

3. She said to me, "How many brothers do you have?"

    = She asked me _____ _____ _____ _____ _____.

B. 다음 문장을 직접화법으로 바꿀 때 빈칸에 알맞은 말을 쓰시오.

1. Ann asked me which bus went downtown.

    = Ann said to me, "_____?"

2. A man asked me where I was from.

    = A man said to me, "_____?"

3. Chris asked us what time the concert started.

    = Chris said to us, "_____?"

C. 다음 주어진 단어들을 바르게 배열하시오.

1. (went, how often, swimming, he)

    → I asked Mike _____.

2. (angry, why, was, I)

    → My mom asked me _____.

3. (found, where, ring, she, my, had)

    → I asked my sister _____.

Grammar Tip

의문사가 주어로 쓰인 경우에는 피전달문을 「의문사＋동사」의 순으로 쓴다.
He said to me, "**Who called Susie?**"
→ He asked me **who had called** Susie.

A. how many 얼마나 많은

의문사가 있는 의문문을 간접화법으로 바꿀 때 what time, how often, how many 등의 의문사는 한 덩어리로 써야 한다.

B. downtown 시내에

C. find 찾다

Unit 77 명령문의 간접화법

• 피전달문이 명령문일 때 간접화법으로 바꾸는 방법

> ① 전달동사 say, say to → 의미에 따라 tell, ask, order, advise 등의 동사로 바꾼다.
> ② 콤마(,)와 인용 부호(" ")를 없애고 피전달문을 to부정사로 바꾼다.
>   긍정명령문 : 「주어＋tell/ask/order/advise＋목적어＋to부정사」
>   부정명령문 : 「주어＋tell/ask/order/advise＋목적어＋not＋to부정사」

The teacher said to them, "Be quiet."
→ The teacher told them **to be quiet.**

He said to me, "Do not take pictures."
→ He asked me **not to take pictures.**

Practice

A. 다음 괄호 안에서 알맞은 것을 고르시오.

1. She asked me (turn / to turn) on the light.

2. I told my brother (not to / to not) make a noise.

3. Sue asked (his / him) to open the windows.

4. The doctor (said / advised) me to eat less sweets.

B. 다음 문장을 간접화법으로 바꿀 때 빈칸에 알맞은 말을 쓰시오.

1. The man said to us, "Don't run fast."
   → The man told _____.

2. Fiona said to me, "Take the subway."
   → Fiona advised _____.

3. My mom said to me, "Get up early in the morning."
   → My mom ordered _____.

C. 다음 우리말과 같은 뜻이 되도록 주어진 단어들을 알맞게 배열하시오.

1. 선생님께서는 내게 많은 책을 읽으라고 조언하셨다.
   (many, to, me, advised, books, read)
   → My teacher _____.

2. 나는 나의 남동생에게 이를 닦으라고 시켰다.
   (brush, his, told, my, teeth, brother, to)
   → I _____.

3. 그녀는 내게 회의에 늦지 말라고 부탁했다.
   (meeting, asked, to, late, me, not, be, the, for)
   → She _____.

Grammar Tip

명령문을 간접화법으로 바꿀 때 피전 달문을 to부정사로 바꾸는데, 부정명령문은 「not＋to부정사」로 바꾼다.

A. less 더 적은

B. subway 지하철

C. meeting 회의
   late for ~에 늦은

148

A. 다음 괄호 안의 단어를 알맞은 형태로 바꿔 쓰시오.

1. We know that Columbus _____ America in 1492. (discover)

2. My teacher taught that the sun _____ in the west. (set)

3. She told me that she _____ ski well. (can)

4. Paul said that he _____ milk every morning. (drink)

B. 다음 문장에서 밑줄 친 부분을 바르게 고치시오.

1. I learned that water <u>froze</u> at 0℃. _____

2. Rachel asked <u>that</u> there was a bookstore nearby. _____

3. I asked Karl where <u>did he live</u>. _____

4. The man told me <u>to not touch</u> paintings. _____

C. 다음 문장을 간접화법으로 바꾸어 문장을 완성하시오.

1. He said, "Kelly is a good cook."
   → He said that _____.

2. Samuel said to me, "Can I borrow your book?"
   → Samuel asked me _____.

3. The teacher said to us, "Do your best."
   → The teacher told us _____.

4. Tom said to me, "Where did you buy the scarf?"
   → Tom asked me _____.

D. 다음 문장을 직접화법으로 바꾸어 문장을 완성하시오.

1. Nell asked them which sport they liked.
   → Nell said to them, "_____?"

2. My dad advised me not to eat anything at night.
   → My dad said to me, "_____."

3. Peter asked if it was snowing.
   → Peter says, "_____?"

4. Tina told you that she couldn't go hiking.
   → Tina said to you, "_____."

Grammar Tip

A. discover 발견하다
   set (해가) 지다

불변의 진리, 현재의 습관은 항상 현재시제로 쓰고 역사적 사실은 항상 과거시제로 쓴다.

B. freeze 얼다
   touch 만지다
   painting 그림

C. cook 요리사
   do one's best 최선을 다하다

D. go hiking 등산하러 가다

1. 다음 빈칸에 알맞은 것을 <u>모두</u> 고르면?

> I think that Monica _____ a good teacher.

① is   ② am
③ was   ④ were
⑤ will be

[2-3] 다음 빈칸에 알맞은 것을 고르시오.

2.
> We learned the earth _____ around the sun.

① go   ② goes
③ will go   ④ went
⑤ had gone

3.
> He said that _____.

① he is very busy
② he will go to the beach
③ he wants to be a model
④ he was cleaning the room
⑤ he is in the hospital

4. 다음 빈칸에 알맞지 <u>않은</u> 것은?

> I knew that _____.

① I was wrong
② the sun rises in the east
③ he had failed the exam
④ Sandra went to school at 8 every day
⑤ Bell invented the telephone

5. 다음 중 어법상 <u>어색한</u> 것은?

① She said that her sister was good at swimming.
② He asked me if I was talking on the phone.
③ The man asked where was a bank.
④ A woman told Sam to close the door.
⑤ Ann told me she had watched the movie.

6. 다음 우리말과 뜻이 같도록 빈칸에 알맞은 것을 <u>모두</u> 고르면?

> 그는 나에게 공포 영화를 좋아하는지 물었다.
> → He asked me _____ I liked horror movies.

① if   ② that
③ to   ④ whether
⑤ what

[7-8] 다음 빈칸에 들어갈 말이 바르게 짝지어진 것을 고르시오.

7.
> Henry said to me, "I can't ride a bike."
> → Henry _____ me that he _____ ride a bike.

① said – can't   ② said – couldn't
③ told – can't   ④ told – couldn't
⑤ asked – can't

8.
> She said to us, "Do you know Sam's phone number?"
> → She _____ us _____ we knew Sam's phone number.

① told – that   ② advised – if
③ asked – if   ④ advised – that
⑤ ordered – whether

9. 다음 우리말을 바르게 영작한 것은?

> Dennis는 내게 언제 떠나는지 물었다.

① Dennis told me when I left.
② Dennis asked me when I left.
③ Dennis asked me when I leave.
④ Dennis asked me when did I leave.
⑤ Dennis asked me when I will leave.

10. 다음 문장을 간접화법으로 바르게 바꾼 것은?

> Vicky said, "I will go to the party."

① Vicky said that she went to the party.
② Vicky said that she will go to the party.
③ Vicky said if she would go to the party.
④ Vicky said that she would go to the party.
⑤ Vicky told that she would go to the party.

11. 다음 괄호 안의 동사를 알맞은 형태로 바꾼 것은?

> I know that the Second World War (break) out in 1939.

① break   ② breaks
③ broke   ④ had broken
⑤ will break

12. 다음 밑줄 친 ①~⑤ 중 어법상 어색한 것은?

> A: I'm going to give a gift ①to Jason.
>   But I don't know ②what Jason liked.
> B: Jason ③told me ④that he ⑤wants
>   to have a blue cap.

13. 다음 문장을 간접화법으로 바꿀 때 밑줄 친 ①~⑤ 중 어법상 어색한 것은?

> Lisa said to me, "I saw Sam at the library."
> → Lisa ①told ②me ③that ④she ⑤saw Sam at the library.

14. 다음 중 간접화법으로 전환이 잘못된 것은?

① She says, "I'm not happy."
→ She says that she's not happy.
② Tony said to me, "Do you like cats?"
→ Tony asked me if I liked cats.
③ I said to Ben, "Where are you going?"
→ I asked Ben where he was going.
④ The man said to us, "Hurry up."
→ The man told us to hurry up.
⑤ Nick said to me, "What time does the train arrive?"
→ Nick asked me what time the train arrives.

15. 다음 문장을 직접화법으로 바르게 바꾼 것은?

> Jane asked me why I was crying.

① Jane said to me, "Why am I crying?"
② Jane said to me, "Why I was crying?"
③ Jane told me, "Why are you crying?"
④ Jane said to me, "Why are you crying?"
⑤ Jane said to me, "Why were you crying?"

16. 다음 문장을 간접화법으로 바꿀 때 빈칸에 알맞은 말을 쓰시오.

> I said to her, "Why are you absent from school?"

→ I _____ her _____ _____ _____ absent from school.

17. 다음 문장에서 어법상 어색한 부분을 찾아 바르게 고쳐 쓰시오.

> My teacher told us that water boiled at 100℃.

_____ → _____

18. 다음 문장을 간접화법으로 바꿔 쓸 때 어법상 어색한 곳을 찾아 바르게 고쳐 쓰시오.

> Paul said to me, "We have to eat out."
> → Paul told me if we had to eat out.

_____ → _____

19. 다음 중 어법상 잘못된 것은?

① He told them not to step on the grass.
  → He said to them, "Don't step on the grass."
② Sean asked me if I had heard the news.
  → Sean said to me, "Did you hear the news?"
③ He asked the woman how much it was.
  → He said to the woman, "How much is it?"
④ Ms. Green told me that he couldn't understand me.
  → Ms. Green said to me, "I can't understand you."
⑤ The doctor advised her that eat more vegetables.
  → The doctor said to her, "Eat more vegetables."

20. 다음 밑줄 친 부분의 쓰임이 나머지 넷과 다른 것은?

① He said that he didn't like baseball.
② I talked to the man that lived next door.
③ The driver told us that there were no seats.
④ My brother said that Sally was in China.
⑤ Peter told me that he had been sick.

21. 다음 문장을 주어진 동사를 이용하여 간접화법으로 바꿔 쓰시오.

> Eric said to me, "Turn down the volume." (tell)

→ _____

22. 다음 문장을 〈보기〉와 같이 바꿔 쓰시오.

> 〈보기〉
> Daniel: How many books do you have?
> → Daniel asked me how many books I had.

Sue: Which bus goes to the theater?

→ _____

23. 다음 우리말과 뜻이 같도록 문장을 영작하시오.

> 나는 그에게 나와 함께 갈 수 있는지 물었다.

→ _____

24. 다음 대화의 내용과 일치하도록 빈칸에 알맞은 말을 쓰시오.

> Susan: Where are you from?
> Lopez: I'm from Mexico.

→ Susan asked Lopez _____ _____ _____ _____. Lopez _____ her _____ he _____ from Mexico.

25. 다음 문장을 직접화법으로 바꿔 쓰시오.

> He asked me what time my swimming class ended.

→ _____

가정법이란 무엇인가?

가정법은 어떤 사실과 반대되거나 일어날 가능성이 적은 일에 대해 가정하여 말하는 것을 뜻한다.

가정법에는 어떤 종류가 있는가?

가정법에는 현재나 미래의 일을 반대로 가정하여 나타내는 가정법 과거가 있고, 과거 사실을 반대로 가정하는 가정법 과거완료가 있다. 현재 사실과 반대되는 소망을 나타낼 때는 「I wish+가정법 과거」로 쓸 수 있고, 과거사실과 반대되는 소망을 나타낼 때는 「I wish+가정법 과거완료」를 쓸 수 있다.

If I **were** rich, I **could** buy a new car. (가정법 과거)

If the weather **had been** better, we **could have played** soccer. (가정법 과거완료)

I **wish** you **were** here. (I wish 가정법 과거)

I **wish** I **hadn't missed** the bus. (I wish 가정법 과거완료)

Chapter 14. 가정법

Unit 78 | 가정법 과거

- 가정법 과거는 '만일 ~라면, …할 텐데'의 뜻으로 현재 사실과 반대되는 일을 가정할 때 쓴다.
  「If+주어+동사의 과거형 ~, 주어+조동사의 과거형(would, could, might)+동사원형 …」의 형태로 나타낸다. be 동사는 인칭에 상관없이 항상 were를 쓴다.

  If I **had** more money, I **could buy** a new car.

  If I **were** a bird, I **could fly** in the sky.

- 가정법 과거를 직설법으로 바꿔 쓸 때는 현재시제로 나타낸다.

  If he **had** much time, he **would travel** to France.

  = **As** he **doesn't have** much time, he **won't travel** to France.

Practice

A. 다음 괄호 안에서 알맞은 것을 고르시오.

1. If I (am / were) you, I would choose this bag.

2. If she (lives / lived) here, we would often meet.

3. If Dennis were rich, he (can / could) buy the house.

4. If I knew your phone number, I (will / would) call you.

B. 다음 우리말과 같은 뜻이 되도록 주어진 단어들을 알맞은 형태로 바꿔 쓰시오.

1. 네가 규칙적으로 운동을 한다면, 살을 뺄 수 있을 텐데. (exercise, lose)
   → If you _____ regularly, you _____ _____ weight.

2. 그가 키가 더 크다면, 농구를 잘할 수 있을 텐데. (be, play)
   → If he _____ taller, he _____ _____ basketball well.

3. 내가 너라면, 그렇게 말하지 않을 텐데. (be, say)
   → If I _____ you, I _____ _____ _____ that.

4. 내가 카메라를 가지고 있다면, 네 사진을 찍어줄 수 있을 텐데. (have, take)
   → If I _____ a camera, I _____ _____ a picture of you.

C. 다음 두 문장이 같은 뜻이 되도록 빈칸에 알맞은 말을 쓰시오.

1. As it isn't cheaper, I won't buy it.
   = _____ it were cheaper, I _____ _____ it.

2. I don't have enough time, so I can't go there.
   = _____ I had enough time, I _____ _____ there.

3. If you wore a muffler, you might not catch a cold.
   = As you don't wear a muffler, you _____ _____ a cold.

Grammar Tip

가정법 과거는 현재 사실과 반대되는 일을 가정한 것이므로 해석할 때도 현재로 한다.

A. choose 선택하다

B. take a picture 사진 찍다

가정법 과거의 직설법 전환 :
(1) if를 as, so, because 등으로 바꾼다.
(2) if절의 과거형을 현재형으로 쓰고, 주절은 「조동사의 현재형+동사원형」으로 쓴다.
(3) 긍정은 부정으로, 부정은 긍정으로 바꾼다.

C. may ~일지도 모른다

79 | 가정법 과거완료

- 가정법 과거완료는 '만일 ~했더라면, …했을 텐데'의 뜻으로 과거 사실과 반대되는 일을 가정할 때 쓴다.
  「If+주어+had+p.p. ~, 주어+조동사의 과거형(would, could, might)+have+p.p. ….」의 형태로 나타낸다.

  If He **had lived** here, I **could have visited** him.

  If you **had finished** your work, you **would have joined** us.

- 가정법 과거를 직설법으로 바꿔 쓸 때는 과거시제로 나타낸다.

  If you **had visited** her, she **would have been** happy.

  = **As** you **didn't visit** her, she **wasn't** happy.

Practice

A. 다음 괄호 안에서 알맞은 것을 고르시오.

1. If I had taken the train, I would (arrive / have arrived) in time.

2. If it had not been rainy, we would (drive / have driven).

3. If he (have / had) had more time, he could have stayed longer here.

4. If Lucy had practiced, she could (succeeded / have succeeded).

B. 다음 빈칸에 알맞은 말을 〈보기〉에서 골라 알맞은 형태로 쓰시오.

〈보기〉 learn	eat	pass	ask

1. 내가 일본어를 배웠다면, 그것을 읽을 수 있었을 텐데.

   → If I _____ Japanese, I could have read it.

2. 네가 그에게 부탁을 했었다면, 그는 너를 도왔을 텐데.

   → If you _____ him, he would have helped you.

3. 우리가 음식을 조금 먹었다면, 배고프지 않았을 텐데.

   → If we _____ some food, we wouldn't have been hungry.

4. 그가 그 시험에 합격했더라면, 그는 행복했을 텐데.

   → If he _____ the exam, he would have been happy.

C. 다음 두 문장이 같은 뜻이 되도록 빈칸에 알맞은 말을 쓰시오.

1. As I didn't have enough money, I couldn't lend you money.

   = If I _____ _____ enough money, I _____ _____ _____ you money.

2. If it had not rained heavily, we _____ _____ _____ outside.

   = As it _____ heavily, we didn't go outside.

3. He broke his leg, so he wouldn't run the marathon race.

   = If he _____ _____ _____ his leg, he _____ _____ _____ the marathon race.

Grammar Tip

가정법 과거완료는 과거 사실과 반대되는 일을 가정한 것이므로 해석할 때도 과거로 한다.

A. drive 운전하다

B. ask 부탁하다

가정법 과거완료의 직설법 전환 :
(1) if를 as, so, because 등으로 바꾼다.
(2) if절의 과거완료형을 과거형으로 쓰고, 주절은 「조동사의 과거형+동사원형」으로 쓴다.
(3) 긍정은 부정으로, 부정은 긍정으로 바꾼다.

C. lend 빌려주다
marathon race 마라톤 경주

80 | I wish 가정법

- 「I wish+가정법 과거」는 '~라면 좋을 텐데'의 뜻으로 현재 사실과 반대되는 소망을 나타낸다. 주어가 He, She 등의 3인칭 단수일 때는 He[She] wishes ~.와 같이 쓴다.

  I wish I **took** piano lessons.　　**She wishes** she **were** taller.

- 「I wish+가정법 과거」는 「I'm sorry+직설법 현재」로 바꿔 쓸 수 있다.

  I wish I **were** here with them. = I'm sorry I'm **not** here with them.

- 「I wish+가정법 과거완료」는 '~했더라면 좋았을 텐데'의 뜻으로 과거 사실과 반대되는 소망을 나타낸다.

  I wish I **had bought** a nice car like you.

- 「I wish+가정법 과거완료」는 「I'm sorry+직설법 과거」로 바꿔 쓸 수 있다.

  I wish I **hadn't lost** my umbrella. = I'm sorry I **lost** my umbrella.

Practice

A. 다음 괄호 안에서 알맞은 것을 고르시오.

1. I wish I (am / were) braver.

2. I wish Fred (doesn't tell / didn't tell) lies.

3. I wish I (have / had) sisters or brothers.

4. Sarah wishes she (visited / had visited) there in childhood.

B. 다음 문장을 우리말로 해석하시오.

1. I wish I understood you.

   → _____

2. I wish I traveled around the world.

   → _____

3. I wish I had followed your advice.

   → _____

C. 다음 두 문장이 같은 뜻이 되도록 빈칸에 알맞은 말을 쓰시오.

1. I wish I practiced the piano harder.

   = I'm sorry I _____ _____ the piano harder.

2. He wishes he had bought new shoes.

   = He is sorry he _____ _____ new shoes.

3. She is sorry she doesn't have breakfast earlier.

   = She _____ she _____ _____ earlier.

4. I'm sorry I spent much money.

   = I _____ I _____ _____ much money.

A. 다음 빈칸에 알맞은 말을 <보기>에서 골라 알맞은 형태로 바꿔 쓰시오.

> <보기> be   try   have   speak

1. If I _____ you, I would forgive her.

2. If she _____ English well, she could talk with a foreigner.

3. If Bob _____ more, he would have win the first prize.

4. If I _____ a lot of money, I could have bought the computer.

B. 다음 문장에서 밑줄 친 부분을 바르게 고치시오.

1. If he <u>is</u> kind, everyone would like him.   _____

2. If I knew his e-mail address, I <u>can send</u> the message.   _____

3. If Erica had done her homework, she <u>would watch</u> the movie.   _____

4. I wish I <u>went</u> shopping yesterday.   _____

C. 다음 우리말과 같은 뜻이 되도록 괄호 안의 단어를 이용하여 문장을 완성하시오.

1. 내가 더 일찍 예약했다면, 콘서트에 갈 수 있을 텐데. (make, go)
   → If I _____ a reservation earlier, I _____ _____ to the concert.

2. 우리가 지하철을 탔다면, 학교에 지각하지 않았을 텐데. (take, be)
   → If we _____ _____ the subway, we _____ _____ _____ late for school.

3. 내가 같은 실수를 다시 하지 않았으면 좋았을 텐데. (make)
   → I wish I _____ _____ the same mistake again.

4. Mike가 소망하기를 그가 배우가 되면 좋을 텐데. (wish, become)
   → Mike _____ he _____ an actor.

D. 다음 두 문장이 같은 뜻이 되도록 빈칸에 알맞은 말을 쓰시오.

1. If it were sunny, we would go to the beach.
   = As it _____ sunny, we _____ _____ to the beach.

2. I didn't tell the truth, so she was very upset.
   = If I _____ _____ the truth, she wouldn't _____ _____ very upset.

3. I'm sorry I don't know that guy's name.
   = I _____ I _____ that guy's name.

Grammar Tip

A. forgive 용서하다
   foreigner 외국인

「I wish + 가정법 과거완료」는 과거 사실과 반대되는 소망을 나타낸다.

B. go shopping 쇼핑하러 가다

C. make a reservation 예약하다
   make a mistake 실수하다

D. upset 화가 난

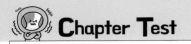

[1-2] 다음 빈칸에 알맞은 것을 고르시오.

1.
> If I _____ you, I would watch that movie.

① am   ② is
③ are   ④ were
⑤ be

2.
> I wish I _____ to New York with my family last year.

① travel   ② traveled
③ has traveled   ④ have traveled
⑤ had traveled

3. 다음 빈칸에 공통으로 알맞은 말을 쓰시오.

> · If I _____ more time, I could stay longer in Jejudo.
> · He would have talked with foreigners if he _____ spoken English well.

4. 다음 빈칸에 들어갈 말이 바르게 짝지어진 것은?

> · I wish I _____ camping last weekend.
> · If Emma _____ the truth, her mom would forgive her.

① went – told
② went – had told
③ had gone – told
④ had gone – had told
⑤ had gone – tells

[5-6] 다음 중 어법상 어색한 것을 고르시오.

5. ① If you had a lot of money, what would you do?
② If I didn't go to the party, Eric would be sad.
③ You might feel better if you got more exercise.
④ If it stopped raining, we could have gone out.
⑤ She wouldn't have bought a coat if it had been expensive.

6. ① I wish I visited Emily yesterday.
② I wish I had something to read.
③ She wishes she knew more people.
④ If he were rich, he would buy a new car.
⑤ Ben would get wet if he didn't take his umbrella.

7. 다음 우리말을 바르게 영작한 것은?

> 내가 지하철을 탔더라면, 길을 잃지 않았을 텐데.

① If I have taken the subway, I wouldn't have been lost.
② If I had taken the subway, I wouldn't have been lost.
③ If I took the subway, I wouldn't be lost.
④ If I had taken the subway, I wouldn't be lost.
⑤ If I took the subway, I wouldn't have been lost.

8. 다음 밑줄 친 ①~⑤ 중 어법상 어색한 것은?

> ①If you ②had practiced ③harder, your team ④could ⑤win the game.

9. 다음 밑줄 친 if의 쓰임이 나머지 넷과 다른 것은?

① I would meet him <u>if</u> I left earlier.

② He told me <u>if</u> I could play the piano.

③ I wouldn't believe him <u>if</u> I were you.

④ She would be healthy <u>if</u> she ate more vegetables.

⑤ I would have gone to the beach <u>if</u> it had been sunny.

[10-11] 다음 빈칸에 들어갈 말로 알맞은 것을 고르시오.

10.

> If you had done your homework,
> _____.

① you go to the party

② you went to the party

③ you can go to the party

④ you could go to the party

⑤ you could have gone to the party

11.

> Chris wishes _____ yesterday.

① he met Susan

② he will meet Susan

③ he has met Susan

④ he had met Susan

⑤ he would meet Susan

12. 다음 밑줄 친 부분을 바르게 고친 것은?

> If she got the ticket, she <u>enjoy</u> the concert.

① enjoys   ② enjoyed

③ will enjoy   ④ would enjoy

⑤ would have enjoyed

13. 다음 우리말과 같은 뜻이 되도록 빈칸에 알맞은 것은?

> 내가 요리를 더 잘하면 좋을 텐데.
> → I wish I _____ better.

① cook   ② cooked

③ have cooked   ④ had cooked

⑤ would cook

14. 다음 문장을 가정법으로 바르게 바꾼 것은?

> As I don't know his birthday, I can't send him a gift.

① If I know his birthday, I can send him a gift.

② If I knew his birthday, I could send him a gift.

③ If I had known his birthday, I could send him a gift.

④ If I had known his birthday, I could have sent him a gift.

⑤ If I knew his birthday, I could have sent him a gift.

15. 다음 문장에서 어법상 <u>어색한</u> 부분을 찾아 바르게 고쳐 쓰시오.

> If Vicky were more careful, she won't break the glass.

_____ → _____

16. 다음 문장을 직설법으로 바르게 바꾼 것은?

> I wish I learned to swim.

① I'm sorry I don't learn to swim.

② I'm sorry I learned to swim.

③ I'm sorry I hadn't learned to swim.

④ I'm sorry I had learned to swim.

⑤ I'm sorry I didn't learn to swim.

[17-18] 다음 두 문장이 같은 뜻이 되도록 빈칸에 알맞은 말을 고르시오.

17.

I didn't have money, so I couldn't buy the camera.
= If I had had money, I _____ the camera.

① could buy
② could bought
③ could have bought
④ couldn't buy
⑤ couldn't have bought

18.

Angela is sorry she is not a movie star.
= Angela wishes she _____ a movie star.

① is
② will be
③ be
④ were
⑤ would be

19. 다음 괄호 안의 동사를 알맞은 형태로 바꿔 쓰시오.

If we (live) in Paris, we could have seen the Eiffel Tower every day.

_____

20. 다음 문장과 의미가 같은 것은?

William didn't follow my advice, so he didn't finish the work.

① If William followed my advice, he would finished the work.
② If William had followed my advice, he would have finished the work.
③ If William has followed my advice, he would finished the work.
④ If William followed my advice, he would have finished the work.
⑤ If William has followed my advice, he would have finished the work.

<서술형 문제>

21. 다음 두 문장이 같은 뜻이 되도록 문장을 완성하시오.

As Amy didn't take medicine, she was sick in bed.

= If Amy _____.

22. 다음 우리말과 뜻이 같도록 괄호 안의 단어들을 바르게 배열하시오.

나의 남동생이 많은 책을 읽는다면 그는 더 똑똑해질 텐데.
(my, if, he, read, be, brother, many, would, books, wiser)

→ _____.

23. 다음 문장을 wish를 이용하여 바꿔 쓰시오.

Anne can't make lots of friends.

→ Anne _____.

24. 다음 대화의 내용과 일치하도록 빈칸에 알맞은 말을 쓰시오.

Andrew: How about going to see a movie?
Julie: Sorry, I can't. I'm very busy now.

→ If Julie _____ _____ _____, she _____ _____ to see a moive.

25. 다음 문장을 <보기>와 같이 바꿔 쓰시오.

<보기>
If I knew how to use this machine,
I could save time.
→ I don't know how to use this machine,
so I can't save time.

If Nicole had gone to bed early, she wouldn't have been tired.

→ _____

A-B-C형 (원형, 과거형, 과거분사형이 각기 다른 형)

원형	과거형	과거분사형
be (am, is)	was	been
be (are)	were	been
bear (낳다)	bore	born
begin (시작하다)	began	begun
bite (물다)	bit	bitten
blow (불다)	blew	blown
break (부수다)	broke	broken
choose (선택하다)	chose	chosen
do (하다)	did	done
draw (그리다)	drew	drawn
drink (마시다)	drank	drunk
drive (운전하다)	drove	driven
eat (먹다)	ate	eaten
fall (떨어지다)	fell	fallen
fly (날다)	flew	flown
forget (잊다)	forgot	forgotten
freeze (얼리다)	froze	frozen
give (주다)	gave	given
go (가다)	went	gone
grow (기르다, 자라다)	grew	grown
hide (숨다)	hid	hidden
know (알다)	knew	known
lie (눕다, 놓여있다)	lay	lain
ride (타다)	rode	ridden
ring (<종을> 울리다)	rang	rung
rise (떠오르다)	rose	risen

원형	과거형	과거분사형
see (보다)	saw	seen
shake (흔들다)	shook	shaken
show (보여 주다)	showed	shown
sing (노래하다)	sang	sung
speak (말하다)	spoke	spoken
swim (수영하다)	swam	swum
take (얻다, 가지고 가다)	took	taken
tear (찢다)	tore	torn
throw (던지다)	threw	thrown
wear (입다)	wore	worn
write (쓰다)	wrote	written

A-B-B형 (과거형과 과거분사형이 동일한 형)

원형	과거형	과거분사형
bring (가져오다)	brought	brought
build (세우다)	built	built
buy (사다)	bought	bought
catch (잡다)	caught	caught
dig (〈구멍 등을〉 파다)	dug	dug
feed (먹이를 주다)	fed	fed
feel (느끼다)	felt	felt
fight (싸우다)	fought	fought
find (찾다)	found	found
get (얻다)	got	got[gotten]
hang (매달다)	hung	hung
have (가지다)	had	had

원형	과거형	과거분사형
hear (듣다)	heard	heard
hold (잡다)	held	held
keep (지키다, 유지하다)	kept	kept
lead (이끌다)	led	led
leave (떠나다)	left	left
lend (빌리다)	lent	lent
lose (잃다)	lost	lost
make (만들다)	made	made
mean (의미하다)	meant	meant
meet (만나다)	met	met
pay (지불하다)	paid	paid
say (말하다)	said	said
sell (팔다)	sold	sold
send (보내다)	sent	sent
sit (앉다)	sat	sat
sleep (자다)	slept	slept
spend (〈돈·시간 등을〉 쓰다)	spent	spent
stand (서다)	stood	stood
strike (때리다)	struck	struck
teach (가르치다)	taught	taught
tell (말하다)	told	told
think (생각하다)	thought	thought
understand (이해하다)	understood	understood
win (이기다)	won	won
wind (감다)	wound	wound

A-B-A형 (원형과 과거분사형이 동일한 형)

원형	과거형	과거분사형
become (~이 되다)	became	become
come (오다)	came	come
run (달리다)	ran	run

A-A-A형 (원형, 과거형, 과거분사형이 동일한 형)

원형	과거형	과거분사형
cost (〈돈이〉 들다)	cost	cost
cut (자르다)	cut	cut
hit (치다)	hit	hit
hurt (다치다)	hurt	hurt
let (시키다)	let	let
put (놓다)	put	put
read[ri:d] (읽다)	read[red]	read[red]
set (설치하다)	set	set
shut (닫다)	shut	shut

Student Book
Answer Key

Chapter 1. 문장의 형식

Unit 01. 1형식과 2형식의 문장
Practice

A. 1. 2형식 2. 1형식 3. 2형식 4. 2형식 5. 1형식

B. 1. strange 2. soft 3. delicious 4. good 5. busy

C. 1. She walked to school.
   2. He is standing next to the door.
   3. The medicine tastes bitter.
   4. Your plan looks possible.

Unit 02. 3형식과 4형식 문장
Practice

A. 1. 3형식 2. 3형식 3. 4형식 4. 3형식 5. 3형식

B. 1. basketball 2. her name 3. her daughter, a doll
   4. a big ball 5. him, the letter

C. 1. Paul found the purse. 2. We left London at five.
   3. She teaches them math. 4. I showed her my album.

Unit 03. 4형식 문장의 3형식 전환
Practice

A. 1. for 2. to 3. for 4. of 5. to

B. 1. us, pizza 2. her, a, card 3. a, favor, of, you

C. 1. Susan made a suit for her brother.
   2. He didn't lend his laptop to her.
   3. I will ask his name of him.

Unit 04. 5형식 문장
Practice

A. 1. to stay 2. happy 3. warm 4. Angel

B. 1. named 2. thought 3. allowed 4. expected

C. 1. her, a star 2. the classroom, clean
   3. to, study, hard

Unit 05. 지각동사와 사역동사
Practice

A. 1. to rise → rise[rising] 2. to cry → cry[crying]
   3. cleaning → clean 4. introducing → introduce
   5. playing → play

B. 1. realize 2. burn 3. dancing 4. smile

C. 1. sit 2. use 3. fly 4. touch

Review Test / Unit 01~05

A. 1. 내 친구가 나에게 편지를 썼다.
   2. 나는 그 상자가 비어 있는 것을 발견했다.
   3. Joe는 그녀가 아름답다고 생각한다.

B. 1. look, dirty 2. felt, tired 3. smells, bad
   4. sounded, interesting

C. 1. became 2. wants 3. passed 4. bought

D. 1. to, me 2. for, me 3. of, her

E. 1. do 2. know 3. sing[singing]

Chapter Test / Unit 01~05

1. ③ 2. ③ 3. ① 4. ② 5. ① 6 ③ 7. ④ 8. ②
9. ①, ③ 10. ① 11. ⑤ 12. ③ 13. to, me 14. for, you
15. ④ 16. ⑤ 17. to call → call[calling] 18. to clean →
clean 19. ② 20. ② 21. I helped her (to) move the box.
22. She asked me to fix the bike. 23. well → good
24. let me know her phone number 25. allowed me to go
back home

1. 감각동사(look, sound, smell, taste, feel) 뒤에는 주격보어로 형용사가 온다.

2. 문장의 형식을 구분할 때는 문장의 필수 요소(주어, 동사, 목적어, 보어)로 구분하며 부사(구)는 영향을 미치지 않는다.

3. like 동사는 목적어를 필요로 하는 동사이다.

4. 보기의 fun은 5형식 문장에서 목적격보어로 사용되었다.

5. 5형식 문장은 「주어+동사+목적어+목적격보어」로 이루어진 문장으로 want는 목적격보어로 to부정사가 온다.

6. 4형식 문장을 3형식 문장으로 바꿀 때 make, buy, get, cook, find 등의 동사는 전치사 for를 사용한다.

7. 4형식 문장은 「주어+동사+간접목적어+직접목적어」로 이루어진 문장으로 간접목적어에는 사람이 온다.

9. see는 지각동사로 지각동사의 목적격보어에는 동사원형이나 현재분사가 온다.

11. 5형식 문장에서 동사 expect는 목적격보어로 to부정사가 온다.

12. 눈으로 보이는 것이므로 동사 look을 사용하여 답한다.

13. 3형식 문장으로 전환할 때, give, send, bring, teach, show, read, tell, write, lend 등의 동사는 전치사 to를 사용한다.

16. 5형식 문장에서 want, ask, tell, order, allow, expect 등의 동사는 목적격보어로 to부정사가 온다.

17. hear는 지각동사로 목적격보어로 동사원형이나 현재분사가 올 수 있다.

18. have는 사역동사로 목적격보어에는 동사원형이 온다.

20. 2형식 문장에서 감각동사는 보어로 형용사가 온다.

Chapter 2. to부정사

Unit 06. 명사적 용법 1
Practice

A. 1. 수영하는 것은(수영하기는)

2. 물을 충분히 마시는 것이(물을 충분히 마시기가)

3. 중국어를 배우는 것이다

4. 디자이너가 되는 것이다

B. 1. It is important for health to eat vegetables.

2. It is interesting to bake bread.

3. It is good for you to go to bed early.

C. 1. is, to, help 2. To, play 3. is, to, collect

4. It, to, prepare

Unit 07. 명사적 용법 2

Practice

A. 1. to stay 2. to teach 3. to ride

B. 1. where to buy 2. when to start 3. how to bake

4. what to do

C. 1. where to put 2. to succeed 3. how to use

Unit 08. 형용사적 용법

Practice

A. 1. 일어날 시간 2. 그것을 살 돈 3. 해야 할 숙제

4. 문을 열 열쇠 5. 먹을 어떤 것 6. 잠을 잘 곳

B. 1. on 2. with 3. in 4. about 5. to

C. 1. write with 2. to have 3. to ask 4. to arrive at

5. something cold

Unit 09. 부사적 용법 1

Practice

A. 1. 피자를 먹기 위해 2. 빨래를 하기 위해

3. 사진을 찍기 위해

B. 1. to buy apples 2. to catch the bus

3. to study history

C. 1. pleased 2. angry 3. sad 4. surprised

Unit 10. 부사적 용법 2

Practice

A. 1. 마시기에 2. 이해하기에 3. 변호사가 되었다

B. 1. to be 2. to remember 3. to wear

C. 1. to be 2. to swim 3. to be 4. to solve

Unit 11. to부정사의 의미상 주어

Practice

A. 1. of 2. her 3. of 4. for

B. 1. of, her 2. for, you 3. of, him 4. for, them

5. for, Amy

C. 1. for, us, to, exercise 2. of, her, to, save

3. for, you, to, go 4. of, him, to, catch

Unit 12. too ~ to, enough to

Practice

A. 1. enough 2. too 3. enough

B. 1. enough, to 2. that, couldn't 3. so, kind 4. too, to

C. 1. too sweet for me to eat 2. hot enough to swim

3. so big that I can put in

Review Test / Unit 06~12

A. 1. The child wanted to eat pizza.

2. He turned on the computer to check the email.

3. My plan is to jog every day.

4. Rebecca hurried to take an airplane.

B. 1. what to buy 2. how to raise 3. when to meet

4. where to put

C. 1. This → It 2. of → for 3. help to → to help

4. painting → paint

D. 1. (a) 2. (c) 3. (d) 4. (b)

Chapter Test / Unit 06~12

1. ③ 2. ⑤ 3. ③ 4. ④ 5. ④ 6. ④ 7. ⑤ 8. ① 9. ② 10. ①
11. ④ 12. ① 13. ② 14. ② 15. (1) of (2) for 16. ④ 17. (a)
too (b) that 18. ① 19. ④ 20. ③ 21. ④ 22. It, to sit on
a chair all day 23. taught me how to skate 24. a cat to
play with 25. was so hard that I couldn't handle it.

1. to부정사가 부사처럼 쓰여 감정의 원인으로 사용될 때는 감정을 나타내는 형용사 뒤에 to부정사가 온다.

2. 문장의 주어와 to부정사의 주어가 일치하지 않을 경우, to부정사 앞에 「for+목적격(행위자)」을 써서 의미상의 주어를 나타낸다.

3. to 뒤에 명사가 올 경우에는 전치사로 '~로, ~에게'의 뜻이다.

5. 「too+형용사/부사+to부정사」는 '…하기에는 너무 ~하다'라는 뜻이다.

6. love, want, wish, start 등의 동사는 목적어로 to부정사가 온다. (명사적 용법)

7. to부정사가 주어로 쓰인 경우에는 주어 자리에 가주어 it을 쓰고 to부정사를 뒤로 보낼 수 있다.

8. it은 대명사 외에도 문장에서 비인칭 주어나 가주어로도 사용된다.

10. 「형용사/부사+enough+to부정사」는 '~할 만큼 충분히 …하다'라고 해석한다.

13. to부정사 앞에 쓰인 명사가 전치사의 목적어가 될 경우 to부정사 뒤에 전치사를 반드시 쓴다.

14. to부정사가 형용사처럼 쓰이는 경우에는 '~하는, ~할'의 뜻으로 형용사처럼 앞의 명사나 대명사를 수식하는 역할을 한다.

15. to부정사가 나타내는 동작, 상태의 주체를 to부정사의 '의미상의 주어'라고 한다. 사람의 성격이나 태도를 나타내는 형용사 뒤에는 「of+목적격」으로 의미상의 주어를 나타낸다.

17. 「too+형용사/부사+to부정사」는 「so+형용사/부사+that+주어+can't/couldn't+동사원형」으로 바꿔 쓸 수 있다.

19. We chatted with some friends.와 같이 '~와 함께'라는 뜻으로 전치사 with가 들어가야 한다.

20. ③번은 의미상 '…하기에는 너무 ~하다'라는 뜻이 되어야 하므로 too가 와야 한다.

22. to부정사가 주어로 쓰인 경우에는 가주어 it을 이용하여 to부정사를 뒤로 보낼 수 있다.

23. '~하는 방법'을 나타낼 때는 how to 동사원형으로 나타낸다.

Chapter 3. 동명사
Unit 13. 동명사의 역할 1
Practice

A. 1. 밤에 수영하는 것은(밤에 수영하기는)
   2. 산책하는 것은(산책하기는)
   3. 가수가 되는 것이다
   4. 택시를 타는 것이다

B. 1. To, be 2. to, invite 3. to, make

C. 1. is, playing 2. Learning 3. is, listening 4. Reading

Unit 14. 동명사의 역할 2
Practice

A. 1. cooking 2. playing 3. being 4. solving

B. 1. winning 2. turning 3. eating 4. helping

C. 1. good, at, playing 2. enjoy, growing
   3. afraid, of, making

Unit 15. 동명사와 현재분사
Practice

A. 1. 동명사 2. 현재분사 3. 동명사 4. 현재분사

B. 1. 음식을 먹는 것은 2. 잠을 자고 있다 3. 일기를 쓰는 것
   4. 춤추는 곰

C. 1. listening to 2. waiting room 3. is playing soccer
   4. girl crying

Unit 16. 동사의 목적어 1
Practice

A. 1. traveling 2. to use 3. answering 4. to learn

B. 1. taking 2. to eat 3. building 4. to come

C. 1. learning 2. to paint 3. cleaning 4. to buy

Unit 17. 동사의 목적어 2
Practice

A. 1. raining[to rain] 2. having[to have]

3. drawing[to draw]

B. 1. meeting 2. putting[to put] 3. playing[to play]

C. 1. 가져오는 것을 잊다
   2. 보냈던 것을 기억하다
   3. 노래 부르는 것을 멈췄다
   4. 합격하기 위해 노력했다

Review Test / Unit 13~17

A. 1. Eating[To eat] 2. visiting[to visit] 3. driving
   4. being 5. running

B. 1. loves reading[to read] comic books
   2. gave up climbing the mountain
   3. stopped talking at the the library
   4. tried to understand other people

C. 1. to be 2. meeting 3. inviting 4. studying[to study]

D. 1. 피아노를 치고 있는 여자 2. 자전거를 타는 것을
   3. 창문을 닫는 것을 4. 그 불쌍한 개를 구하기 위해

Chapter Test / Unit 13~17

1. ③ 2. ⑤ 3. ⑤ 4. ② 5. ② 6 ⑤ 7. ③ 8. ② 9. ② 10. ④
11. seeing 12. meet, to meet 13. ② 14. to arrive 15. ③
16. ⑤ 17. walking 18. ④ 19. ②, ③ 20. ③ 21. Getting up early is not easy. 22. Remember to take your umbrella
23. finished doing the dishes before 24. (1) to play, playing
(2) being, to be 25. to call his dad

1. 동명사와 to부정사는 '~하는 것이다'라는 뜻의 보어 역할을 한다.

2. 전치사의 목적어 역할을 할 때는 동명사가 와야 한다.

3. plan은 to부정사를 목적어로 취하는 동사이다.

4. <보기>와 ②의 동명사는 목적어 역할을 한다.

5. give up은 동명사를 목적어로 취하는 동사이다.

6. ⑤는 be동사와 함께 쓰여 현재진행형을 만드는 현재분사이다.

7. 동명사와 to부정사는 '~하는 것은, ~하기는'의 뜻의 주어 역할을 하고, 전치사의 목적어 역할을 할 때는 동명사가 온다.

8. promise는 to부정사를 목적어로 취하는 동사이다.

9. finish는 동명사를 목적어로 취하는 동사이다.

10. keep은 동명사를 목적어로 취하는 동사이다.

11. '~했던 것을 기억하다'는 「remember+동명사」로 나타낸다.

12. expect는 to부정사를 목적어로 취하는 동사이다.

13. hope는 to부정사를 목적어로 취하는 동사이다.

14. '~하려고 노력하다'는 「try+to부정사」로 나타낸다.

15. ③은 명사를 수식하는 현재분사이고 <보기>와 나머지는 용도의 의미로 쓰인 동명사이다.

16. 과거에 한 일에 대해 잊었을 때는 forget 뒤에 동명사를 쓴다.

17. '~하는 것을 멈추다'는 「stop+동명사」로 나타낸다.

18. 「remember+동명사」는 과거에 한 일에 대해 기억하는 것을 뜻한다.

19. 동명사와 to부정사는 문장에서 주어 역할을 하고, 동명사나 to부정사가 주어로 쓰일 때는 단수 취급하므로 동사도 단수형을 써야 한다.

20. 「stop+동명사」는 '~하는 것을 멈추다'의 뜻이고, 「stop+to부정사」는 '~하기 위해 멈추다'라는 뜻이다.

23. finish는 동명사를 목적어로 취하는 동사이다.

Chapter 4. 현재완료

Unit 18. 현재완료의 쓰임과 형태

Practice

A. 1. seen 2. lived 3. lost 4. finished

B. 1. have, studied 2. has, been 3. has, gone
   4. have, eaten

C. 1. have, met 2. have, learned 3. has, lost
   4. has, been

Unit 19. 현재완료의 용법

Practice

A. 1. 경험 2. 결과 3. 계속 4. 완료

B. 1. has fallen 2. have lost 3. has gone

C. 1. have studied Spanish 2. has lost his violin
   3. have tried Thai food

Unit 20. 현재완료의 부정문과 의문문

Practice

A. 1. arrived 2. never 3. Have 4. Has

B. 1. never eaten 2. stopped 3. haven't 4. moved

C. 1. I haven't finished the report.
   2. Has she bought a new bracelet?
   3. Wendy hasn't watched the Lion King.

Unit 21. 과거시제와 현재완료의 차이점

Practice

A. 1. had 2. have known 3. has reduced 4. ate

B. 1. have worked 2. lived 3. have joined

C. 1. has gone 2. have read 3. visited

Unit 22. 과거시제와 현재완료에 쓰이는 표현

Practice

A. 1. once 2. When 3. three hours ago 4. since

B. 1. has rained 2. arrived 3. lost 4. has learned

C. 1. have, just, finished 2. have, watched, before
   3. bought, yesterday

Review Test / Unit 18~22

A. 1. have been 2. have read 3. have practiced
   4. heard

B. 1. have never raised 2. built 3. for
   4. Have you ever seen

C. 1. Yes, I've visited there three times.
   2. I've studied English for six years.
   3. No, I haven't finished it yet.

D. 1. has he lived here
   2. have just arrived here
   3. has lost her wedding ring
   4. have never been abroad

Chapter Test / Unit 18~22

1. ⑤ 2. ④ 3. ④ 4. ③ 5. ② 6 ④ 7. ④ 8. ⑤ 9. ④ 10. ②
11. bought 12. ③ 13. ② 14. has read 15. ② 16. ① 17. ②
18. ③ 19. have stayed 20. has gone 21. She has lost her new cap. 22. hasn't, played 23. I have never seen a polar bear. 24. We have just finished baking cookies.
25. (1) be → been (2) have visited → visited

1. 현재완료는 과거의 특정 시점을 나타내는 말과 함께 쓸 수 없다.

2. 컴퓨터 수리를 아침에 시작했지만 아직 끝내지 못했다는 의미가 되어야 하므로 현재완료 부정문 「haven't[hasn't]+과거분사」으로 나타낸다.

3. 3년 동안 캐나다에서 살고 있다는 뜻이 되어야 하므로 현재완료가 알맞다.

4. last winter는 과거의 특정 시점을 나타내는 말이므로 과거시제를 써야 한다.

5. 현재완료는 「have+과거분사」의 형태로 나타낸다.

6. since는 '~한 이후로'라는 뜻으로 현재완료와 함께 쓰인다.

7. 〈보기〉와 ④는 계속의 의미를 나타내는 현재완료이다.
① 완료 ② 경험 ③ 결과 ⑤ 경험

8. 〈보기〉와 ⑤는 완료의 의미를 나타내는 현재완료이다.
① 경험 ② 경험 ③ 결과 ④ 계속

9. 현재완료의 의문문은 「Have[Has]+주어+과거분사 ~?」의 형태로 쓴다.

10. 현재완료의 의문문은 「Have[Has]+주어+과거분사 ~?」의 형태로 쓴다.

11. last summer는 과거시제에 쓰이는 부사구이다.

12. 현재완료의 의문문에 대한 대답으로 긍정일 때는 「Yes, 주어+have[has].」로, 부정일 때는 「No, 주어+haven't[hasn't].」로 답한다. 의미상 긍정의 대답이 알맞다.

13. ten years ago는 과거시제와 함께 쓰이고, since는 현재완료와 함께 쓰인다.

14. 이틀 전부터 책을 읽기 시작했고 지금도 계속 읽고 있으므로 현재완료 시제로 써야 한다.

15. have been to는 '~에 가 본 적이 있다'라는 뜻이고 have gone to 는 '~로 가버렸다'라는 뜻이다.

16. 현재완료의 부정문에서 never는 보통 have와 과거분사 사이에 쓴다.

17. 언제 책을 읽었는지 물어보고 있으므로 두 번 읽었다고 답한 것은 어색하다.

18. last week는 과거시제와 함께 쓰인다.

19. since는 현재완료 시제에 쓰인다.

20. 일본에 가서 현재 여기에 없으므로 현재완료의 결과를 나타내는 문장으로 써야 한다.

22. 현재완료의 부정문은 「haven't[hasn't]+과거분사」로 나타낸다.

24. 현재완료에 쓰이는 just는 보통 have와 과거분사 사이에 쓴다.

Chapter 5. 조동사

Unit 23. can, could
Practice

A. 1. solve 2. can 3. use 4. Can

B. 1. am, able, to 2. could 3. were, able, to
   4. Is, able, to

C. 1. can ski well 2. could not sleep well
   3. Could I turn on

Unit 24. will, be going to
Practice

A. 1. go 2. help 3. Are 4. study

B. 1. carrying → carry 2. not will → will not
   3. are → be 4. rains → rain

C. 1. will, clean 2. Will[Would], do
   3. am, going, to, go

Unit 25. must, have to
Practice

A. 1. has to 2. had to 3. must 4. don't have to

B. 1. must 2. don't have to 3. must not

C. 1. don't have to 2. must 3. must not 4. had to

Unit 26. may, should
Practice

A. 1. should 2. should not 3. may 4. may

B. 1. not should → should not 2. loses → lose
   3. play may → may play 4. is → be

C. 1. 너는 다른 사람들의 말을 들어야 한다.
   2. 그녀는 학교에 지각할지도 모른다.
   3. 내가 너의 펜을 빌려도 될까?

Unit 27. 관용 표현
Practice

A. 1. b 2. a 3. c

B. 1. plays → play 2. used → used to
   3. had not better → had better not

C. 1. used to exercise in the morning
   2. Would you like to go
   3. had better drink lots of water

Review Test / Unit 23~27

A. 1. visit 2. Is 3. turn 4. should not

B. 1. isn't, able, to 2. have, to 3. may 4. would, like, to

C. 1. You must not go to bed late.
   2. You had better take an umbrella.
   3. You don't have to order anything.

D. 1. had, to, clean 2. may, be 3. used, to, have

Chapter Test / Unit 23~27

1. ① 2. ① 3. ② 4. ③ 5. has, to 6. ④ 7. ③ 8. ① 9. ⑤
10. ② 11. ⑤ 12. must 13. ⑤ 14. ⑤ 15. had not better
→ had better not 16. ⑤ 17. ③ 18. ② 19. ①, ④ 20. ④
21. must not 22. He couldn't[wasn't able to] ride a bike
yesterday. 23. I used to play soccer after school.
24. should eat vegetables, should not[shouldn't] watch TV
late at night 25. has to turn off her cell phone

1. '우리는 늦었으니 서둘러야 한다.'의 의미가 되어야 하므로 must가 알맞다.

2. had better 뒤에는 동사원형이 와야 한다.

3. '과거에 ~하곤 했다'라는 뜻의 「used to+동사원형」을 써야 한다.

4. should의 부정문은 should not[shouldn't]으로 나타낸다.

5. '~해야 한다'라는 뜻의 의무를 나타내는 must는 have to로 바꿔 쓸 수 있는데 주어가 3인칭 단수이므로 has to로 써야 한다.

7. ③은 '~임에 틀림없다'라는 뜻의 강한 추측을 나타내고 나머지는 '~해야 한다'라는 뜻의 의무를 나타낸다.

8. ①은 '~해도 좋다'라는 뜻의 허락을 나타내고 나머지는 '~할 수 있다'라는 뜻의 능력, 가능을 나타낸다.

9. don't have to는 '~할 필요가 없다'라는 뜻이고 must not은 '~해서는 안 된다'라는 뜻이다.

10. '~해도 좋다'라는 뜻의 허락을 나타내는 조동사는 can 또는 may를 쓴다.

11. '~해야만 하니?'라는 의문에 대한 대답은 must not이나 don't have to로 답할 수 있는데 여기서는 '우산을 가져갈 필요가 없다'라는 의미가 되어야 한다.

12. '피곤함에 틀림없다'라는 의미가 되어야 하므로 must가 알맞다.

13. 나머지는 도서관에서 먹지 말라는 의미이지만 ⑤는 먹을 필요가 없다는 의미이다.

14. '~일지도 모른다'라는 뜻의 추측을 나타내는 may가 알맞다.

15. had better의 부정형은 had better not으로 쓴다.

16. 체중을 줄이고 싶다는 말에 대한 충고로 물을 많이 마시지 말라고 하는 것은 알맞지 않다.

17. '~해야 했다'는 had to로 쓴다.

18. 첫 번째 빈칸에는 지루해 보이므로 흥미있는 것을 찾는 게 좋겠다는 충고하는 내용이 적절하고, 두 번째 빈칸에는 뒤에 지금은 할 수 있다는 내용이 왔으므로 전에는 할 수 없었다는 과거시제가 와야 한다.

19. '~해도 좋다'는 can 또는 may로 쓴다.

20. ④는 '지각해서는 안 된다'라는 의미가 되어야 하므로 don't have to 대신에 shouldn't나 must not으로 쓴다.

21. '~하지 마'라는 뜻의 부정명령문은 '~해서는 안 된다'라는 의미로 바꿔 쓸 수 있다.

23. '(과거에) ~하곤 했었다'는 used to로 나타내고 뒤에 동사원형을 쓴다.

24. 상황에 따라 should(~하는 게 좋겠다) 또는 should not(~해서는 안 된다)으로 표현한다.

Chapter 6. 분사

Unit 28. 현재분사의 쓰임
Practice

A. 1. taking 2. walking 3. dancing 4. flying
B. 1. 동명사 2. 현재분사 3. 동명사 4. 현재분사
C. 1. is writing a diary 2. The smiling woman is
   3. is sleeping on the floor

Unit 29. 과거분사의 쓰임
Practice

A. 1. Baked 2. used 3. broken 4. smiling
B. 1. boiled 2. written 3. covered 4. made
C. 1. sent 2. locked 3. cooked

Unit 30. 분사의 명사 수식
Practice

A. 1. ② 2. ② 3. ② 4. ②
B. 1. 뜨고 있는 태양 2. 책을 읽고 있는 남자
   3. 100년 전에 지어진 이 집
C. 1. is cleaning up the broken vase
   2. need a used bicycle
   3. The girl eating pizza is
   4. books written in English

Unit 31. 감정을 나타내는 분사
Practice

A. 1. surprised 2. amazing 3. interested
   4. disappointing
B. 1. boring 2. excited 3. interesting 4. shocked
C. 1. satisfying → satisfied 2. excited → exciting
   3. interested → interesting 4. tiring → tired

Unit 32. 분사구문
Practice

A. 1. Hearing the news 2. Having a headache
   3. Eating lunch
B. 1. Because Jimmy was busy
   2. While I was reading a comic book
   3. If you study harder
C. 1. 피곤했기 때문에 2. 밝게 웃으면서 3. 왼쪽으로 돌면

Review Test / Unit 28~32

A. 1. swimming 2. baked 3. used 4. throwing
B. 1. The man sitting on that sofa
   2. some poems written in Spanish
   3. the girl taking a piano lesson
   4. those broken plates
C. 1. amazing 2. interesting 3. excited 4. bored
D. 1. not having enough money 2. Drinking cold water
   3. Cleaning the room 4. Coming home

Chapter Test / Unit 28~32
1. ③ 2. ④ 3. ③ 4. ② 5. ③ 6. ④ 7. disappointing 8. ②
9. ④ 10. ④ 11. ③ 12. ② 13. ⑤ 14. ③ 15. ② 16. ②
17. ① 18. Being 19. ② 20. ④ 21. The man playing
soccer is a famous actor. 22. interested → interesting
23. I like this chocolate cake made by my mom.
24. Listening to music, he cooked dinner. 25. Because
she had a bad cold, she had to get some rest.

1. '커피를 마시고 있는'의 진행의 의미가 되어야 하므로 현재분사가 알맞다.

2. '깨진'이라는 뜻의 수동의 의미가 되어야 하므로 과거분사가 알맞다.

3. 첫 번째 빈칸에는 현재분사가 be동사와 함께 쓰여 진행의 의미가 되어야 하고, 두 번째 빈칸에는 수식어구와 함께 명사 뒤에서 명사를 수식하므로 현재분사가 알맞다.

4. ②는 목적어 역할을 하는 동명사이고 나머지는 현재분사이다.

5. 첫 번째 빈칸에는 주어가 감정을 느끼고 있으므로 과거분사가 알맞고, 두 번째 빈칸에는 주어가 감정을 유발하므로 현재분사가 알맞다.

7. '실망스러운'의 뜻으로 주어가 감정을 유발하므로 현재분사가 알맞다.

8. 분사가 수식어구와 함께 쓰여 명사를 수식할 때는 명사 뒤에 위치한다.

9. 분사가 단독으로 쓰여 명사를 수식할 때는 명사 앞에 위치한다.

10. '삶아진 달걀'이라는 수동의 의미가 되어야 하므로 과거분사가 알맞다.

11. 주어가 감정을 느끼고 있으므로 과거분사가 알맞다.

12. ②는 주어가 감정을 유발하므로 tiring이 알맞다.

13. 과거분사가 수식어구와 함께 쓰여 명사를 수식하는 형태가 되어야 한다.

14. 부사절의 접속사와 주어를 생략하고 동사를 현재분사로 만들어 분사구문의 형태로 바꿔 쓸 수 있다.

15. '산책을 하면서'라는 뜻의 분사구문이므로 while이 있는 부사절로 바꿔 쓸 수 있다.

16. 분사구문은 부사절의 접속사와 주어를 생략하고 동사를 현재분사로 바꿔서 만든다.

17. '만들어진'이라는 뜻의 수동의 의미가 되어야 하므로 과거분사가 알맞고, 수식어구와 함께 쓰여 명사를 수식하므로 명사 뒤에 위치한다.

18. 분사구문은 부사절의 접속사와 주어를 생략하고 동사를 현재분사로 바꿔서 만든다.

19. 주어가 감정을 유발하므로 현재분사가 알맞다.

20. '피곤했기 때문에 집에 일찍 왔다.'라는 뜻이 되는 것이 자연스럽다.

21. '~하고 있는'의 의미로 진행을 나타내므로 play는 현재분사 형태로 바꾸고, 수식어구와 함께 명사를 수식하므로 명사 뒤에 위치한다.

22. 주어가 감정을 유발하므로 현재분사가 알맞다.

23. 과거분사가 수식어구와 함께 쓰여 명사 뒤에서 수식하며 수동의 의미를 나타낸다.

24. 분사구문은 부사절의 접속사와 주어를 생략하고 동사를 현재분사로 바꿔서 만든다.

25. 분사구문은 「접속사＋주어＋동사」의 부사절을 간단히 한 것이며 주절의 시제에 유의해서 문장을 바꿔 써야 한다.

Chapter 7. 수동태

Unit 33. 수동태의 쓰임과 형태
Practice

A. 1. loved   2. made   3. used   4. written

B. 1. he → him   2. grew → grown
   3. washing → washed

C. 1. was repaired by Alex   2. was cleaned by him
   3. invented the telephone   4. found Jim's backpack

Unit 34. 수동태의 시제
Practice

A. 1. were baked   2. will be released   3. was built
   4. will be painted

B. 1. The parcel will be sent by Susan.

   2. Some sandwiches were made by my mom.

   3. This song is loved by many young people.

C. 1. is, visited   2. will, be, published   3. was, found
   4. was, saved

Unit 35. 수동태의 부정문과 의문문
Practice

A. 1. are not grown   2. were not solved
   3. was not invited   4. is not taken

B. 1. Was, eaten   2. Was, fixed, wasn't
   3. When, was, sent

C. 1. The drama was not[wasn't] written by Shakespeare.
   2. Was the light bulb invented by Edison?
   3. When was the mushroom soup made by Lisa?

Unit 36. 조동사가 있는 수동태
Practice

A. 1. should be   2. be played   3. should not

B. 1. is → be   2. be not → not be   3. save → saved
   4. is will → will be   5. is → be

C. 1. A lot of flowers will be used for the wedding.
   2. The truck may be sold by an old man.
   3. The task should be finished by her.
   4. The rules must be followed by students.

Review Test / Unit 33~36

A. 1. built   2. played   3. used   4. told

B. 1. is loved → love   2. his → him   3. hold → held
   4. protect → protected

C. 1. Is English spoken
   2. Where was my cell phone found
   3. was not written by Charles
   4. can be taken by foreigners

D. 1. These cars are made by
   2. This machine should not be touched
   3. The rabbit was caught by him
   4. The project will be finished by

Unit 37. 4형식 문장의 수동태
Practice

A. 1. for me   2. was given   3. made   4. to her

B. 1. taught   2. cooked   3. asked   4. shown

C. 1. were told an interesting story by her,
      was told to us by her
   2. was given a nice gift by Robert,

was given to me by Robert

Unit 38. 5형식 문장의 수동태
Practice
A. 1. Ken is believed honest by the people.
   2. He was called a genius by my parents.
   3. Amy was helped to carry the desk by us.

B. 1. was made to copy the book
   2. were asked to solve the problem by me
   3. was seen to cry by me

C. 1. was, kept, warm
   2. was, advised, to, exercise
   3. was, seen, swim

Unit 39. 동사구의 수동태
Practice
A. 1. off by 2. looked after 3. off by 4. at by

B. 1. was turned on by Sam
   2. was run over by a car
   3. is looked up to by students

C. 1. Her nephew was brought up by her.
   2. The game was given up by our team.
   3. My little brother is taken care of by me.
   4. A new house was looked for by us.

Unit 40. by + 행위자 생략
Practice
A. 1. by people 2. by someone 3. by us

B. 1. with 2. at 3. for 4. of 5. about

C. 1. filled, with 2. made, from
   3. was, disappointed, with

Review Test / Unit 37~40
A. 1. for → to 2. doing → to do 3. run → to run
   4. from → of

B. 1. was called a hero
   2. were heard to sing
   3. was cooked for us by him
   4. is taken care of by her aunt

C. 1. is, known, for
   2. is, crowded, with
   3. were, satisfied, with
   4. was, surprised, at

D. 1. The actor was laughed at by some people.
   2. A bike was bought for me by my uncle.

   3. We are made happy by his song.
   4. He was watched to play the piano by his parents.

Chapter Test / Unit 33~40
1. ④ 2. ② 3. ⑤ 4. ④ 5. ⑤ 6 ④ 7. ④ 8. ③ 9. ④ 10. ⑤
11. ① 12. ④ 13. ③ 14. ④ 15. born 16. ⑤ 17. ① 18. ⑤
19. ③ 20. Eric honest 21. This city is known for strawberries. 22. (1) A smartphone is used by me. (2) A smartphone is not[isn't] used by me. (3) Is a smartphone used by me? 23. was given the comic book by Lisa, was given to Tony by Lisa 24. Was, wasn't, by 25. fall → to fall

1. 콜럼버스에 의해 발견이 되었으므로 수동태로 써야 하는데 과거의 일이므로 과거시제가 알맞다.
2. 수동태의 부정문은 be동사 뒤에 not을 붙인다.
3. be filled with: ~로 가득 차다. be covered with: ~로 덮여 있다
4. '제주도에서 찍혔다'는 의미가 되어야 하므로 수동태 were taken이 알맞다.
5. 행위자가 일반적이거나 알 수 없는 경우에 「by+행위자(목적격)」는 생략할 수 있다.
6. tomorrow가 있으므로 미래시제를 쓴다. 미래시제의 수동태는 「will be +과거분사」로 쓴다.
7. 조동사가 있는 문장의 수동태는 조동사 뒤에 「be+과거분사」를 쓴다.
8. 5형식 문장의 수동태를 만들 때는 능동태의 목적격보어를 그대로 수동태 동사 뒤에 쓴다.
9. 직접목적어가 주어로 쓰인 4형식의 수동태로 give, tell, teach, show 등의 동사는 간접목적어 앞에 전치사 to를 쓴다.
10. 사역동사가 쓰인 5형식 문장이므로 목적격보어인 동사원형은 수동태에서 to부정사로 바꿔야 한다.
11. be made of: ~로 만들어지다(물리적 변화), be interested in: ~에 관심이 있다
12. 수동태의 의문문은 「be동사+주어+과거분사~by+목적격?」의 형태로 나타낸다.
13. 동사구가 있는 문장의 수동태는 동사구를 하나의 동사로 취급하여 쓴다. 시제가 현재시제이므로 are looked up to가 알맞다.
14. 동사 make가 쓰인 4형식 문장의 수동태는 직접목적어를 주어로 써서 만들고 간접목적어 앞에 전치사 for를 쓴다.
15. 수동태가 되어야 하므로 과거분사 born이 알맞다.
16. 조동사가 있는 수동태 문장의 부정문은 조동사 뒤에 「not+be+과거분사」를 쓴다.
17. 지각동사가 있는 문장의 수동태는 목적격보어인 동사원형을 to부정사로 바꿔 쓴다.
18. ①~④는 Sarah가 내게 영어를 가르쳤다는 의미이고, ⑤는 내가 Sarah에게 영어를 가르쳤다는 의미이다.
19. ③에서 능동태 문장의 시제가 과거이므로 수동태도 과거시제가 되어야

한다. Where was your dog found by you?가 알맞다.

20. 목적격보어로 형용사가 쓰인 5형식 문장의 수동태이다.

24. 의문사가 없는 수동태의 의문문은 「be동사+주어+과거분사 ~?」의 형태이다.

25. 지각동사가 있는 문장의 수동태는 동사원형인 목적격보어를 to부정사로 쓴다.

Chapter 8. 대명사

Unit 41. one, some, any
Practice

A. 1. one 2. one 3. ones 4. one 5. it

B. 1. Some 2. any 3. some 4. some, any

C. 1. any 2. it 3. some 4. one 5. ones

Unit 42. all, both, each, every
Practice

A. 1. Every 2. Both 3. All 4. Each 5. is

B. 1. members 2. has 3. rabbit 4. are 5. was

C. 1. Every, student 2. Both, are 3. Each, has
4. All, are

Unit 43. 부정대명사의 표현
Practice

A. 1. One 2. the others 3. another 4. the other

B. 1. Some, others 2. Some, the others 3. each other

C. 1. another → the other 2. the others → another

Unit 44. 재귀대명사의 용법
Practice

A. 1. himself 2. herself 3. myself 4. themselves

B. 1. themselves 2. itself 3. herself 4. myself

C. 1. 강조 용법 2. 재귀 용법 3. 재귀 용법 4. 강조 용법

Unit 45. 재귀대명사의 관용 표현
Practice

A. 1. Help, yourself 2. enjoyed, themselves 3. of, itself
4. beside, ourselves

B. 1. 그는 이 집에서 혼자 산다.
2. 그 아기는 혼자 힘으로 그 상자를 열었다.
3. 그 전등은 저절로 떨어졌다.

C. 1. usually has breakfast by himself
2. must hang the picture for myself
3. Help yourself to the cake

Review Test / Unit 41~45

A. 1. All 2. ones 3. Every 4. one 5. any

B. 1. It → One 2. another → the other
3. the other → the others/others
4. one another → each other

C. 1. herself 2. ourselves 3. himself 4. themselves

D. 1. for, yourself 2. enjoyed, himself 3. Help, yourself
4. by, myself

Chapter Test / Unit 41~45

1. ② 2. ③ 3. ③ 4. sandals 5. ① 6. ④ 7. ① 8. ② 9. ③
10. ④ 11. ⑤ 12. ⑤ 13. enjoyed, themselves 14. country,
has 15. one, ones 16. ⑤ 17. play → plays 18. one,
another 19. ③ 20. ② 21. another, the other 22. Every
student has to follow the school rules. 23. Monica learned
Korean for herself. 24. (1) some, any (2) themselves, itself
25. (1) Some, the, others (2) All, One, the, others

1. 앞에 언급된 사물과 같은 종류의 것을 가리키므로 one이 알맞다.

2. '5명의 소녀 모두를 알고 있다.'는 의미가 되어야 하므로 all이 알맞다.

3. 「some ~, the others ...」는 정해지지 않은 범위에서 '일부는 ~이고, 나머지 전부는 ...이다'의 의미이다.

4. 앞에 나온 샌들과 같은 종류의 대상을 가리키고 복수이므로 ones로 쓰였다.

5. ①은 재귀대명사의 강조 용법이고 나머지는 재귀 용법으로 쓰였다. ③의 themselves는 hurt의 목적어이므로 생략할 수 없다.

6. each는 단수 취급하므로 동사도 단수형인 has가 와야 한다.

7. '혼자서'라는 뜻에 해당하는 재귀대명사의 관용 표현은 by oneself이고, 주어가 Julia이므로 by herself가 알맞다.

8. 권유문에서는 some을 쓰고 정해지지 않은 범위에서 '일부는 ~이고, 또 다른 일부는 ...하다'는 「some ~, others ...」로 쓴다.

9. 재귀대명사가 강조 용법으로 쓰인 경우에는 생략할 수 있으나, 동사나 전치사의 목적어 역할을 하는 재귀 용법에서는 생략할 수 없다.

10. '둘 다'는 both로 표현하고 항상 복수 취급한다.

11. 주어를 강조하는 재귀대명사가 와야 하고, 주어가 David and his friends이므로 themselves가 알맞다.

12. 셋 중에서 하나는 one, 또 다른 하나는 another, 나머지 하나는 the other로 나타낸다.

14. all 뒤에 셀 수 있는 명사가 올 때는 복수명사가 오고, every 뒤에는 「단수명사+단수동사」가 와야 한다.

15. 앞에 나온 사물과 같은 종류를 가리키므로 one으로 쓴다. 단수일 때는 one, 복수일 때는 ones로 쓴다.

17. each는 단수 취급하므로 동사도 단수형인 plays가 와야 한다.

18. 셋 이상에서 '서로'는 one another로 표현한다.

20. all은 '모두'의 뜻으로 뒤에 셀 수 있는 명사의 복수형이나 셀 수 없는 명사의 단수형이 오는데 명사의 수에 동사의 수를 일치시킨다.

21. 셋 중에서 하나는 one, 다른 하나는 another, 나머지 하나는 the other로 표현한다.

23. '혼자 힘으로'는 for oneself로 표현하는데 주어가 Monica이므로 재귀대명사는 herself가 알맞다.

24. each는 단수 취급하므로 itself가 알맞다.

25. '일부는 ~이고, 나머지는 …하다'의 의미일 때는 「some ~, the others …」이 알맞다. '모든'을 나타내는 말은 all과 every가 있는데 뒤에 복수형이 왔으므로 all이 알맞다.

Chapter 9. 형용사와 부사
Unit 46. 형용사와 부사의 쓰임
Practice

A. 1. tall 2. exciting 3. expensive
B. 1. slowly 2. hot 3. Luckily 4. sour
C. 1. I never wake up early in the morning.
   2. Kate usually goes swimming in her free time.
   3. Fred is always tired on Mondays.

Unit 47. 수량형용사
Practice

A. 1. much 2. questions 3. little 4. lots of 5. a little
B. 1. a little 2. Few 3. many 4. books 5. little
C. 1. (1) 그녀는 돈을 약간 저축한다.
      (2) 그녀는 돈을 거의 저축하지 않는다.
   2. (1) 교실에 학생들이 몇 명 있었다.
      (2) 교실에 학생들이 거의 없었다.

Unit 48. -thing + 형용사 / the + 형용사
Practice

A. 1. new, shoes 2. something, cold 3. soft, towel
   4. anything, wrong
B. 1. 그녀는 병원에서 아픈 사람들을 도왔다.
   2. 이 음식은 젊은이들에게 인기 있다.
   3. 그는 집 없는 사람들을 위해 그 집을 지었다.
C. 1. Did you find anything strange?
   2. I met someone famous yesterday.
   3. It is helpful for the elderly.

Review Test / Unit 46~48

A. 1. a few 2. little 3. a little 4. few
B. 1. much 2. always eat 3. someone special
   4. perfect
C. 1. 그는 정원에 몇 송이의 꽃을 심었다.
   2. 그녀는 결코 학교에 지각하지 않는다.

3. 나의 엄마는 아픈 사람들을 도와주셨다.
4. 그 당시에 Eva는 음식이 거의 없었다.

D. 1. This steak smells good.
   2. I found something important on the desk.
   3. There is a lot of salt in the bowl.
   4. The young are the hope of the future.

Chapter Test / Unit 46~48

1. ⑤ 2. ③ 3. ④ 4. ④ 5. ④ 6 ② 7. ② 8. ④ 9. few
10. ④ 11. always, drinks 12. Many, people 13. ⑤ 14. ⑤
15. ③ 16. ⑤ 17. the, old 18. a few, a little 19. something,
spicy 20. ② 21. drives, carefully 22. We often go camping
on Saturday. 23. I saw someone strange at the park.
24. many, much[a lot of, lots of] 25. to the poor

1. '시간이 조금 있니?'라는 뜻으로 셀 수 없는 명사 time이 있으므로 a little이 알맞다.

2. '치마를 좋아하지 않아서 거의 없다.'는 뜻으로 셀 수 있는 명사 skirt가 왔으므로 few가 알맞다.

3. 첫 번째 빈칸에는 '할 일이 많다'라는 뜻으로 셀 수 없는 명사 work가 있으므로 much, a lot of, lots of가 알맞다. 두 번째 빈칸에는 '얼마나 많은'의 뜻으로 셀 수 있는 명사 egg가 있으므로 many가 알맞다.

4. snow는 셀 수 없는 명사이므로 few는 알맞지 않다.

5. -thing, -one, -body로 끝나는 대명사를 수식할 때는 형용사가 뒤에 위치한다.

6. 빈도부사는 be동사나 조동사의 뒤, 일반동사의 앞에 위치한다.

7. the rich는 '부유한 사람들'이라는 뜻으로 복수 취급한다.

8. '쉽게 만들 수 있다'라는 의미가 되어야 하므로 부사 easily가 알맞다.

9. '거의 없는'의 수량형용사는 few와 little이 있는데 people이 셀 수 있는 명사이므로 few가 알맞다.

10. '거의 없는'의 뜻으로 셀 수 있는 명사 앞(seats)에는 few가 와야 한다.

11. '항상'이라는 뜻의 빈도부사는 always이고 일반동사 앞에 위치한다.

12. lots of는 '많은'의 뜻으로 셀 수 있는 명사와 셀 수 없는 명사 앞에 모두 쓰인다. people은 셀 수 있는 명사이므로 many와 바꿔 쓸 수 있다.

13. -thing, -body, -one으로 끝나는 대명사는 형용사가 뒤에서 수식한다.

14. I got something sweet for you.가 되어야 한다.

15. To help the poor is not difficult.가 되어야 한다.

16. ⑤의 house는 셀 수 있는 명사이므로 a little이 알맞지 않다.

17. 「the+형용사」는 「형용사+복수 보통명사」로 바꿔 쓸 수 있다.

18. '약간'의 뜻으로 셀 수 없는 명사에는 a little을 쓴다.

19. -thing으로 끝나는 대명사를 수식할 때는 형용사가 뒤에 위치한다.

20. 「the+형용사」는 「형용사+복수 보통명사」의 뜻으로 '~하는 사람들'의 의미이다.

22. 빈도부사는 일반동사의 앞이나 be동사, 조동사의 뒤에 위치한다.

Chapter 10. 형용사와 부사의 비교

Unit 49. 비교급, 최상급의 규칙 변화

Practice

A. 1. smaller, smallest 2. fatter, fattest
   3. more slowly, most slowly 4. busier, busiest
B. 1. faster 2. more difficult 3. biggest 4. most famous
C. 1. hotter 2. more, popular 3. tallest 4. heaviest

Unit 50. 비교급, 최상급의 불규칙 변화

Practice

A. 1. better, best 2. less, least 3. more, most
   4. worse, worst
B. 1. best 2. worse 3. less 4. most
C. 1. 나는 Jenny보다 더 많은 책을 가지고 있다.
   2. 네 휴대전화는 내 것보다 더 좋다.
   3. 그는 최악의 가수였다.

Unit 51. as + 원급 + as

Practice

A. 1. fast 2. old 3. as 4. smart
B. 1. bigger → big 2. more → many
   3. is as not → is not as 4. so → as
C. 1. as, slowly, as 2. as, easy, as
   3. not, as[so], cold, as 4. not, as[so], heavy, as

Unit 52. 비교급 + than

Practice

A. 1. higher, than 2. lighter, than 3. more, beautiful, than
   4. less, careful, than
B. 1. less, interesting 2. less, hot 3. taller, than
C. 1. Health is even more important than money.
   2. A plane is much faster than a car.
   3. This bike is a lot cheaper than that one.

Unit 53. the + 최상급

Practice

A. 1. the longest 2. most popular 3. of 4. in
B. 1. the, most, delicious 2. the, strongest
   3. the, most, difficult 4. the, prettiest
C. 1. the, richest, of 2. the, oldest, in
   3. the, most, exciting, of

Unit 54. 비교 구문 1

Practice

A. 1. high 2. long 3. older, weaker 4. colder, colder

B. 1. 나는 그녀보다 두 배 더 많은 책들을 가지고 있다.
   2. Ben은 점점 더 똑똑해졌다.
   3. 너는 더 열심히 공부할수록, 더 나은 점수를 얻을 것이다.
C. 1. as, loudly, as, possible 2. bigger, than
   3. as, they, could

Unit 55. 비교 구문 2

Practice

A. 1. one, of, the, greatest 2. One, of, the, busiest
   3. one, of, the, oldest
B. 1. students 2. is 3. stronger 4. country
C. girl, young, as, No, other, younger, than, any, other

Review Test / Unit 49~55

A. 1. bigger 2. warm 3. the highest 4. coldest
B. 1. of 2. as 3. the earlier 4. big
C. 1. one, of, fastest, girls 2. More, and, more
   3. as, expensive, as 4. sweeter, than
D. 1. less, heavy 2. twice, larger 3. he, can
   4. any, other, bridge

Chapter Test / Unit 49~55

1. ② 2. ② 3. ① 4. ① 5. ⑤ 6. ③ 7. ③ 8. ② 9. ②
10. ④ 11. ④ 12. twice, as 13. cold and cold → colder
and colder 14. are → is 15. ④ 16. ⑤ 17. she, could
18. ③ 19. ③ 20. ④ 21. the worst 22. No, great, as,
than, any, other, artist 23. The earth is four times bigger
than the moon. 24. Health is one of the most important
things of our life. 25. (1) much, as (2) the, least (3) the,
most (4) less, than

1. 「단모음+단자음」으로 이루어진 형용사나 부사의 비교급과 최상급은 자
음을 한 번 더 쓰고 -er/-est를 붙인다. thin – thinner – thinnest
2. '~보다 더 …한[하게]'의 의미는 비교급이 알맞다.
3. '~만큼 …한[하게]'의 뜻은 「as+형용사나 부사의 원급+as」로 나타낸
다.
4. '가능한 ~한[하게]'는 「as+원급+as+주어+can[could]」 또는 「as+
원급+as+possible」로 쓸 수 있다. 동사가 현재형이면 can을, 과거형이면
could를 쓴다.
5. 3음절 이상의 형용사나 부사, -ing, -ed, -ly, -ful 등으로 끝나는 형용사
나 부사의 비교급 앞에 more를 붙인다.
6. 비교급을 강조할 때는 비교급 앞에 much, far, even, still, a lot 등을
쓴다.
7. 최상급 앞에는 the를 붙이고, '~할수록 더 …한'은 「the+비교급, the+
비교급」으로 표현한다.

8. '~만큼 …하지 않는'은 「not as[so]+형용사나 부사의 원급+as」로 나타내고 '~보다 덜 …한'의 열등비교는 「less+형용사나 부사의 원급+than」으로 나타낼 수 있다.

9. '다른 ~보다 …한'의 최상급 표현은 「비교급+than any other+단수명사」로 나타낼 수 있다.

10. in 뒤에는 장소나 범위를 나타내는 말이 오고, of 뒤에는 비교 대상이나 기간을 나타내는 말이 온다. ④는 of가 알맞고 나머지는 in이 알맞다.

12. 배수사를 이용한 비교급은 「배수사+as+형용사나 부사의 원급+as」 또는 「배수사+비교급+than」으로 나타낼 수 있다.

13. '점점 더 ~한'의 뜻을 나타낼 때는 「비교급+and+비교급」으로 나타낸다.

16. '다른 ~보다 …한'의 최상급 표현은 「비교급+than any other+단수명사」로 나타낼 수 있다.

19. 〈보기〉는 '자전거가 자동차보다 더 싸다.'라는 뜻이므로 '자동차는 자전거만큼 싸지 않다.'라는 뜻으로 바꿔 말할 수 있다.

20. 과학 점수가 가장 낮은 것을 알 수 있다.

21. '모든 것 중에서 최악'이라는 뜻이 되어야 하므로 최상급이 알맞다.

24. '~한 것 중의 하나'는 「one of the+최상급+복수명사」로 나타낸다.

25. (1) Paul은 Lisa만큼 돈을 썼다. (2) Kate는 셋 중에서 가장 적은 돈을 썼다. (3) Kate는 셋 중에서 가장 많은 책을 읽었다. (4) Lisa는 Kate보다 책을 덜 읽었다.

Chapter 11. 접속사

Unit 56. and, but, or
Practice

A. 1. and 2. or 3. but 4. and

B. 1. She is not pretty but very popular.
   2. You can pay by cash or credit card.
   3. Leave now, and you can catch the bus.

C. 1. Read, many, books, and 2. Take, a, break, or

Unit 57. 접속사 that
Practice

A. 1. × 2. ○ 3. × 4. ○

B. 1. That 2. that 3. that 4. that

C. 1. I hope that you will pass the exam.
   2. That Sally speaks Japanese well is true.[It is true that Sally speaks Japanese well.]
   3. I think that we should protect the earth.

Unit 58. 시간 접속사 1
Practice

A. 1. while 2. when 3. As 4. while

B. 1. 나는 준비가 될 때 나갈 것이다.
   2. 내가 샤워를 하는 동안 전화벨이 울렸다.
   3. 내가 집에 도착했을 때 비가 내리기 시작했다.

C. 1. He will come to the party when he finishes his work.
   2. While they were playing soccer, someone called them.
   3. As I opened the door, I dropped my mug.

Unit 59. 시간 접속사 2
Practice

A. 1. before 2. since 3. until 4. after

B. 1. after I come back home 2. before the movie started
   3. until I lose weight

C. 1. before you go out 2. until he fell asleep
   3. since I moved here

Unit 60. 이유 접속사
Practice

A. 1. because I felt hungry 2. as the traffic was bad
   3. since it was so noisy 4. because of a cold

B. 1. 수학 시험 때문에
   2. 그가 그의 휴대전화를 잃어버렸기 때문에
   3. 그 영화가 흥미롭기 때문에

C. 1. We couldn't arrive on time since we missed the train.
   2. As he was weak, he decided to exercise.
   3. The bank was closed because it was Sunday.

Unit 61. 결과 접속사
Practice

A. 1. Jake felt tired, so he came back early.
   2. I was very busy, so I couldn't go see a movie.
   3. We won the first prize, so we are all happy.

B. 1. so, sick, that 2. so, hot, that 3. so, boring, that

C. 1. Because[As/Since] I need to ask you something
   2. because[as/since] he didn't wear a coat
   3. so the bus couldn't arrive in time

Unit 62. 조건 접속사
Practice

A. 1. you eat too much sweets 2. you hurry
   3. you want to read it

B. 1. Unless you have breakfast
   2. if you don't wear the raincoat
   3. unless you are careful

C. 1. if you have any questions
   2. unless you are busy
   3. if it is cloudy

Unit 63. 양보 접속사

Practice

A. 1. Though she is over 50 years old, she doesn't look old.
   2. Although I don't speak English well, I will travel to Canada.
   3. Even though Andy is young, he is very brave.
   4. Even if you have lots of money, you should not waste it.

B. 1. Although, Eric, was, short
   2. though, she, told, a, lie
   3. even, if, it, is, cold

C. 1. Though this is an old car
   2. Even if tomorrow is a holiday
   3. even though it is bad for health

Unit 64. 상관 접속사

Practice

A. 1. and 2. or 3. either 4. but

B. 1. either buy or borrow the book
   2. Both she and I like
   3. Not only you but also Alice
   4. is not only hungry but also tired

C. 1. is → are 2. has to → have to
   3. don't → doesn't 4. enjoys → enjoy

Review Test / Unit 56~64

A. 1. since 2. while 3. that 4. or

B. 1. Though[Although/Even though/Even if]
   2. When 3. and 4. because of

C. 1. until her mother came back
   2. either cheese cake or ice cream
   3. so cold that many people are wearing
   4. Not only I but also she is

D. 1. so 2. unless 3. before

Chapter Test / Unit 56~64

1. ③ 2. ① 3. ② 4. ⑤ 5. ② 6. ①, ③, ⑤ 7. ① 8. ①
9. that 10. ⑤ 11. ③ 12. ① 13. after 14. Both, and
15. ② 16. are, is 17. will meet, meet 18. ③ 19. ③
20. since 21. Unless, wear, a, coat, or, you'll, catch, a, cold 22. Either Brad or Sam is good at running.
23. Even though his computer is in good condition, he wants to buy a new one. 24. because[as/since] her cell phone is broken 25. (1) when (2) that (3) if

1. '그래서'라는 뜻의 결과를 나타내는 접속사가 알맞다.

2. '~해라, 그러면 …할 것이다'라는 의미가 되어야 하므로 「명령문, and …」로 나타낸다.

3. 「either A or B」: 'A 또는 B 둘 중 하나'
「명령문, or …」: '~해라, 그렇지 않으면 … 할 것이다'

4. because 뒤에는 「주어+동사」의 절이 와야 하고, because of 뒤에는 명사나 구가 온다.

5. 목적어 역할을 하는 명사절을 이끄는 that은 생략할 수 있다.

6. '~ 때문에'라는 뜻의 이유를 나타내는 접속사는 because, since, as 등이 있다.

7. 첫 번째 빈칸에는 '비록 ~이지만'이라는 뜻의 양보의 접속사가 필요하고, 두 번째 빈칸에는 '~하기 전에'라는 뜻의 접속사가 필요하다.

8. '~할 때까지'는 until로 나타내고 시간의 부사절에서는 미래를 의미하더라도 현재시제를 쓴다.

9. 첫 번째 빈칸에는 목적어 역할을 하는 명사절을 이끄는 접속사가 필요하고, 두 번째 빈칸에는 '너무 ~해서 …하다'라는 뜻의 「so+형용사」나 「부사+that」의 형태가 알맞다.

10. ①~④는 명사절을 이끄는 접속사이고 ⑤는 지시형용사이다.

11. 「either A or B」는 B에 맞춰서 동사를 결정하므로 knows가 알맞다.

12. '~해라, 그러면 …할 것이다'라는 뜻이 되어야 하므로 「명령문, and …」로 나타낸다.

15. 〈보기〉와 ②는 '~ 때문에'라는 뜻으로 이유를 나타내고 ①은 '~대로', ③~⑤는 '~할 때'라는 뜻으로 시간을 나타낸다.

16. 「not only A but also B」는 B에 맞춰서 동사를 결정한다.

17. 시간의 접속사가 이끄는 절에서는 미래의 의미를 나타내더라도 현재시제를 쓴다.

18. '추웠지만 많은 사람들이 스키 타는 것을 즐겼다.'는 뜻이 되어야 하므로 양보의 접속사가 알맞다.

19. '바빠서 콘서트에 갈 수 없었다.'는 뜻이 되어야 하므로 「so+형용사나 부사+that」의 형태로 쓴다.

21. '만약 ~하지 않는다면, … 할 것이다'라는 접속사 unless 또는 「명령문, or …」로 나타낼 수 있다.

22. 「either A or B」: 'A나 B 둘 중 하나'

23. even though: 비록 ~일지라도, ~임에도 불구하고

24. 휴대전화가 고장 나서 전화할 수 없다는 내용이 되어야 하므로 이유의 접속사를 쓴다.

25. (1)은 '~할 때'라는 뜻의 접속사가 필요하고 (2)는 목적어 역할을 하는 명사절을 이끄는 접속사 that이 필요하고 (3)은 '만약 ~한다면'이라는 뜻의 접속사가 필요하다.

Chapter 12. 관계사
Unit 65. 관계대명사 who

Practice

A. 1. who 2. whose 3. whom 4. who

B. 1. who 2. whose 3. whom[who] 4. whom[who]
C. 1. There are many girls who are playing badminton.
   2. He is the boy whose mother is a famous actress.
   3. Ms. Green is a teacher whom[who] everyone respects.

Unit 66. 관계대명사 which
Practice

A. 1. Fred has a dog whose name is Molly.
   2. They climbed the mountain whose top is covered with snow.
   3. This is the song which many people like.
   4. We need a house which has a beautiful garden.
B. 1. which → whose 2. whose → which
   3. whose → which 4. who → whose
C. 1. It has a long neck.
   2. They watched it yesterday.
   3. Its color is pink.

Unit 67. 관계대명사의 수 일치
Practice

A. 1. is 2. is 3. fits 4. doesn't
B. 1. is 2. is 3. are 4. is
C. 1. whom Sam likes is Jennifer
   2. which I wanted to read was sold out
   3. who work at the office are kind

Unit 68. 관계대명사 that
Practice

A. 1. whose 2. who, that 3. which, that 4. that
B. 1. who 2. which 3. whom[who] 4. which
C. 1. that discovered America in 1492.
   2. that I've ever eaten
   3. that were crossing the street
   4. that matches this blouse

Review Test / Unit 65~68
A. 1. which 2. who 3. whose 4. whom[who]
B. 1. who 2. which 3. whom[who] 4. which
C. 1. whose 2. is 3. was 4. that
D. 1. who[that] is playing in the garden
   2. which[that] Henry is wearing
   3. whom[who/that] Jim likes
   4. who[that] come from Japan

Unit 69. 관계대명사 what
Practice

A. 1. What 2. who 3. what 4. which
B. 1. what I really want to have
   2. what I heard from Susie
   3. What I ate for dinner
C. 1. What, The thing that[which]
   2. what, the thing that[which]
   3. what, the things that[which]

Unit 70. 관계대명사의 생략
Practice

A. 1. that 2. which 3. which is 4. who are
B. 1. This is the portrait which[that] I drew for myself.
   2. I know the boy who[that] is taking a nap on the bench.
   3. She is the hair desiger whom[who/that] Ann wants to work with.
   4. He read the book which[that] was written in Korean.
C. 1. Look at the boys who[that] are swimming in the pool.
   2. This is the chair which[that] is made of glass.
   3. Can you see the woman who[that] is eating sandwich?

Unit 71. 관계부사 1
Practice

A. 1. when 2. where 3. when 4. where
B. 1. where we stayed was very dirty
   2. the time when the train arrived
   3. the bakery where we can buy some pies
C. 1. the day when he comes back
   2. the place where we spent our vacation
   3. the area where the climate is warmer

Unit 72. 관계부사 2
Practice

A. 1. why 2. how 3. the way 4. why
B. 1. This is how I can stay healthy.
   2. He explained (the reason) why he stopped smoking.
   3. I am learning how I knit a sweater.
C. 1. Can you tell me the reason why you don't like Sally?
   2. This is the town where I want to visit someday.
   3. I'll never forget the day when we first met.

Review Test / Unit 69~72

A. 1. what 2. why 3. where 4. when

B. 1. What 2. the way[how] 3. where 4. when

C. 1. which 2. who is 3. where 4. which are

D. 1. what, I, like 2. what, he, bought
   3. how, you, solved 4. reason, why, you, cried

Chapter Test / Unit 65~72

1. ③ 2. ① 3. ④ 4. ① 5. ⑤ 6. ④ 7. ② 8. ②, ③ 9. ①
10. that 11. ③ 12. ① 13. ② 14. ① 15. ② 16. is, are
17. that, what 18. where 19. ① 20. ② 21. I saw old
ladies (who[that] were) talking together in the park.
22. I don't know the time when the airplane arrived.
23. What I like most is playing the violin. 24. This is
the watch which[that] Joe bought for me. 25. (1) whose,
who[that] (2) when, why

1. the girl이 선행사이고 명사가 이어지므로 소유격 whose가 알맞다.

2. 선행사가 시간을 나타내는 the time이므로 when이 알맞다.

3. 선행사가 사물이나 동물일 때 주격과 목적격 관계대명사는 which를 쓴다.

4. 선행사가 사람이고 주격 관계대명사이므로 who가 알맞다.

5. 방법을 나타내는 선행사 the way는 how와 바꿔 쓸 수 있다.

6. 사물이 선행사이고 소유격 관계대명사이므로 whose가 알맞다.

7. 첫 번째 빈칸에는 사람을 선행사로 하는 목적격 관계대명사 whom[who/that]이 필요하고, 두 번째 빈칸에는 선행사를 포함한 관계대명사 what이 필요하다.

8. '하는 것'이라는 뜻의 선행사를 포함한 관계대명사는 what을 쓰고 the thing(s) that[which]으로 바꿔 쓸 수 있다.

9. 관계부사의 선행사가 특정 정보가 없는 일반적인 경우에는 생략할 수 있다.

10. 선행사가 사람 또는 사물일 때 주격과 목적격 관계대명사로 that을 공통으로 쓸 수 있다.

11. 목적격 관계대명사나 「주격 관계대명사+be동사」는 생략할 수 있다.

12. 빈칸 앞에 선행사가 장소를 나타내는 the country이므로 관계부사 where가 이끄는 절이 알맞다.

13. 목적격 관계대명사로 문장을 연결할 때 관계대명사절에서는 목적어를 따로 쓰지 않는다.

14. 목적격 관계대명사를 이용해서 연결해야 하는데 선행사가 the pictures로 사물이므로 which나 that이 알맞다.

15. ①, ④는 사물이나 동물을 선행사로 하는 목적격 관계대명사 which[that]가 들어가고, ③, ⑤는 주격 관계대명사 which[that]가 들어간다. ②는 소유격 관계대명사 whose가 들어간다.

16. 주어가 the flowers 복수이므로 동사도 복수형으로 써야 한다.

17. 선행사를 포함한 관계대명사는 what이다.

18. 관계부사는 「전치사+관계대명사」로 바꿔 쓸 수 있는데 선행사가 장소

를 나타내는 the place이므로 where가 알맞다.

19. ①은 명사절을 이끄는 접속사이고 나머지는 관계대명사이다.

20. 선행사가 장소를 나타내는 the city이므로 관계부사 where가 알맞다.

21. 선행사가 사람이므로 관계대명사 who[that]를 써야 하고 「주격 관계대명사+be동사」는 생략할 수 있다.

22. 선행사가 시간을 나타내고 있으므로 관계부사 when으로 연결한다.

23. '~하는 것'의 뜻으로 선행사를 포함한 관계대명사는 what이다.

24. 목적격 관계대명사 which나 that이 이끄는 절이 선행사 the watch를 수식하는 문장이다.

25. 사람을 선행사로 하는 주격 관계대명사이므로 who나 that이 알맞고, 선행사가 the reason으로 이유를 나타내므로 관계부사 why가 알맞다.

Chapter 13. 일치와 화법
Unit 73. 시제일치
Practice

A. 1. was 2. goes 3. invented 4. is

B. 1. is 2. broke 3. rises 4. has

C. 1. they would agree with my opinion
   2. light travels faster than sound
   3. Leonardo Da Vinci painted the *Mona Lisa*

Unit 74. 평서문의 간접화법
Practice

A. 1. said 2. told 3. that 4. didn't

B. 1. says, she, is, going 2. told, he, couldn't
   3. said, he, liked 4. said, he, had, seen

C. 1. I can 2. said, to, I, am 3. it's, raining

Unit 75. 의문사가 없는 의문문의 간접화법
Practice

A. 1. asked, if[whether], I, liked
   2. asked, if[whether], we, had, been
   3. asked, if[whether], it, was

B. 1. Can, you, ride
   2. Are, you, tired
   3. Do, you, know

C. 1. if he watched the movie
   2. if the cap was expensive
   3. whether I would join them

Unit 76. 의문사가 있는 의문문의 간접화법
Practice

A. 1. asked, where, I, lived
   2. asked, who, had, told

3. how, many, brothers, I, had

B. 1. which bus goes downtown
   2. Where are you from
   3. What time does the concert start

C. 1. how often he went swimming
   2. why I was angry
   3. where she had found my ring

Unit 77. 명령문의 간접화법
Practice

A. 1. to turn 2. not to 3. him 4. advised

B. 1. us not to run fast
   2. me to take the subway
   3. me to get up early in the morning

C. 1. advised me to read many books
   2. told my brother to brush his teeth
   3. asked me not to be late for the meeting

Review Test / Unit 73~77

A. 1. discovered 2. sets 3. could 4. drinks

B. 1. freezes 2. if[whether] 3. he lived 4. not to touch

C. 1. Kelly was a good cook
   2. if[whether] he could borrow my book
   3. to do our best
   4. where I had bought the scarf

D. 1. Which sport do you like
   2. Don't eat anything at night
   3. Is it snowing
   4. I can't go hiking

Chapter Test / Unit 73~77

1. ①, ③, ⑤ 2. ② 3. ④ 4. ④ 5. ③ 6. ①, ④ 7. ④ 8. ③
9. ② 10. ④ 11. ③ 12. ⑤ 13. ⑤ 14. ⑤ 15. ④ 16. asked,
why, she, was 17. boiled, boils 18. if, that 19. ⑤ 20. ②
21. Eric told me to turn down the volume. 22. Sue asked
me which bus went to the theater. 23. I asked him if
[whether] he could go with me. 24. where, he, was, from,
told, that, was 25. He said to me, "What time does your
swimming class end?"

1. 주절의 시제가 현재일 때 종속절은 모든 시제가 가능하다.
2. 종속절의 내용이 일반적인 사실을 나타낼 때는 항상 현재시제를 쓴다.
3. 주절의 시제가 과거일 때 종속절의 시제는 과거나 과거완료가 되어야
한다.
4. 현재까지 계속되는 습관은 항상 현재시제로 쓴다.

5. 의문사가 있는 의문문의 간접화법은 「의문사+주어+동사」의 어순으로
쓴다.
6. 의문사가 없는 의문문의 간접화법은 if나 whether를 쓴다.
7. 평서문의 간접화법은 say to를 tell로 바꾸고, 전달동사가 과거일 때 피
전달문의 현재시제는 과거로 바꾼다.
8. 의문사가 없는 의문사의 간접화법은 say to를 ask로 바꾸고, if나
whether를 써서 연결한다.
9. 의문사가 있는 의문문의 간접화법은 said to를 ask로 바꾸고, 「의문사
+주어+동사」의 어순으로 쓴다.
10. 평서문의 간접화법은 say는 그대로 쓰고 that으로 연결한다. 전달동사
가 과거일 때 피전달문의 현재시제는 과거로 바꾼다.
11. 역사적 사실은 항상 과거시제를 쓴다.
12. 간접화법의 전달동사 told가 과거시제이므로 wants도 과거시제가 되
어야 한다.
13. 직접화법에서 전달동사의 시제가 과거일 때 피전달문의 현재시제는 과
거시제로, 과거시제는 과거완료가 되어야 하므로 had seen이 알맞다.
14. 직접화법에서 전달동사의 시제가 과거일 때 피전달문의 현재시제는 과
거시제가 되어야 하므로 arrived가 알맞다.
15. 간접화법의 asked는 said to가 되고 피전달문의 과거시제는 현재로
되어야 한다.
16. 의문사가 있는 의문문의 간접화법에서 동사는 ask로 고치고 「의문사+
주어+동사」의 어순으로 쓴다.
17. 일반적인 사실을 말할 때는 항상 현재시제로 쓴다.
18. 평서문의 간접화법에서 주절과 피전달문을 연결할 때 that을 쓴다.
19. 명령문의 간접화법은 피전달문을 「to+동사원형」의 형태로 쓴다.
20. ②는 주격 관계대명사이고, 나머지는 간접화법에 쓰인 접속사 that이
다.
22. 의문사가 있는 의문문의 간접화법에서 동사는 ask로 고치고, 「의문사
+주어+동사」의 어순으로 쓰는데 의문사가 주어로 쓰일 때는 「의문사+동
사」의 어순이 된다.
23. 의문사가 없는 의문문의 간접화법은 동사를 ask로 바꾸고 피전달문
앞에 if나 whether를 써서 연결한다.
25. asked는 said to가 되고, 피전달문의 과거시제는 현재시제가 되어야
한다.

Chapter 14. 가정법
Unit 78. 가정법 과거
Practice

A. 1. were 2. lived 3. could 4. would

B. 1. exercised, could, lose
   2. were, could, play
   3. were, would not[wouldn't], say
   4. had, could, take

C. 1. If, would, buy 2. If, could, go 3. may, catch

Unit 79. 가정법 과거완료

Practice

A. 1. have arrived   2. have driven   3. had
   4. have succeeded

B. 1. had learned   2. had asked   3. had eaten
   4. had passed

C. 1. had, had, could, have, lent
   2. would, have, gone, rained
   3. had, not, broken, would, have, run

Unit 80. I wish 가정법

Practice

A. 1. were   2. didn't tell   3. had   4. had visited

B. 1. 내가 너를 이해하면 좋을 텐데.
   2. 내가 세계 여행을 하면 좋을 텐데.
   3. 내가 너의 충고를 따랐으면 좋았을 텐데.

C. 1. don't, practice   2. didn't, buy
   3. wishes, had breakfast   4. wish, hadn't, spent

Review Test / Unit 78~80

A. 1. were   2. spoke   3. had tried   4. had had

B. 1. were   2. could send   3. would have watched
   4. had gone

C. 1. made, could, go   2. had, taken, wouldn't, have, been
   3. hadn't, made   4. wishes, became

D. 1. isn't, won't, go   2. had, told, have, been
   3. wish, knew

Chapter Test / Unit 78~80

1. ④ 2. ⑤ 3. had 4. ③ 5. ④ 6. ① 7. ② 8. ⑤ 9. ②
10. ⑤ 11. ④ 12. ④ 13. ② 14. ② 15. won't, wouldn't 16. ①
17. ③ 18. ④ 19. had lived 20. ② 21. had taken medicine,
she wouldn't have been sick in bed 22. If my brother read
many books, he would be wiser. 23. wishes she could
make lots of friends 24. were, not, busy, could, go
25. Nicole didn't go to bed early, so she would be tired.

1. 주절의 동사가 would watch이므로 가정법 과거가 되어야 한다. 가정법 과거에서 be동사는 주어에 상관없이 were를 쓴다.
2. 과거 사실과 반대되는 소망을 나타내므로 「I wish+가정법 과거완료」가 되어야 한다.
3. 첫 번째 빈칸은 가정법 과거 문장으로 '더 많은 시간이 있다면'의 뜻이 되어야 하므로 had가 알맞고, 두 번째 빈칸은 가정법 과거완료 문장이므로 if절에 「had+p.p.」의 형태가 되어야 한다.
4. 첫 번째 빈칸은 과거 사실과 반대되는 소망을 나타내므로 「I wish+가

정법 과거완료」가 되어야 하고, 두 번째 빈칸은 가정법 과거 문장이므로 if절에 과거 동사가 와야 한다.
5. 가정법 과거이므로 「조동사 과거형+동사원형」의 형태가 되어야 한다.
6. 과거 사실과 반대되는 소망을 나타내므로 「I wish+가정법 과거완료」가 되어야 한다.
7. '~했더라면 …했을 텐데'라는 뜻의 가정법 과거완료 문장으로 완성해야 하므로 「If+주어+had+p.p. ~, 주어+조동사 과거형+have+p.p. …」가 되어야 한다.
8. 가정법 과거완료의 문장이므로 「조동사 과거형+have+p.p.」의 형태가 되어야 하므로 have won이 알맞다.
9. ②는 평서문의 간접화법에 쓰인 if이고, 나머지는 가정법에 쓰인 if이다.
10. 가정법 과거완료 문장이므로 「If+주어+had+p.p. ~, 주어+조동사 과거형+have+p.p. …」가 되어야 한다.
11. 과거 사실과 반대되는 소망을 나타내므로 「I wish+가정법 과거완료」가 되어야 한다.
12. 가정법 과거이므로 「조동사 과거형+동사원형」의 형태가 되어야 한다.
13. 현재 사실과 반대되는 소망을 나타내므로 「I wish+가정법 과거」가 되어야 한다.
14. 현재 사실과 반대되는 일을 가정하므로 가정법 과거가 되어야 한다.
15. 가정법 과거이므로 「조동사 과거형+동사원형」의 형태가 되어야 한다.
16. 「I wish+가정법 과거」는 현재 사실과 반대되는 소망을 나타낸다.
17. 가정법 과거완료 문장이므로 「If+주어+had+p.p. ~, 주어+조동사 과거형+have+p.p. …」가 되어야 한다.
18. 현재 사실과 반대되는 소망을 나타내므로 「I wish+가정법 과거」가 되어야 한다.
19. 가정법 과거완료 문장이므로 「If+주어+had+p.p. ~, 주어+조동사 과거형+have+p.p. …」가 되어야 한다.
23. 현재 사실과 반대되는 소망을 나타내므로 「I wish+가정법 과거」로 쓴다.
24. 바빠서 영화를 보러 갈 수 없다는 내용이므로 현재 사실과 반대되는 가정을 나타내는 가정법 과거를 쓴다.
25. 가정법 과거완료이므로 과거 사실과 반대되는 가정을 나타낸다.